T0355805

UNCONDITIONAL

Also by Samra Zafar

A Good Wife

UNCONDITIONAL

BREAK THROUGH PAST LIMITS
TO TRANSFORM YOUR FUTURE

DR. SAMRA ZAFAR

with Kim Pittaway

Collins
An imprint of HarperCollins Publishers

Published by HarperCollins Publishers Ltd

First edition

This book does not give individual medical, therapeutic
or other professional advice and cannot be held to do so. The author
encourages readers to consult their own competent practitioners
concerning any matters of health and wellness raised in the book.

This book draws on the author's own experiences.
Certain names and other details in the book have been changed.

HarperCollins books may be purchased for educational, business,
or sales promotional use through our Special Markets Department.

HarperCollins Publishers Ltd
Bay Adelaide Centre, East Tower
22 Adelaide Street West, 41st Floor
Toronto, Ontario, Canada
M5H 4E3

www.harpercollins.ca

Library and Archives Canada Cataloguing in Publication

Title: Unconditional : break through past limits to transform your future / Dr. Samra Zafar with
Kim Pittaway.
Names: Zafar, Samra, author.
Description: First edition. | Includes bibliographical references.
Identifiers: Canadiana (print) 20240517040 | Canadiana (ebook) 20240518292 | ISBN 9781443470469
(softcover) | ISBN 9781443470476 (Ebook)
Subjects: LCSH: Zafar, Samra—Mental health. | LCSH: Self-actualization (Psychology) | LCSH:
Self-realization. | LCSH: Self-acceptance.
Classification: LCC BF637.S4 Z34 2025 | DDC 158.1—dc23

Printed and bound in the United States of America
24 25 26 27 28 LBC 5 4 3 2 1

First and always, for my daughters, Kinza and Saarah.

*And for every woman who has felt "not enough" or "too much,"
who has pushed against the boundaries put in place to keep us
"less than," who has been scolded for dreaming: This is your time
to soar, to become who you are meant to be—unconditionally!*

Our lives equip us with unique experiences and perceptions. In the pages that follow, we explore issues related to a wide range of life situations and circumstances, including some that may be triggering to some readers. If you encounter material that is challenging or upsetting for you, or causes you discomfort, I encourage you to seek support.

CONTENTS

Unlearning

I t was August 2020. I was alone in an igloo-shaped bubble tent nestled among tall pines, the scent of needles adding fragrance to the nighttime breeze. A few yards away, the waves lapped gently on the shores of Lake Masson in rural Quebec. Darkness surrounded me, only broken when I gazed up through the tent's transparent ceiling to where the stars shimmered in a clearing in the branches above me.

I was at a crossroads. The road I'd travelled to get here had had many twists and turns, peaks and valleys. I'd been a child bride trapped in a forced marriage, emotionally and physically abused and controlled by my husband.[1] As a young mother, I'd earned money by babysitting, taken courses online to finish my high school diploma and applied to university, eventually escaping my husband's violence and control.

When I left my marriage, I expected my biggest challenges would be to learn new things: the knowledge I needed to build a career, the practical things I needed to know to create a home for my daughters and me, the social skills I needed to navigate friendships and dating. While I didn't think it would be easy, I'd always been an excellent student, a quick study. And since leaving, I *had* managed to create a new future for my two daughters and me, completing a graduate degree in economics and entering the world of banking.

When I embarked on my new life with my girls, I started telling people my story, sharing what I'd escaped, what I'd survived, first in talks to small groups where I hoped to reach women who were trapped as I had been, then in a magazine article and eventually in a book. When that book, *A Good Wife*, was published, I believed I would continue on the path I had found out of my abusive marriage and into independence, climbing the corporate ladder in banking, making a difference in the world by speaking out about what I'd been through while keeping my girls safe and secure.

The financial institutions I worked for put me on posters promoting diversity and invited clients to speeches I delivered on equity and inclusion. But back at the office, my boss didn't seem to know what tasks to assign me as she said my "sexy" speaking engagements were causing my co-workers to resent me.

In my personal life, my ex-husband and I continued to clash over raising our daughters. As a mom, my relationship with Kinza and Saarah was stronger than ever, but my relationship with my widowed mother, always challenging, had fallen into a pattern of long silences punctuated by angry phone calls. And while I'd hoped to forge a healthy romantic relationship, that, too, seemed to elude me.

To others, I may have looked successful. But my old beliefs continued to haunt me. Perhaps I'd never find love. *You're not worthy of it*, those old voices whispered. *God is punishing you for leaving*. When I struggled, they spoke up again: *You don't have what it takes*. And they aimed newly sharpened doubts at my psyche as well. Had I been promoted in the corporate world as a diversity token? Had the choices I'd made to distance myself from unhealthy family relationships isolated my children? Was I now all the family they had? Had the trauma

I'd been through irreparably damaged me, made me unable to be happy? Maybe I still didn't deserve to be loved.

It seemed so strange. In escaping my marriage and starting over, I'd done something that had seemed impossible, Herculean. Yet I was still confined in ways I hadn't anticipated. As I stared up into the night sky over Lake Masson, I realized that while my circumstances had changed, I remained constricted by the beliefs I'd been trained to accept as normal. Not all these beliefs originated in my marriage. Some had been with me since childhood: the notion that I had to earn the love of my parents and others, the idea that I had to be perfect to be considered worthy, the belief that I was a black sheep for dreaming of a life and education those around me said was reserved for boys. I struggled to believe that I deserved to be loved, even—perhaps most especially—by myself. I had been conditioned to believe that I shouldn't have a self at all because my role was to be selfless, to lose myself in serving others. That's what good girls, good daughters, good mothers, good wives did: they became ghosts in their own lives, visible only as they served to make their families look good, their husbands shine, their children happy, their employers successful, their communities stronger.

I'd stepped into my new life ready to learn. But I wasn't prepared for the unlearning I needed to do: deconstructing the limiting beliefs, the cultural conditioning and the societal expectations threatening to trap me anew in unconscious cycles of shame, stigma and self-sabotaging behaviour. It was becoming clear that my journey was not all about learning: the hardest work would be in unlearning the false beliefs holding me back.

I knew I wasn't alone in my struggle. We all want to be true to ourselves, to be accepted, respected and loved for who we are. Yet we live in a world where we are surrounded by messages, subliminal and direct, telling us that who we are is either not enough or too much. We aren't attractive enough, or smart enough, or funny enough, or strong enough. Or we're too loud, too flamboyant, too outspoken, too emotional. Those messages are especially strident for those of us outside the dominant white culture: immigrants, women of colour, gender non-conforming people or anyone else whom society marginalizes and for whom role models can be harder to find. The voices of "not enough" and "too much" whisper and shout, doing their best to convince us we need to be someone other than who we are.

I carried those voices within me. But when I escaped the windowless room of my marriage, I also carried within me the seed of another belief, a belief in myself, a hardy kernel that survived despite a lack of warmth and nourishment, a small nugget of truth, telling me that things shouldn't be as they were, that my daughters and I deserved more. And as I rebuilt my life, I worked hard to nurture that seed.

By the time I arrived in the bubble tent by the lake, I'd spent hours and hours in therapy, on my own and with my daughters, untying the knots of trauma, untangling emotions distorted by shame, anger and sadness, learning to listen for the voice of my authentic self and to trust its insights, needs and desires. I'd consumed dozens of psychology and self-help books, first looking for ways to help my girls cope with the lingering effects of the abuse they'd witnessed and then seeking answers for myself.

I knew I'd made the right decision—for me and my girls—in leaving my marriage. But while the path I'd taken in my career provided security, I was more and more convinced it wasn't the path I was meant to follow. I'd had conversations with colleagues, talked it over again and again with friends, but still had no answers. Stick it out and climb the corporate ladder, counselled some—I made good money, after all. Follow your heart, advised others. But I wasn't sure what my heart actually wanted—at work or in some of my personal relationships—and so the road ahead of me remained hazy, the twists and turns blanketed in the fog of unknowing.

Just drive, whispered a voice deep inside me. Learning to drive had been one of my early steps in escaping my marriage. My husband and I shared a home with his parents, and I'd convinced my mother-in-law that the two of us should take driving lessons together so we could go shopping without relying on the men in the household. I'd passed my driving test; she hadn't. And while that meant I became her driver, she also, over time, allowed me to run errands on my own, affording me precious moments of independence and autonomy. In the years since, I'd done some of my clearest thinking, tackled some of my toughest decisions, while behind the wheel.

An idea began to form: I'd been trying to find my answers in listening to others. I needed to listen to myself. What did I want? What did I need? I wasn't sure. Maybe intuition was like a muscle, mine rusty from disuse. What if I set off on a trip with the goal of listening to my inner voice? No predetermined destination, no advance booking, just me behind the wheel, going down whichever roads my intuition thought looked interesting.

My girls were old enough to stay on their own with an adult friend checking in on them, but still I wanted to be within a day's drive home in case of emergency. A solo trip through our home province would be simple but perhaps too comfortable: pushing myself outside my comfort zone seemed like a more promising challenge. I don't speak French, had never driven through Quebec except on the highway to Montreal. And so I set off on a road trip through Quebec, serendipity as my guide. I had no plans other than my vow to trust my intuition and open myself up to possibility. I would follow the roads that looked promising, hoping I'd find answers.

That's how, early in my trip, I'd arrived at Lake Masson.

As I stared up into the night sky, I could see no answers written in the stars. Still, I fell asleep comforted. I'd recognized that something wasn't right in my life, and even if the path forward remained unclear, that awareness was the first step in finding my way. I couldn't wait to see what I'd discover in the days ahead.

Why I've Written This Book

I'm a reader, a studier, a magpie for information and inspiration. On my journey, I've sought the wisdom of other writers, other women, other thinkers. I've shared my wisdom, too, in the pages of my first book and in the hundreds of speeches I've given in the past decade, since I set out to remake a life for myself and my daughters. Those speaking engagements have taken me around the world, to Ivy League universities, villages in rural Kenya, the executive towers of Toronto's Bay Street and elsewhere. I've spoken about resilience, trauma, racism, allyship, unconscious bias, the healing power of vulnerability and gratitude, self-care, empathy, finding your purpose, the power of giving back and more. And while the topics vary widely, at their core, they all involve talking about what I've learned and what I've had to unlearn to change my life for the better.

On the pages that follow, I share those lessons, exploring the core beliefs that conditioned me to limit my freedom, my happiness and my potential. They are the beliefs about love, work, parenting, self-sufficiency, perfectionism, trauma, shame and self-love that cut across our many identities—gender, race, religion, ability, sexuality and more. Unlearning limiting beliefs has been key to allowing me to connect to my authentic self, to tap into the power of unconditional self-love and self-acceptance, to evolve and grow—and to set the example I hope will inspire my daughters to seek an authentic and empowering path as they too evolve and grow throughout their lifetimes.

The details of your life are undoubtedly different from mine. But at their core, our journeys are similar, as we try to find our way back to ourselves and then step out into the world to be our truest selves.

I know the beliefs that limited me also constrain so many of us. As I've worked to dismantle them in my own life, I have come to believe that the tools I've used and the lessons of my journey can inspire others to unlearn as well. Since leaving corporate finance, I've trained as a medical doctor, further bolstering my lived experience as I've explored the biology, psychology and science of trauma, change and mental health. All of this has led me to the conviction that we do not have to live lives limited by the unhealthy beliefs imposed on us by family, culture, religion and society. We can release ourselves from the shame and blame and self-sabotage we have internalized. The healing that follows is magical, allowing us to reclaim what we thought we'd lost to trauma in an even more beautiful way as we learn to be who we were born to be and to live—and love—unconditionally.

On the Road Again

As I continued my drive along the Gaspé coast, I replayed Dr. Bessel Van Der Kolk's audiobook *The Body Keeps the Score: Brain, Mind, and Body in the Healing of Trauma.*[1] His insights inspired me, as I connected them to the impact of trauma in my own life. But more than that, his work inspired me, his ability to touch so many lives so profoundly with the knowledge that he'd gained as a psychiatrist and researcher. It was work that made a difference in the world, work that made the world better.

I'd once dreamed of being a doctor, imagined myself as a healer. But those dreams had disintegrated, replaced first with a marriage I didn't want to a man I didn't know and then later with the security of a career in finance. Now, as I sought a new path, a question floated to the surface, whispered in the voice of the girl I'd been, a girl with big dreams: *Is it too late?* she asked.

I knew McMaster University had a program that welcomed applicants with non-traditional backgrounds—students whose undergraduate degrees weren't in the sciences. *Maybe?* I wondered, as I paused Dr. Van Der Kolk's audiobook and pulled over to the side of the road to search the university's site on my phone. The application deadline was just weeks away. I'd have to find a way to write the MCAT (Medical College Admission Test) Critical Analysis and Reasoning section, a requirement for entry. It was impossible.

And yet . . . that voice whispered in my head. *Maybe?*

I searched for MCAT exam slots: not an open one anywhere in Canada in time for the McMaster deadline. I hit refresh—and a slot opened in Calgary. I grabbed it. I'd have just weeks to prepare, and if I passed, I would barely squeak through in time for McMaster's application deadline.

Maybe?

When I set out on this road trip, I'd promised myself I would follow where my intuition took me. That I'd listen to my inner voice. That I'd welcome serendipity. As I stared at the phone in my hand, the confirmation of my MCAT appointment on the screen, I wondered. Did I trust myself enough to listen to the voice inside me that so wanted my attention? Did I trust the universe?

I had to try.

A month later, I wrote the MCAT and applied to McMaster. In spring 2021, I was one of more than five hundred applicants selected for an interview. Then I learned I would be one of just over two hundred admitted to classes that summer. It was the beginning of another journey, and I had found my first steps on a road trip alone with my intuition.

Building Your Tool Kit

"I'm not really a therapy person."

The woman sitting across from me in the hospital examination room said the words as if she had failed a test and was confessing her low mark, the same way you might say "I'm not really a math person," or "I'm not very artistic," as if therapy were a skill for which she had no inborn aptitude. But just as with math and art, our skills for self-reflection and psychological growth aren't something we're born either with or without, they're abilities we foster and develop over time. Yes, some may have interests or aptitudes that give them an edge, while others may face circumstances and barriers complicating their efforts, but all of us have the capacity to look within, to come to understand ourselves, our actions and reactions and to take steps to modify the behaviours and habits we wish to leave behind.

"What makes you say that?" I asked gently.

"Well, it's expensive, and I don't really have the money to spare," she eventually said, not meeting my eyes. She seemed worried I might judge her for not finding the money. "And I tried a free support group, but I didn't really like it."

Her concerns were legitimate: therapy can be expensive. But there are alternatives, and over the next hour together, we came up with a plan: programs she could check out and resources she could access.

It will likely come as no surprise that I think that anyone can benefit from working with the right therapist. I know I have, as have my daughters. And I wouldn't be working now in the mental health field if I didn't strongly believe in the power of talk therapy, and yes, where appropriate, the right medication. But I also know that good, effective therapy and medical treatments aren't affordable or available to everyone. It can be especially challenging for those of us seeking culturally sensitive, trauma-informed professional help, whether we're looking for a counsellor whose background resembles ours or one who has done the work to develop cross-cultural competency.

But that doesn't mean you have to remain stuck.

Whether you're seeking therapy or going solo for now—and even if you are working successfully with a therapist—there are steps you can take to support your own wellness journey. I think of them as three different types of fuel.

1. Insights

I'm always on the lookout for wisdom to inspire me, advice that strikes a chord and stories that help me see my situation a bit more clearly through the experiences of others. I'm happy to find those insights in all kinds of places—popular psychology books and articles, peer-reviewed studies, conversations and even social media posts.

There are a handful of books I've found especially insightful and inspirational on my journey. You'll see some of them referenced on the pages of this book, including:

- *The Body Keeps the Score: Brain, Mind, and Body in the Healing of Trauma* by Dr. Bessel Van Der Kolk.[2] Based on Dr. Van Der Kolk's lifetime of research and work with survivors of trauma, this book is a deep dive into the science of trauma and the powerful possibility of recovery. It is an inspiring, hope-filled guide.
- *The Myth of Normal: Trauma, Illness and Healing in a Toxic Culture* by Dr. Gabor Maté with Daniel Maté.[3] Dr. Maté mas-

terfully examines the interconnections of emotional and physical health in a book that offers both understanding and compassion for our journeys to whole health.

- *Set Boundaries, Find Peace: A Guide to Reclaiming Yourself* by Nedra Glover Tawwab:[4] Counsellor Tawwab's book provides clear and powerful advice on establishing healthy boundaries and expressing our needs.
- *Good Morning, I Love You: Mindfulness and Self-Compassion Practices to Rewire Your Brain for Calm, Clarity, and Joy* by Shauna Shapiro:[5] A compelling and compassionate exploration of the power of self-kindness by a leading scientist studying the effects of mindfulness on the brain.

Whether you're a reader or, like me, an audiobook listener, or whether you find inspiration on Instagram, podcasts, TikTok or elsewhere, it can be easy to let a moment of insight slip away as another crowds into the queue behind it. I'm a big believer in the power of collecting the insights I connect with into a central spot. For me, it's the notes folder on my phone. For you, it might be voice notes, a computer file, a journal—or even scribblings on the pages of the books you read. Whatever you choose, I guarantee the insights you find will work harder for you if you do the work of pausing to reflect, connect and record them in some way (and I'd be delighted to see your marked-up version of the book you hold in your hands now!).

2. Accountability

The best intentions in the world may not amount to much without follow-through—and accountability is follow-through's rocket fuel. We can be accountable to ourselves or to someone else; our accountability can be public or private; it can be motivated by external guidelines or inner values. One element of therapy's effectiveness is that in committing to therapy, we're making an accountability commitment to ourselves and to our therapist. But we can also commit to accountability in group support settings; one-to-one with peers, friends or family members who are supporting us or with whom we're engaged in mutual support; and to ourselves.

The "ourselves" commitment can be tricky in that it can be easy to let ourselves off the hook—or to forget exactly what we've committed to or even how we felt in a past situation. As with insights, putting our commitments down on the page is a powerful tool to lock in accountability. This doesn't have to be complicated or require a particular format or document: like your insights, you can record them whatever way suits you. My suggestions for inclusion in your records:

- When you're committing to a change, honestly acknowledge your starting point. This will make assessing what you've accomplished easier.
- Not sure you want to make a change or what change you could make? Jot notes about how things are now. You might notice patterns coming up you hadn't noticed before.
- Arguing with yourself in your head? Put it down on the page. Giving voice to your reluctance, frustration or other barriers can help bring to the surface insights—and parts of yourself—you're ignoring and help you find your way through that internal conflict.

3. Joy

You might not expect to see joy on a list of mental health tools. Trying to address trauma and its impact on our lives, putting in the effort to make positive change, is hard work. A frank therapy session, journaling, attending to a mental health book or podcast that makes you think about your life or relationships in new ways, preparing for and having a tough conversation with a loved one: each one of these steps is like a gym workout for the psyche. It stretches us, works our emotional muscles and sometimes pushes us to the brink. No one can sustain that kind of effort without refuelling, and to my mind, joy is one of the most powerful fuels for change that we can tap into.

A caution, of course: not everything that makes us feel good brings us joy. Satisfying addictive or other negative urges can feel good in the moment, but won't cause us joy in the longer run. Joy enhances our well-being; joyful activities bring us delight that lasts beyond the moment. And joy is different from happiness: the way I see it, joy is the in-the-moment feeling of being whole, at one with yourself and the universe, while happiness is the accumulation of those joyful moments.

Think about what brings you joy and how you might add some joy to your life. For me, in the toughest moments of my marriage, I found joy in small freedoms, walking with my daughters in their stroller, pausing on a pathway under the Credit River Bridge near my home that was sheltered from view, where I could remove my hijab and feel the breeze in my hair. More recently, on a trip to Hawaii, I rose at two in the morning—not joyful!—for an excursion to the edge of the Haleakala volcano, the largest dormant volcano in the world. As the sun's first rays crested over the crater, the colours in the sky changed from black to blue to orange, pink and purple, the clouds drifting by like a slow waterfall. It was magic. Pure joy. The distance between the young mother I had been and the medical student I was that day in Hawaii seemed immeasurable. But I would never have experienced the soul-expanding joy of that mountaintop if twenty-something me hadn't first allowed herself a minute or two of joy in the summer breeze on a pathway under a bridge all those years ago.

Having trouble finding your joy? Think about what made you happiest as a child. What did you get lost in? Look for "joy signals" in your current life as well. What parts of your daily rhythms and rituals do you look forward to? Maybe it's the pleasure of putting together a great outfit, a few minutes spent on a hobby, or time talking with a friend. Can you find a way to inject even a bit more of that source of happiness into your day today?

How to Use This Book

In the pages that follow, I cover many aspects of life and living, informed by my experiences, wide reading, spirited discussions with friends and colleagues, and learnings from leaders in the fields of trauma, mental health, psychology and psychiatry, and further developed by my more recent studies as a medical student. As of writing this book, I've completed my MD, and as of the book's publication, I expect to be partway through my first year of residency work to further specialize in psychiatry. What you'll find on these pages are my insights and learnings, though my words do not constitute medical advice.

I learn best by listening, and so I love to listen to audiobooks, using audio bookmarks to note meaningful sections and typing notes on my phone for later reference. Others love the printed page, and will underline, highlight, and jot notes in the margin. And for some, e-books are the way to go. There is no one best way to navigate the pages that follow: do what works for you—but do the work, and it *will* work for you.

Some sections may cover issues that are central to you, others may be of little concern (at least for now). You can start from the beginning and read straight through or jump into the sections that matter most to you right now. I've organized each section to make connecting with its tools and insights as helpful, meaningful and accessible as possible. Here's how each section unfolds:

I START WITH STORIES BECAUSE STORIES ARE STICKY. They help us see new connections, forge new insights and shift our thinking. Each chapter digs deep into a specific set of beliefs: about love, parenting, perfectionism, rebellion, religion, connection, diversity and allyship and more—and they all start with stories. I'll explore each chapter's issues through stories from my own experience, weaving in research, science and other wisdom to help shed light on why we believe and behave as we do. I'll describe the tools that have helped me, the therapeutic approaches and modalities I've found useful, both in my own therapy and with others as a doctor and mental health practitioner. I'll share insights grounded in both experience and science on how we can shift our thinking to break free of what's holding us back to allow us to embark on a healthier, happier life. And because I've also benefited from the guidance of friends and colleagues, I've included their "whispered wisdom" in special call-outs in each chapter as well.

I INCLUDE SUMMARIES BECAUSE SUMMARIES HELP US HOLD ON TO INSIGHTS. As a life-long learner, I know summaries help me anchor the insights that bubble to the surface as I read. Record the ones that resonate most for you and review the key takeaways in the Summary section of the Unconditioning Workbook at the end of each chapter, where you may also find new examples to further illuminate and new tactics to consider for tackling the challenges related to the chapter's themes.

I SUGGEST REFLECTIONS BECAUSE REFLECTION MAKES IT YOURS. The beliefs limiting your life may be different from mine, and the Reflection section of the Unconditioning Workbook at the end of each chapter is the place to explore this. Here you'll find questions to consider as you reflect on what you want to unlearn. You're free to answer these questions in the way that works best for you—on these pages or elsewhere—but I promise you they will be most helpful if you take the time to capture your answers somehow. I'm certain you give your time and attention to others throughout your day; make space and time for your journey to give yourself the attention you deserve.

SHARE YOUR INSIGHTS, BECAUSE BY SHARING, WE LEARN AND HEAL TOGETHER. You may wish to share your experiences with loved ones, a therapist or other trusted people in your life, talking through what you're learning and how you're growing. I'd love to hear your experiences too! There are many ways to connect with me and share your insights, lessons and triumphs. Go to samrazafar.com to find out how.

I WELCOME YOU. UNCONDITIONALLY.

Therapy's Alphabet Soup: CBT, DBT, ACT, and More

There are many approaches to psychotherapy, with some practitioners adhering to a single method and others employing a blend. I fall firmly in the blend camp: in my experience as both a patient and a clinician, I have found pathways of understanding and strategies for change in a variety of practices—some work better for some problems. In the pages ahead, you'll see the following therapeutic approaches referenced, and you'll recognize threads from each interwoven into the practices and strategies I recommend along the way.

Cognitive Behavioural Therapy (CBT): One of the most common forms of therapy, CBT is based on the idea that changing thought patterns— cognition—will help you change how you act—behaviour. CBT has been widely researched and its effectiveness is supported by many studies. According to the American Psychological Association, core principles of CBT affirm that psychological problems are based both in faulty ways of thinking and in learned patterns of unhelpful behaviour.[6] CBT places greater emphasis on where you are in your life now as opposed to digging deeply into your history and the causes of your current ways of coping. Learning to face fears, self-calm, recognize distorted thinking, understand why others act as they do and develop better problem-solving skills are all strategies employed in CBT.

Dialectical Behaviour Therapy (DBT): A form of cognitive behaviour treatment, DBT blends CBT with mindfulness practices and has a greater focus on helping with emotional regulation. According to the Cambridge Dictionary online, *dialectical* means "discovering what is true by considering opposite theories." DBT teaches people the apparently opposing strategies of acceptance and change: to accept their experiences and actions as valid while also recognizing the need to make positive changes to manage their emotions and move forward as they strengthen their interpersonal skills.[7] One common strategy in DBT is to replace the word *but* with *and*. For instance, I can be a happy person AND still feel sad. I can feel grateful for my life AND still grieve what was taken from me. I can be a good mother AND still make mistakes that make me cringe. When we get locked into the word *but*, we tend to distance ourselves from uncomfortable emotions. Rather than acknowledging that we can feel sad, we get stuck on saying "but I'm a happy person." Or when confronted with a parenting mistake, we respond with "but I'm a good mother!" Replacing that *but* with *and* allows us to open space to the reality that we can be two opposing things at once: we can be happy people and feel sad sometimes, and we can be good mothers and still make mistakes.

Acceptance and Commitment Therapy (ACT): ACT is an approach that starts from the idea that every life is touched by pain, but that long-term suffering is the result of becoming too focused on our suffering and then also trying to avoid sources of pain, or control and suppress the feelings that arise from pain. Essentially, say proponents of ACT, our lives become constructed around avoidance of pain rather than attraction to what engages and delights us. ACT is grounded in exploring the values and goals by which we wish to live our lives, accepting that we and others are imperfect in our interactions, while committing ourselves to change problematic behaviour. Separating behaviour from shame and blame is key, since those two negative impulses can be part of what keeps us stuck in avoidance. At the same time, acceptance and commitment must be linked: acceptance of behaviour that causes pain to ourselves or others without a commitment to change is simply a way to let oneself off the hook, to dodge responsibility. Linked with a commitment to behave differently in the future, though, acceptance becomes a key step in achieving healthy behaviours and aligning our actions with our values and goals.[8]

Parts Work Therapy: Parts Work Therapy is an umbrella term that applies to a range of therapeutic methods, including Internal Family Systems (IFS), Gestalt Therapy, Ego State Work and others. These therapeutic approaches suggest that we each have a number of sub-personalities, or parts, that affect how we behave and interact with others. These aren't multiple personalities. Rather, they're all parts of one larger self, with none of those parts intrinsically "bad." (Richard Schwartz's book *No Bad Parts: Healing Trauma and Restoring Wholeness with the Internal Family Systems Model* is very helpful in understanding this.[9]) Parts Work Therapy posits that the parts we disown or distance ourselves from can be sources of ongoing pain or missed opportunities for joyful connection.

For instance, disowning our artistic side because we grew up in a family that viewed art as flaky might result in being judgmental towards others who are artistic, even disparaging our own children's artistic interests, and rob us of the chance to connect with pursuits that could bring enjoyment. As well, finding that we are "stuck" when we try to change unhealthy or unhelpful behaviour can be the result of not giving voice to and engaging with a part of ourselves that fears the change we say we want. For instance, saying we want to be more assertive at work while ignoring the part of ourselves that fears being blamed for decisions can lead us to self-sabotage. That inner blame-avoider won't simply disappear, but if we pause to listen to her, we are more likely to find a way forward that holds space for her fear.

Whispered Wisdom

One of the biggest lessons I've learned is: JUST BE YOU. By staying true to who you are, you embrace your strengths, quirks, and imperfections included. This leads to genuine happiness, fulfillment, and a more meaningful life journey.

AZADEH YARAGHI, BRAND STRATEGIST, GOGO TELUGO CREATIVES INC.

CHAPTER ONE:

You Are Here

The two-lane rural road stretched ahead of me. The first days of my Quebec road trip had been spent on busier routes, divided highways of fast-moving eighteen-wheelers and cars filled with summer travellers. It had been easy to get lulled into simply following the traffic, speeding past one exit after another behind vehicles heading to more well-known destinations like Montreal and Quebec City. *Come on*, the traffic whispered to me. *It'll be faster if you stick with us.*

I'd set out on this trip vowing to follow my instincts, promising myself I'd opt for the less travelled roads, but I could feel the highway's urgency tugging me along. I was literally going with the traffic's flow, ignoring the side routes I'd said I would follow. *Nope*, I thought, as I signalled my lane change and headed to the exit, circling back and pointing the car in the direction I'd just come from. I'd been tempted by the last turn-off but blasted past it. If my plan to build my intuitive muscles was going to work, I had to not just hear my gut but act on it too.

That first turn-off didn't yield much: a meander down a side road before circling back up to the highway. But the next one I followed led me to a route closer to the striking vistas of the St. Lawrence, and now, a few days into my journey, another "follow that sign" urge struck me along a quieter two-lane road. "Les Jardins de Métis" said the marker. A rest stop perhaps or community garden, I thought, as I steered the car towards my spur-of-the-moment destination. Instead what I discovered was a twenty-acre oasis, the northernmost garden in eastern North America, filled with azaleas, blue poppies, roses and more.

I'd set out on my journey feeling lost. And now look what I'd found: respite and beauty.

Lost and Found

Have you ever gotten lost in a mall or amusement park? Finding the site map, with its starred "you are here" locator can be a sanity-saver: you can't find your way out until you know where you are. But there are other keys to getting unlost: looking around to see what surrounds you, stopping to consider where you've travelled from (where did you park the car?), thinking about where you want to go and even knowing what supplies you have or what you can get (where's the coffee shop?) to sustain you along the way. And if you've got others with you—thirsty kids or tired companions—you'll take that into account in planning your next steps as well.

That context matters because "lost" and "found" aren't two distinct points on the map. We can be lost anywhere. And found isn't a place, it's a state of mind, a confidence in choosing which road we'll travel—even if we don't know exactly where we'll end up.

For some of us, that feeling of being lost is threatening, scary, like a wave crashing into us, threatening to sweep away all that is familiar and safe. For others, it is a dull ache, a sense that something in our lives isn't quite right. And sometimes being lost is so familiar that we don't even "feel" it until something in our lives shifts, making us aware that all isn't as it should be.

Why Now?

Just a few months before my road trip, in spring 2020, I was standing in front of my bathroom mirror in my downtown Toronto apartment, straightening my hair with the blow dryer and brush, when a flashback overtook me. I felt like I'd time travelled a decade into the past, to a moment when my husband stands over me, twisting my arm in rage because I asked for money to buy diapers for our daughter. My heart pounds, I can't catch my breath, and I have to sit down. A week later, as I ordered food from a local restaurant to be delivered to the apartment, a wave of guilt washed over me. I could hear my ex-mother-in-law's voice in my head, criticizing me as she used to when we shared a house and kitchen during my marriage, telling me how wasteful I was to consider ordering out, how selfish I was to choose dishes I enjoyed or to express any desires of my own at all. It wasn't so much a memory as it was a re-experiencing, the anxiety I felt as intense as it had been in that moment years before.

These weren't the first flashbacks I'd had. A few weeks earlier, the green binding of my expired Pakistani passport, its cover lettered in gold, caught my eye as I cleaned out my closet. On the laminated interior page, next to the photo of sixteen-year-old me, my occupation was listed: housewife. It had been a decade since I'd broken free from my child marriage and built a new life for me and my daughters. I'd shared my story hundreds of times since, in speeches and interviews. I'd even written a damn book about it. But in that moment, in that closet, none of that mattered. A tsunami of pain and grief engulfed me, and for the next several minutes, I sobbed uncontrollably on my closet floor.

"What the hell is going on?" I asked my therapist at my next appointment. We were still in pandemic lockdown, and so we were meeting on Zoom. I rarely had flashbacks anymore, but suddenly, they'd become frequent visitors. Why was this happening now? My marriage was long over. My children and I were safe. *Why now?*

"When was the last time you couldn't leave your house?" he asked. "When was the last time you were this isolated?"

The answer clicked into place: in my marriage. I knew that lockdown and the isolation of my marriage were two different times, two different circumstances, but there were echoes of similarity. My intellect hadn't connected them. But my psyche had.

At the time, I would never have shared this, wouldn't have talked about it in my speeches onstage either. I would have hidden my tears and fears and told no one about what happened in the closet, in the bathroom or as I'd ordered food. I had survived being beaten and abused. I didn't want anyone to think I was broken.

It wasn't the first time I'd asked my therapist the "why now?" question. It had been one of the questions I'd posed when I started working with him a few years earlier. From the outside, I looked happy and safe then: I'd left my husband, gotten a university education and embarked on a successful career, supporting my daughters and our life independently. Things seemed better than they ever had. But as I tried to move on, troubling memories from my childhood were bubbling to the surface, and I was exhausted from working to keep all of it—my feelings of insecurity and inadequacy, my childhood memories—under control. Why, I asked him, was this all happening now, when I should be happier than ever?

"When else could you have coped with it?" he had responded. "When you were holding down four jobs, raising two girls and going to university? When you were trying to dig yourself out of a financial hole and finally get some security? Or when you were a kid trying to keep yourself alive and safe? Your brain knew you couldn't cope with it then, so it put a lid on it and locked it away."

Even more challenging, though, is that traumatic memories often aren't like regular memories. It's as if our brains packed them in a hurry, not taking the time to process, examine or understand them, and so when they resurface, they overwhelm us with their immediacy, bringing us back into a moment that feels like it's happening now rather than in some distant, past "then." Think of it this way: revisiting memories we've processed is a bit like flipping through a photo album from the comfort of a living room couch. Re-experiencing traumatic, unprocessed memories is more like being dropped into the middle of a 3-D virtual reality universe, complete with full sensory experience. Even if you know you're sitting safely on the couch, your heart starts pounding, your hands get clammy, you suddenly have trouble breathing and you feel ready to fight or run.

It wasn't until I was in a safer place—literally and psychologically—that my brain finally said, *Okay, things are pretty stable now, so let's start dealing with that stuff we packed up.* I guess I should have said, *Thanks for waiting, brain.* But what I really wanted to say was *Are you fucking kidding me?*

Understanding Trauma

My marriage wasn't the only trauma I'd faced. When I left my marriage, people in my community called me shameless; people in my family told me I was a bad mother. When I started sharing my story to help break the silence on gender-based abuse, others accused me of defaming my culture and religion for self-promotion.

We live in cultures that praise our strength in putting up with abuse, that see nobility in suffering in silence. As women, we are heralded as superwomen when we are perceived as having "overcome" trauma—a label that can lead us to believe we must continue to overcome without complaint. But when we break that silence and give voice to our trauma, it doesn't take long for those around us to expect us to get over it, get past it—perhaps because it makes them uncomfortable or reminds them of their own trauma—to do whatever it takes to just stop talking about it. If we struggle to move on? Our inability to cope with our trauma is to blame. If we thrive? Our trauma gets the credit for our success: everything happens for a reason, we're told, and we should be grateful that what happened made us stronger.

But we are not here today *because* of what happened to us. We are here *in spite of* what happened to us. And by examining and understanding the impact of trauma on our lives, we can equip ourselves to continue to heal and to ultimately live lives of authenticity, creativity and hope. To do so, we need to explore how we got here, what challenges we face and what new skills we need to build to live healthy, happy lives.

Much of the work around trauma and its impact on mental health has focused on events such as childhood sexual abuse, intimate partner violence, experiences of war or other violence, the aftermath of injury or other significant loss. But as Dr. Gabor Maté so compellingly and compassionately explains in his book *The Myth of Normal*, while not all of us have experienced what he calls capital-T traumas, many more have experienced small-t traumas: hurtful comments, bullying, neglect—not just "bad things happening . . . but also good things not happening."[1] Whether as a result of capital-T or small-t trauma, our connections to our family, our community and wider society are disrupted, and we become disconnected from ourselves in important ways. We carry an emotional wound that either scars over and causes diminished feelings—perhaps numbing or less joy and happiness—or becomes a source of ongoing emotional pain and infection, like an open wound, so we are more volatile and angry.

The results of the pain, fear and sadness that bubble up may be varied: we may seek to soothe ourselves through addictions or other means, we may inflate our egos as a defence against the smallness we feel at our core, we may overcompensate by becoming super-achievers or super-healers trying to save the world, we may become hyper-independent and feel we have to do everything for ourselves or we may adopt the habit of invisibility, erasing ourselves so we don't draw the attention or ire of others. While our specific responses may vary widely, at its root, trauma impairs our "capacity to experience gratitude for the beauty and wonder of life."[2]

Of course, we're rarely adopting these coping strategies consciously: because the wounds often happen in childhood (though some may certainly happen in adulthood), our coping mechanisms cause distortions in our emotional development. But how we cope becomes "normal" to us at least, just part of who we are. Our brain isn't trying to screw us up; it's simply doing the best it can in that moment to protect us. And coping mechanisms developed in childhood emerge from a child's understanding and utilize the limited emotional skills of a child, creating what might look like solutions but become problems as they persist, while coping mechanisms developed in response to adult trauma may reflect the limited options we perceived at the time of the trauma.

It's also important to note that while the trauma instigates the process that leads to emotional disruption, the trauma itself is not the only key to our later problems. Our response to it is also vital. If this sounds like victim blaming, it's not. In fact, it opens up a powerful opportunity for victim empowerment. Because while we can't change what happened to us—the traumatic events of the past—we can, over time and with insight and support, change our reactions to those events. We don't have to remain locked into a child's coping mechanisms or an adult's perceived limited options: as we know and understand more, we can use our more developed emotional skills to choose a better path forward—and we can extend compassion to ourselves, for coping as best we could with the skills and insights we had at the time.

Think of it this way: if you expressed this as a math equation, it wouldn't be "Experience = Outcome." It would be "Experience × Response = Outcome." And being able to change your emotional response means you can change the outcome.

Getting Inside Your Head

It also helps to understand what's happening in the brain when we experience trauma, especially as children. The various parts of our brains have different functions or specialities. The amygdala, for instance, is part of the limbic system, the most primitive part of the brain that helps us deal with emotion and responses to emotion. The amygdala is believed to help detect danger and respond to threats, giving it a central role in processing and responding to fear, anxiety and aggression.

You've likely heard about the differing roles of the left and right sides of the brain: for most people, the right being more concerned with vision, spatial reckoning, tactile sensations, emotion and intuition, while the left side is more analytical, specializing in language and sequence. You could say the right side of the brain experiences or feels life while the left side of the brain knows how to talk about it. When we're born, our right brain is more highly developed, and our left brain gets to work as we start to learn language. There's plenty of communication between the two hemispheres as they are highly connected by brain fibres, and contrary to popular myth, there is no "dominant side." The neurons in our brain are busily creating networks and pathways to coordinate what we're feeling and how we respond to and understand the information flowing into our heads from all our senses. In those early years, the brain is developing at a dizzying speed: by the time we're three years old, our brains are almost 80 percent of their adult size.[3] But they're still far from fully developed. The human brain continues to change, grow and strengthen through two more decades, reaching maturity in our mid to late twenties.

So what happens if we experience trauma in our early years? Our neural pathways can become over-focused on responding to trauma, leading to lower development in other areas. To use an absurd image, it's a bit like having your body decide it needs to put most of its energy into growing your left leg and, as a result, leaves fewer resources for your right leg's growth. The fact that you have trouble later isn't just caused by your brain's overdevelopment in its trauma response— your longer left leg—it's also compounded by underdevelopment in other areas—your shorter right leg. In real terms, trauma in our early years can disrupt our ability to form stable, healthy attachments with others, delay our cognitive development and impair our ability to regulate our emotions, while trauma in our teen years can hinder our learning, social relationships and educational success.[4]

Things are further complicated by the fact that trauma in childhood may have occurred before we had the language skills to describe what we were experiencing, and almost certainly before we had the emotional or analytical skills to understand it. As well, as children, we often didn't have the ability to fight (we were powerless) or flee (especially if the trauma was inflicted by a loved one, such as a parent). So our dominant response becomes to "freeze"—we dissociate. We learn to be outside our own bodies and to detach from our feelings, boundaries and intuition. That's why childhood trauma is so detrimental to our connection with ourselves: detachment and dissociation become our dominant emotional roadmap, and we don't know how to fight for ourselves, set effective boundaries, make good decisions about who to trust or act on our intuition.

And even if our trauma happened in adulthood, the fear or other strong emotions it provoked may have resulted in powerful fight, freeze or flee responses that overpower our capacity to reason our way through what we experienced and what we re-experience when triggered.

How we coped with that fear in the past may have allowed us to survive, but it may not be effective in coping with today's fears, today's real life. When I was growing up, my parents' relationship was volatile. They were locked in a cycle of violence that followed a typical circular pattern: a blow-up, followed by remorse, which cycled into a honeymoon period, followed by a slow build-up of tension and another explosion—and so on and so on, over and over again. Very early on, I became attuned to spotting the telltale signs of an imminent eruption, and when I did, I would do my best to try to cajole my father into a better mood, protect my sisters during the fights and comfort my mother in the aftermath. I was like a lighthouse keeper, always watching the horizon for storm clouds, ready to jump into action and try to save those around me from the crashing waves and howling winds. As an adult, I carried these coping mechanisms with me, becoming adept at spotting and heading off problems.

Or so I thought. In reality I was focused on trying to spot and prevent trouble, expending my energy on fear—solving problems that truly weren't problems yet—and it left me little energy to enjoy life. The skills I'd used to survive as a child were not the skills I needed to thrive as an adult.

It was as if I were living in a house with shaky foundations. I wanted to make the house mine, create a space that was healthy and happy for my daughters and me, but until I addressed the cracked basement walls, I couldn't move forward. Sure, I could try to paper over the cracks, but I'd just be putting off the problems—and costing myself more in the long run. And here's the thing: with a real-life renovation, you can move out of the house while you get the work done. When your life is the house, you've got no choice but to keep living in it.

Like I said, *Thanks, brain.*

Emotions in Search of an Explanation

When we haven't done the emotional work to heal our past trauma, those overdeveloped neural pathways connected to trauma are easily triggered. As Dr. Bessel Van Der Kolk puts it in his book *The Body Keeps the Score*: "When something reminds traumatized people of the past, their right brain reacts as if the traumatic event were happening in the present. But because their left brain is not working very well, they may not be aware that they are reexperiencing and reenacting the past—they are just furious, enraged, ashamed or frozen."[5] The emotions we experience in this situation can be very powerful, even overpowering, because they are responding to something traumatic. And when our fear or anger is triggered, our brains look for something to attach that emotion to: we're angry because our partner forgot to pick up the milk, we're afraid because our high-school-aged daughter is fifteen minutes late getting home. But our responses are out of proportion to what we're attaching them to—the forgotten milk is not the problem, the echo of the past that triggered our fear is.

Early in the pandemic, after lockdown had ended, I'd needed to fly to a speaking engagement. I'd always loved travel, but now things felt . . . off. A day or two before my scheduled flight, I noticed I was booked on a Boeing 737 Max, the model that had been grounded in 2019 after two crashes. The planes had been declared airworthy and were back in service. But my gut told me no way. Rebooking my route was enormously expensive—it rang in at almost $3,000—and meant multiple connections. But I was ready to pay any price necessary to avoid a flight I was certain was going to crash.

That 737 I'd been booked on did not drop from the sky. Sure, my rebooked flight brought me safely to my destination—but I was exhausted and $3,000 poorer than I'd have been if I'd stuck with my original booking.

But aren't we told to trust our intuition? After all, we've all heard the stories of people who trusted their gut, rebooked their flight and avoided the crash, right? Still, the reality is that planes don't crash that often. And while I'm certain I'm not the only person to rebook a flight that didn't crash, I might be the only one you've heard admit it.

So what was really going on the day I rebooked that flight? The pandemic's free-floating fear was still everywhere. Things at the airport—a place I'd always felt comfortable before—were bound to be weird: I knew the procedures on the day of my flight would be different than they had been pre-pandemic, and that knowledge provoked more tension. I also hadn't done a live speaking engagement in several months, and so that anxiety bubbled below the surface.

I was swimming in fear and my amygdala was on high alert. And that fear triggered the neural pathways in my brain connected to my past traumas—my childhood, my marriage. The specific underlying fear triggered was that if something happened to me, my girls would be sent back to their father and pushed into forced marriages. It was a possibility that had terrified me when I'd been married, but now, even though we were independent and safe, it lurked in the background. The thought of my children being left powerless—as I had once been—haunted me. Rather than sharpening my ability to cope, those misfiring neurons clouded it, and panic bubbled up. I was afraid. *What is making me afraid and what can I do to resolve that fear?* my panicked brain wondered, as it noticed "Boeing 737 Max" on my itinerary. *That's it!* shouted my brain, as rebooking the ticket became the obvious—and costly—solution.

My childhood had taught me to scan for danger and jump into action to head it off. But as an adult, I needed to unlearn that impulse.

What should I have done before scrambling to rebook my flight? I needed to hit pause and sit with my fear, to get my conscious brain to understand where the fear response was coming from and to consider whether that fear was warranted by the current situation or was being triggered by a past pattern or event. In my case, the flight itself wasn't the main issue. What was bubbling up was a deep-seated fear I'd had for years about leaving my kids alone. I needed to hear that fear clearly, so that I could speak back to it clearly: my daughters were not powerless. I was no longer in a marriage where they could be taken away from me and married off as children. I had already created a new life for them that was safe and empowering. I had raised them to be independent, strong-minded, intelligent young women who know how to stand up for themselves. And I had travelled the world by myself and returned home safe and sound after every trip.

Yes, some situations do require immediate action, but in many instances, pausing to assess what we're really feeling rather than rushing to purge the emotion is essential. Making decisions when the past is clouding the present is like driving in the fog: it's easy to take a wrong turn.

You Can't Heal What You Hate

Think of the language we use to describe past trauma: the skeleton in the closet, the monster in the box, the demons of the past. And while recalling traumatic events can be scary, these images draw at least some of their power from the shame we attach to them. That power expands when we blame ourselves for being weak. It becomes scarier when we shame ourselves for being afraid. It controls us when we hate ourselves for not being able to control it.

And ironically, when it comes to abuse suffered at the hands of parents or caregivers, we can be quicker to extend compassion to them—"they did their best"—than we are to extend compassion to our childhood selves. We're often understanding of the adults who failed us, while we carry into our own adulthood the shame and blame for our childhood inability to protect ourselves, to stand up for ourselves, to save ourselves or even, illogically, to stop the bad things from happening at all.

But we can't heal what we hate, especially when that hate ends up directed at ourselves. An example: As we were preparing to publish my memoir, *A Good Wife*, my book editor sent me a mock-up of the cover the publisher was proposing. I remember staring at the image: the bejewelled face of seventeen-year-old me on my wedding day stared back at me, my husband's torso towering above, fist clenched, his face hidden behind the book's title. My stomach churned as a wave of disgust overtook me—not aimed at him, but at her. I didn't want her—that abused girl, that naive child who'd been forced into marriage—on the cover of my book. That girl in a red and gold headscarf wasn't me: she was my "before." I was the successful "after": the confident raven-haired woman in a banker's power-blue dress who'd appeared in *Toronto Life* magazine.

I didn't like the cover. I wanted to forget I'd once been that girl, to pretend she was no longer part of me.

"Take a few days and think about it," my editor responded after receiving my lengthy "why we should redesign the cover" email.

But wait, I can hear you saying, *hadn't you just written a book about that girl and what she'd gone through? Surely you'd worked through your trauma?*

Ah, the power of denial is strong.

Yes, I'd written about what I'd been through—but my focus was on sharing what I'd overcome in my marriage. I wasn't ready to dig deeply into the trauma preceding my marriage, and so I buried the memories of my parents' explosive relationship under what Dr. Maté calls the "bushel of compassion." My portrayal of my parents, their marriage and our childhood home as largely positive in my book wasn't a lie: it was how I perceived it at that time in my life. My father had struggled with employment and finances. My mother had struggled with my father. I told myself things weren't that bad growing up, especially compared to how they'd been in my marriage.

I wasn't ready to share stories of standing naked in the shower, my childhood body being beaten with coat hangers. I wasn't ready to give voice to my father's violent explosions and emotional manipulations in turning me against my mother or to expose my mother's constant withholding of love, the way my sisters and I were bullied into subservience and compliance.

Perversely, I didn't attach the shame I felt to my family—I attached it to me, to the child who'd endured it. And so I was doing my best to do what my parents and husband had done to her as well: to abandon her, shaming her as if she were the one to blame. I didn't think of her as an extension of me—I thought of her as someone I had left behind.

In the days following my email to my editor about the book cover, I travelled to Ottawa for a speaking engagement at a high school graduation ceremony. In the speech—written before receiving the cover proof—I spoke about accepting yourself, loving yourself, being yourself. As the sixteen-, seventeen- and eighteen-year-olds paraded across the stage to receive their diplomas, stopping for selfies with me as they passed, high-fiving each other, I was struck by how young they were, how beautiful they were, how much I wanted to protect them. What if they'd gone through what I'd experienced at their age? Would I be disgusted by them? Would I not want them on a book cover? Of course not! I'd feel compassion for them, want to hug and celebrate them.

That evening, I sat in my hotel room, staring at the photo of seventeen-year-old me. I realized that I was abandoning her as others had, and I couldn't stop my tears. I wanted to reach into the cover and embrace her, to tell her I love her and am proud of her. "Thank you for fighting back," I said to her. "Thank you for believing in your dreams. Thank you for not giving up. Thank you for doing the best you could. Because if you had given up, I wouldn't exist today. You are safe. You are me, and you will always be part of me."

I'd shared what had happened in my marriage. And while I still wasn't fully ready to share publicly what had happened in my childhood home, I was ready to extend compassion and care to the girl I'd been then, the girl who lived on inside me.

"You're right," I told my editor when we spoke. "That seventeen-year-old girl is the real hero of my story. Because if she hadn't done what she did, I wouldn't exist. She should be on the cover."

Tackling Trauma

In the early days of tackling my past traumas, my therapist used a technique to help me manage unpacking the past without having it take over my whole life. At the beginning of each session, he would guide me through a visualization exercise, where I would choose which box of memories and experiences to open that day. Then, at the end of the session, we'd do the reverse, packing the box back up and locking it in his office so that I could go out into the world and deal with the rest of my life—at home with my girls, at work and in the other important relationships in my life. I needed to deal with the past, but I also needed to live in the present.

That image of file boxes has stuck with me. Think of your memory as a file room, filled with shelves of boxes. Some are orderly. Some are filled with photos and memorabilia we're happy to revisit. But others are messy, scary, taped shut, bulging. And sometimes, when something changes in our world, the ground shakes and a big ugly box falls off a shelf. We might try to reshelve it, walk around it, stack other stuff on top of it, but odds are, it's going to remain an obstacle until we unpack it, process it and put it in a better, more orderly box.

It can be tempting to just wait until a box tumbles off a shelf, forcing us to deal with it. But it's also possible to make deliberate choices about tidying our file rooms, choosing which boxes to open and when and getting some help with the heavy lifting and some advice on improving our filing system. We have the power to develop healthy skills and strategies to process our losses and heal our emotional wounds. It can be sweaty, hard work, but it's worth it.

- **RECOGNITION IS THE FIRST STEP:** Acknowledging that we need to make changes is a significant, essential and brave first step. It takes resolve and commitment to continue our journey of growth and transformation, but pause to pat yourself on the back for taking this first step.

- **THERAPY DOESN'T HAVE TO BE IN A THERAPIST'S OFFICE (OR ZOOM ROOM):** Professional help can be enormously helpful in finding our way, but it's not accessible to all. If you're able to afford—and find—the right professional help for you, it can be life-changing. I was fortunate to work with a trauma psychologist for five years who was instrumental in helping me reclaim myself. My daughters and I have benefited from group therapy. But I've also walked away from therapists who weren't quite right. And I've found insights on the pages of books and healing in moments of joy sparked by doing the things I love: cooking, travelling and driving.

- **HEALING IS HUSTLE:** I'm not going to lie. Healing the wounds of the past requires effort and perseverance. It's like exercise— no matter what the charlatans tell you, there's no quick way to get physically or emotionally fit. But the good news is that the strength you build today will help you leap over the challenges you'll face tomorrow.

- **YOU CAN'T FIX WHAT YOU DON'T FACE:** Around the world, many countries are engaged in national truth and reconciliation processes. Here in Canada, that process is focused on grappling with Canada's relationship with Indigenous peoples. And again and again, as atrocities such as the unmarked graves of children who died while in residential schools and the effects of intergenerational trauma and other realities are discussed, inevitably a chorus of "Can't we just move on?" emerges. But whether our goal is to heal relationships across cultures, across communities, across kitchen tables or within ourselves, we cannot heal what remains hidden. Recognition and remorse are essential to reconciliation.

- **HEALTHY SKIN, NOT ARMOUR:** It can be tempting to think that emotional health after trauma will be like a coat of armour you put on. But armour is heavy, inflexible, sweaty and hard—not a great model for emotional health! Emotional trauma can be compared to a physical wound or infection. Sometimes that wound needs to be cleaned out or stitched up. Sometimes there will be scars. But what we're aiming for isn't emotional armour: it's healthy emotional skin, a remarkably flexible, soft and yet powerful barrier that keeps us healthy while still allowing us to feel.

- **BE CAREFUL ABOUT INTELLECTUALIZING TRAUMA:** Our bodies carry both trauma and the wisdom to heal. Often, through therapy and reading, we intellectualize trauma. It can help to explore therapies that allow emotions to move through our bodies: yoga, massage, bodily soothing, grounding, breathing and other forms of bodywork. For example, I often feel heaviness in my shoulders and I've realized that by saying things like "all these responsibilities rest on my shoulders," I may be exacerbating the feelings.

- **WITH PRACTISE AND PATIENCE, WE CAN LEARN TO OBSERVE OUR EMOTIONS AND CHOOSE WHEN TO ACT:** Emotion doesn't have to equal immediate action, and as we grow emotionally, we can learn to pause, assess and choose our course of action. You'll hear some trumpet the value of trusting your instincts, but for those of us whose instincts have been distorted by trauma, we need to learn to trust our insights as well. Yes, pay attention when emotion bubbles up, but recognize you may need to sit with that emotion before it reveals the truth of what it's trying to tell you—and then you'll be ready to act.

- **COMPASSION AND ACCOUNTABILITY ARE KEY:** In our relationships with others, compassion without accountability makes us doormats, while accountability without compassion makes us despots. We need to extend both compassion and accountability to ourselves, as well, forgiving our human failings while striving to be better tomorrow than we are today.

- **HEALING OUR PAST TRAUMA OPENS US TO TODAY'S JOYS AND TOMORROW'S POSSIBILITIES:** Trauma's habits can steal joy from our lives even if we find a safe harbour, as we end up focusing on heading off tomorrow's potential disaster rather than enjoying today's calm seas. Doing the work to unlearn trauma's faulty lessons allows us to more clearly see where we are, do what needs doing, and connect with life's beauty and joy.

Voices from the Past

As fear, pain or other powerful emotions—even joy and excitement—course through our brains, our ability to cope with them may be further complicated by the chattering of voices offering their opinions on what we're doing or are about to do. My mother-in-law berating me for ordering takeout food during the pandemic wasn't the only voice from my past whispering in my ear. My ex-husband's voice disparaged my ambition: "Who do you think you are?" My mother's voice berated me for the clothes I wore, cautioned me not to view my successes as my own: "If you disappoint Allah by showing your skin, He will take away all your successes and burn your skin over and over again for eternity." A former boyfriend told me no man would love a woman whose success outshone his own: "You make men feel small."

Even when we manage to distance ourselves from those who have caused us harm, physical disconnection doesn't necessarily equal emotional disconnection. People can be out of our lives but still live in our heads. As clinical psychologist Steven C. Hayes, one of the originators of Acceptance and Commitment Therapy (ACT), and his co-authors Kirk D. Strosahl and Kelly G. Wilson put it, we may finally be in the driver's seat but still have a busload of passengers chattering behind us, doubting our choices, discounting our successes, telling us we are headed in the wrong direction.[6]

On good days, I can turn down the volume—but on days when I feel low or discouraged, they seem to sense it, their voices rising in a chorus of undercutting. My response in the past? To try to fill the air with other voices affirming my value, to work harder—the most socially acceptable addiction of all—accruing awards and accolades in the hope that voices praising my success would drown them out.

And still, their damaging chatter echoed in my ears.

Whispered Wisdom

Honour the person you were meant to be, not the person others want you to be. Do what you are passionate about. Not sure? Be still. Look back. You have always known.

DR. ELIZABETH CHARLES, PH.D.

What Skills Do We Need?

I should be able to handle this. I'd been in a low mood all day, not really aware of why until my irritation spiked when I saw again the voicemail indicating a message from my ex-husband. I'd listened to it earlier in the day but neglected to delete it. We'd been divorced for years and communicated only when necessary to address issues related to our daughters. But despite my efforts to limit our contact, each time I heard his voice, I was thrown into a funk, sometimes experiencing flashbacks or nightmares as a result. If a friend had told me she was having this experience, my advice would have been simple: *Tell him not to call you. Of course his voice is triggering—you spent years listening to him criticize and abuse you!*

But when it came to setting my own boundaries, I hesitated. *Shouldn't I be able to manage hearing his voice? Shouldn't I just grow up? Why am I so weak?*

The voice in my head berating me sounded more and more like him. Why did I believe I just had to put up with it, when there were other ways to draw boundaries that would mean I didn't have to hear his voice at all?

Setting boundaries is a skill. And in the chaotic household I grew up in, where emotional manipulation was the way my family related to each other, there were no boundaries. As a child-bride, I entered a relationship with my husband and his family in which boundaries were not mine to draw: I was to obey the lines others set down.

"It's so much harder to learn boundary setting as an adult," my therapist told me as he countered my self-blame. "And when you're learning a new skill, you will fail. You're not at one hundred percent— no one is. But you're going to keep learning, and you'll be stronger."

And he was right.

Trauma robs us of so many skills: boundary setting, emotional regulation, clear judgment about our own needs and the needs of others. But we can build those skills as adults, with support, courage and self-compassion. And I'll show you how in the pages that follow.

Hearing my ex-husband's voice made me feel awful. And there was no need for me to hear it. It was okay—even healthy!—for me to draw a clearer line. I started communicating by email and text and he followed my lead, responding via those same platforms.

No one is ever 100 percent. I know I'm not. But like you, I'm a work in progress, working at progressing.

Whispered Wisdom

When I have an encounter with
self-honesty, I am faced with two choices:
either honouring the truth and being willing to pay
the cost for that choice or, ignoring it, remain in
the status quo and continue betraying myself.

DR. ANDREA ALVAREZ, MD, FRCPC,

PSYCHIATRIST, ASSISTANT CLINICAL PROFESSOR,

McMASTER UNIVERSITY

The Trauma Olympics

When we talk about trauma, it can be easy to fall into comparing or min-imizing. We rank our trauma compared to others' and use that ranking to decide who is entitled to sympathy and whose behaviour should be excused because of past difficulties. Or we dismiss trauma—our own or others'—because it has been "survived." *You're all right now*, goes the thinking, *so it couldn't have been that bad.* "Look where you are today," my mother has told me more than once. "All that you went through was Allah's way of getting you where you are."

What doesn't kill you makes you stronger, goes the saying. And I call bull-shit. What doesn't kill you doesn't make you stronger—it harms you, it robs you of joy, it makes your life more difficult than it should be.

If you are stronger after trauma, YOU deserve the credit for doing the hard work to survive, heal and thrive, not the trauma. And if you are struggling? Don't blame yourself. Seek the help you need, from people who believe you and believe *in* you. Emotional healing is possible, for all of us.

What About Changing the World We Live In?

There's an inspirational saying that keeps popping up in my Instagram feed: "Keep calm and stay strong." The first time I saw it, my immediate response was "Hell no—raise hell and change the world!"

And then I thought, *Well, yes. But, no.*

Clear as mud, right? Here's what I mean. I get my energy from speaking onstage, from connecting with people, from taking part in projects and events that change the way people think and act. I want to speak the truth and change the world! But I can't do that without focusing on my own healing as well—by keeping calm and staying strong. It's the old "put on your own oxygen mask first" rule of life and airline safety: you're unlikely to save others if you don't save yourself.

And even then, you're not required to safely land the plane. We live in a culture that places enormous pressure on people who've experienced trauma to not only survive and thrive, but do the work of making the world a better place while they're at it. And that's just bullshit. If, as you are working to make yourself whole and healthy after trauma, you feel inclined to take on some of the work of trying to change your corner of the world, bravo! I see you, sister (and brother), and I thank you. But it's also perfectly okay—indeed, essential—for you to focus on your own healing: to keep calm and stay strong. Which is world-changing in its own way too.

Unconditioning Workbook

- "Lost" and "found" aren't two distinct points on your emotional map. You can be lost anywhere, even in circumstances that look to others as if they are ideal. And found isn't a place, it's a state of mind, a confidence in choosing your path forward.

- We are not here today *because* of what happened to us. We are here *in spite of* what happened to us. And by examining and understanding the impact of trauma on our lives, we can equip ourselves to continue to heal and to ultimately live lives of authenticity, creativity and hope.

- Trauma in our early years can disrupt our ability to form stable, healthy attachments with others, delay our cognitive development and impair our ability to regulate our emotions, while trauma in our teen years can hinder our learning, social relationships and educational success. Even if our trauma happened in adulthood, the fear or other strong emotions provoked by what happened may have resulted in powerful fight, freeze or flee responses that overpower our capacity to reason our way through what we experience when triggered.

- The skills we used to survive as children may not be the skills we need to thrive as adults. Our childhood selves did their best: they deserve our compassion and our thanks as our adult selves take over the work required to heal and move forward.

- Making decisions when the past is clouding the present is like driving in the fog: it's easy to take a wrong turn.
- Trauma's power expands when we blame ourselves for being weak. It becomes scarier when we shame ourselves for being afraid. And it controls us when we hate ourselves for not being able to control it. We can't heal what we hate, especially when that hate is directed at ourselves.
- People can be out of our lives but still live in our heads. Physical disconnection doesn't necessarily equal emotional disconnection.
- Emotion doesn't have to equal immediate action. As we grow emotionally, we can learn to pause, assess and choose our course of action.
- Trauma robs us of many skills: boundary setting, emotional regulation and clear judgment about our own needs and the needs of others. But we can build those skills as adults, with support, courage and self-compassion. Doing the work to unlearn trauma's faulty lessons allows us to more clearly see where we are, do what we need to do and connect with life's beauty and joy.

Reflection: Why Won't They Just Say They're Sorry?

"I just want my parents to see how they hurt me."

"He needs to say he's sorry!"

"I don't understand why she just doesn't get it!"

When we've been harmed by someone—a parent, a caregiver, a lover or friend—it's easy to get locked into wanting to hear "I'm sorry." Sometimes we make it our mission to make them realize what they did was wrong, as if we need them to validate our pain. It's a natural impulse: as children, we sought validation from our parents when we were hurt, turned to them for a kiss to make it better, an acknowledgement of our pain. And when our parents or others diminished our pain, told us to stop our whining or worse or didn't believe us when we told them someone hurt or violated us? We learned to suppress our hurt and doubt our responses—and sometimes got trapped in a toxic pattern of seeking the approval and validation of those who hurt us or denied our distress, hoping validation from the person who harmed us would heal us. But should someone who has used their power to hurt us be trusted to heal us? We don't need to let them continue to have that hold over us: with work, we can find the power to heal within ourselves.

You might be expecting me to counsel forgiveness. And if that feels like the right route for you, go for it. Forgiving someone can be a powerful way to release *ourselves* from the toxicity of rage, hatred or resentment. As Maya Angelou once explained to Oprah, sometimes forgiveness involves saying "I'm finished with you."[7] But know this too: forgiveness isn't necessary for you to move on.

These are some things to think about when considering forgiveness:

- **FORGIVENESS IS A GIFT YOU ARE NOT OBLIGED TO GIVE:** It is perfectly okay to opt not to forgive someone who has hurt you. The key is to unlock yourself from the disruptive emotions connected to them and the harm they caused so they no longer hijack your emotions and attention. This takes work, and therapy can help. You know what else can help? Creative cursing: "May their nose hairs be ingrown, their banking details shared on the dark web, their sleep interrupted at 2:47 a.m. for eternity, and their organs attacked by disruptive but non-deadly disorders." Creative characterizations can help as well. One accomplished friend, a woman of colour who has often been a trailblazer in her field, has faced road-blocking haters and underminers in her professional career. "I just think of them as the chlamydia of my existence, the flies on my ass," she told me. "Nasty attitude infections that you need to blast with mental antibiotics!" Therapy is still an option. But the cursing and characterizing can help too.

- **YOU CAN CHOOSE TO FORGIVE—AND STILL LOCK THE DOOR:** You may decide forgiving someone for the harm they've caused feels right for you, but you're under no obligation to let that person back into your life. "I forgive you— but you're not welcome here" is a perfectly reasonable response, especially—but not only—in situations where someone has shown themselves to be unwilling or incapable of changing behaviour that places you or those you care about in harm's way. Forgiveness isn't a free pass to cause future harm.

- **YOU MAY OPT FOR RECONCILIATION:** When is forgiveness necessary? If your intention is to maintain a relationship. Holding a grudge within an ongoing relationship locks you into unproductive, unhealthy patterns. If you're committed to the relationship, seek help in finding your way to forgiveness, with compassion and accountability on both sides.

- **FORGIVENESS SHOULD NOT BE USED AS AN ENDLESS DEBT:** If you've forgiven someone, it's not fair to bring that forgiveness up again and again in subsequent disagreements to shame or manipulate them. That's toxic behaviour. Still, neither is it healthy to completely forget what happened, especially if the pattern of behaviour continues. Let's say a partner cheats on you and after working through the betrayal, you decide to forgive. While it's unfair to bring up that past cheating in every argument afterwards, it's also harmful to tolerate new episodes of cheating. Forgiveness that doesn't move on is false—but so is an apology that doesn't result in changed behaviour.

- **FORGIVENESS ISN'T A DESTINATION, IT'S A PATH:** Forgiveness is a dynamic, continuous practice of letting go of resentment. You may choose to forgive someone and still find yourself triggered to feel anger towards them for the harm caused, especially if some of those impacts aren't immediately apparent. That's okay: anger is a valid response to recognizing that a boundary has been violated. But pushing anger down or burying it inevitably increases resentment and undermines our efforts to forgive. As emotionally healthy adults—or those striving to be—we can choose how to channel our anger in productive, positive ways. Give yourself the space and time to listen to and decode your anger. What is your anger telling you? What is it trying to reveal to you? It may be telling you that you need extra help or a conversation with the other person, or that you need to work to identify your triggers. In an ongoing relationship, it is healthy and reasonable to let someone know that, while you are committed to forgiving, you sometimes struggle with it. This isn't the same as using forgiveness as an excuse for ongoing shaming: the focus isn't on making the other party feel awful, but rather is on recognizing the emotional challenges you are grappling with, being honest about that and seeking their help in coming up with a joint strategy to build a healthier relationship.

Explore your options with these exercises:

- **Craft a creative curse:** If you've chosen not to forgive, give yourself permission to move on and allow yourself the satisfaction of a final absurdly creative curse. What's yours?

May their _____ become _____;
their _____ end up _____; and their
_____ turn into _____.

- **You're forgiving, not forgetting:** Sometimes it can be tempting to ignore why we've chosen to cut someone out of our lives. If you're opting to forgive and lock the door, write down your reasons for severing your ties—in case you're tempted to unlock the door.

I am locking the door to _____ because _____
_____.

- **You've chosen to travel Reconciliation Road:** What are your reasons for extending the gift of compassion and forgiveness? What accountability do you require—of yourself and the person you are forgiving?

I am forgiving _____ for _____ _____
_____ because _____
_____. The accountability I need from _____
is _____. I'm holding
myself accountable within this relationship by _____
_____.

CHAPTER TWO

A Real Mother

How does a nineteen-year-old, isolated in a new country and trapped in an abusive marriage, parent? A crying baby might anger her husband, and so she rushes to push a pacifier into her baby's mouth at the first sign of whimpering. She trains her baby to play quietly in the basement bedroom so no one else in the house is disturbed. Later, because a child's misbehaviour in public means a mother's punishment in private, Mom gives in at the first sign of a tantrum so her toddler stays calm and quiet—but also stuffs a scary clown mask into the diaper bag, telling her little girl that if she acts up, the monster in the bag will be mad at her. She quizzes her child on her colours and numbers and alphabet, desperate to prove to her parents-in-law that she's a good mom by showing how smart her little one is. Later, she keeps the girl up past her bedtime doing spelling bee drills to ensure she takes first prize in a grade school competition, turning learning into a test of endurance. She doesn't see anxiety's tentacles wrapping around her daughter's psyche, won't know until later the clown is her daughter's nightmare visitor well into her teens.

How does a twenty-seven-year-old with an angry husband, two young daughters and no income of her own parent? She thinks her girls are safe as long as her husband's venomous words and punishing hands seek her as their target, her gaze so focused on him she doesn't see her eight-year-old huddled under the coffee table, her younger daughter hiding in the closet praying to God to make her daddy stop hitting her mommy. Later, as the young mother cries in the kitchen, her eight-year-old wraps her arms around her. "Mommy, are you staying because of me and Saarah?" the girl asks. The twenty-seven-year-old is stunned. She has started to think about leaving but is still too overwhelmed by the questions she doesn't have answers to: Where would they live? How would she support them? Could they survive? "What do you mean?" she asks her daughter. "Please don't stay because of us, Mommy. We won't be happy until you're happy."

How does a twenty-nine-year-old single mom holding down multiple jobs while studying for her university exams parent? She declares her ten-year-old her best friend and partner, praising her maturity as she relies on the preteen to help make life manageable. She calls her five-year-old the family cheerleader, not seeing the younger girl's impulse to keep the peace and cheer people up might mask less sunny emotions. And while she drifts from the faith she was raised in, she makes sure her girls memorize passages of religious text, fulfilling her husband's separation agreement demands.

How does a thirty-three-year-old junior banking professional parent when her teenager tells her she's never had a childhood? "You should be grateful," she hears herself shouting. "I was almost married at your age!"

"Just because you had different problems doesn't mean my problems aren't real," the teen shouts back. It will be months later that the mother discovers her daughter is self-harming.

How did I parent?

Fearfully.

Protectively.

Imperfectly.

As best I could.

Whispered Wisdom

Give yourself permission to not feel "okay" or "good" all the time. Often there is a perceived pressure to skip over the tough times and reclaim a sense of normalcy as fast as possible. But it's only once we genuinely pause and allow ourselves time to honour our emotions that we begin to heal through self-compassion, resiliency, and authenticity.

EMMA HARASETH, DIVERSITY & INCLUSION LEADER

On-the-Job Training

How do we learn to be parents? Our earliest teachers are our own parents. From our first hours, we learn. Do our parents pick us up when we cry? Are we fed and warm? Are we changed when we need to be? Does someone gaze into our eyes with love, smile at us, laugh? Are we comforted when we're sad, cheered on for our accomplishments? Are our interests nurtured? Our curiosity welcomed?

These early days and months of our lives—and later, our children's lives—are crucial to emotional and psychological development. We are wired to seek and make connections. That need for attachment is grounded in what is, from an evolutionary point of view, the most ancient part of our brain: our brainstem. Our need for interactions with others originates in the same part of our brain where we crave food, according to a recent MIT study.[1] Other research has found that we "feel" social exclusion and rejection through the same physiological mechanisms triggered by physical pain.[2]

The pattern established between a child and their primary caregiver can set the course for how that child engages with the world and the people in it. Dubbed "attachment theory" by twentieth-century psychiatrist and psychoanalyst John Bowlby, these patterns are characterized as being "secure" or "insecure." As their needs for food, connection, warmth and other life necessities are met, children who have secure attachment to their primary caregiver come to understand that they are protected, a feeling allowing them to cope with fear and explore their worlds knowing they can return to the safe base of the person looking after them. Children whose emotional and physical needs are not met, or whose needs are inconsistently met, may develop insecure attachment patterns. While there are a number of subtypes of insecure patterns, essentially they all affect children's ability to cope with fear and stress, to manage their own emotions, to connect with others and to feel able—or not—to explore the world around them. While later life experiences and insights may mean that those who experience insecure attachment can still lead emotionally healthy lives, children who benefit from secure attachment as youngsters have an emotional head start.

But children and parents don't exist in isolation: they are also part of communities and cultures that can influence approaches to parenting and childhood emotional development. Some cultures may prize independence while others emphasize close mother-child bonds. Parenting in some conservative religious traditions may value obedience and subservience while approaches in more liberal settings may rate children's autonomy and decision-making more highly.

Of course, we're not destined to parent as our communities expect or as our parents parented. We might react against the parenting approach we grew up with, replacing strictness with a more relaxed approach—or an anything-goes attitude with a clearer set of rules. We're influenced by the partner we choose, by the social circles we move in, by the culture around us. We learn, too, from our children themselves, shifting our responses as parents according to how our children behave, and, if we have more than one child, to what we've learned by parenting our other children. For those of us who are immigrant or first-generation parents trying to bridge cultures, the push and pull of how we were raised with "how it's done here" can present its own challenges.

And so sometimes our learning means unlearning: unravelling the impact of damaging patterns established in our family of origin, pushing back against unhealthy influences in our adult relationships and grappling with our own parenting mistakes and failures along the way.

If this sounds like a lifetime of opportunities to screw things up . . . well, it can be. And so some of us opt for a parenting approach based on never having to admit we were wrong, while those of us weighed down with mommy guilt end up feeling like we're trapped in an endless loop of saying we're sorry. Neither are great options.

Past Due

The email from my lawyer pinged in my inbox as I sat down in the deck chair overlooking the St. Lawrence River from my hotel balcony. I grimaced, the beauty of my view no longer holding my attention as I scrolled through his message. I'd been pursuing my ex-husband for support payments he'd missed and additional assistance for Kinza's university tuition, and for months he'd been delaying. My lawyer's advice was direct: File with the courts. That would force my ex to finally come to the table.

I hated this back and forth. Worry had settled like a low background hum in my brain for months now, and even my road trip hadn't managed to dislodge it. Maybe I should just drop it, I thought. Carrying the costs myself wasn't always easy, but the girls and I were managing. Was the emotional turmoil worth whatever money we might eventually be awarded? Was I holding my ex accountable or letting him lock me into a toxic dance?

Later, before bed, I talked with Kinza on the phone. "I'm thinking of giving up on asking your dad for the support he owes," I told her. There was a pause as she absorbed my words. "Mom, I'm okay with whatever you decide," she said, "but here's my take: he chose to have kids and that responsibility doesn't disappear just because his wife stops putting up with his abuse."

Now the pause was on my side of the conversation as I considered my daughter's words. She was right. The internal voice I'd been hearing was me a decade earlier, when I'd first left my marriage—the young mother who couldn't afford a lawyer, didn't know her rights and settled for less than she should have. I was older and wiser now, as was my daughter. I needed to be empathetic towards the part of me that was afraid of another fight over support payments, while reminding myself that I was no longer powerless and broke. I had knowledge, autonomy and the ability to hold him accountable and stand up for my daughters. This wasn't a fight over what he owed me. It was about what he owed them.

In the weeks ahead, I would return to Kinza's words as my lawyer and I negotiated with my ex-husband about his missed support. Eventually we came to an agreement that saw him settle the account and agree to new terms, continuing to share our daughters' education and health expenses. These conversations were difficult, but the outcome was a fair one.

A Broken Circle

Months earlier, I had stood in front of a room full of social workers, lawyers, mediators, judges and others who worked in the family court system. "I want to tell you a story," I said, looking out at the audience gathered in the auditorium of the Toronto Public Library. "My eldest daughter and I like to go out for Ultimate Endless Shrimp at Red Lobster—it's one of our traditions. When she was sixteen, as we were making our way through our third kind of shrimp, she looked up at me and said, 'Mom, can I share something with you?' Naturally, I said yes. And this is what she said:

"'I keep having this memory from when I was four or five years old. I'd made a card for Dad, and I wanted to give it to him, but I knew he might not be in a good mood, so I asked you if I should. You told me to wait, but I was excited about the card, and so I went to give it to him anyway, and I interrupted him watching TV. And he just started yelling, and then he threw something at you and you were crying, and then you took me to my room so we could play there, away from him. And I just wanted to say, I'm sorry for making you cry and for making him do that to you.'"

Turning to the screen behind me in my speech, I pushed the

projector button on the control I held in my hand, and an illustration titled "The Cycle of Violence" appeared. Also often called "The Power Wheel," it showed two adults in a circular image, with points on the circle labelled "romantic pursuit," "honeymoon period," "build-up phase," "stand-over phase" and "explosion and remorse," repeating in an endless loop.

"You've seen this image before," I said as dozens among the attendees bobbed their heads affirmatively. "And usually we talk about what it looks like from the point of view of the adults in this cycle. But we don't often talk about it from the perspective of the four-year-old who thinks that explosion is her fault. Or the teenager who, years later, still blames herself for making Dad mad and Mom cry."

I told the audience that when I left my marriage, taking my girls with me, I thought I'd saved them. Their father hadn't hit them, he'd hit me. I told myself that I was the one who'd been abused, that I'd managed to protect them, that they hadn't been hurt.

I was wrong.

A Mother's Intuition

It had been five years since I'd left my marriage. I'm not sure what made me get up in the middle of that night to check on Kinza: Mom's spidey sense maybe? But as I stepped into the living room, I could see my now-teenaged daughter on the couch, arms bared and showing the telltale signs of self-harm.[3]

In the days that followed, she was receiving mental health treatment, and I tumbled into a spiral of self-blame. Breaking the generational cycle of abuse to provide a better life for my daughters was my biggest motivation for leaving my marriage. When I'd separated from my husband, he'd told me I was ruining our daughters' lives. And while I knew rationally that he was wrong, emotionally I became trapped in trying to project the image of the perfect family. I was fine. My daughters were happy.

I made my girls attend religious classes even though some of the teachings didn't match the values I'd come to hold, telling myself that giving them a solid religious foundation was what a good mother did. (Later, I'd realize my impulse wasn't unique to Muslim mothers. Women from Christian, Jewish and other traditions shared stories with me of similar disconnects between their values and what the more conservative voices in their religious communities counselled.) When Kinza's high school grades started slipping, I stepped in and completed her assignments, telling myself I didn't want her to fail. In truth, I was at least as much concerned about looking like a failure as the mother. Behind the "we're okay" facade, I still felt we were a broken family and that my job was to hide the brokenness, to prove my ex-husband wrong.

And Kinza was buckling under the pressure. From the time she was born, my in-laws had treated me more like a nanny than a mother, criticizing my parenting and doing their best to disrupt my connection to my daughter. I loved Kinza deeply, but the emotional life in our home was toxic. Years later, Kinza would say she grew up with two emotional role models: her raging father and her despairing mother. Her earliest years were spent watching me sit crying at the kitchen table as I tried to figure out what to do, how to escape. Later, in school, she'd do the same, spending recess with her head down, crying at her desk, not knowing how else to express her fear, sadness or insecurity.

It was different with Saarah, my youngest. By the time she was born, I'd started standing up for myself, slowly figuring out how to extricate us from my marriage, gradually building my confidence. Because Saarah wasn't the first-born or a grandson, my in-laws weren't especially interested in her, so Saarah and I had room to bond, to laugh and play and be with each other in ways Kinza and I never had. Later, I would see that I had parented Kinza with my fearful mind, while I'd connected to Saarah with my brave heart. Where Saarah knew I loved her for who she was, Kinza grew up feeling I loved her only when she did well, and so she spent her teen years swinging back and forth between wanting to please me and wanting to piss me off.

And the truth was, we hadn't dealt with the fallout from what my girls had seen growing up. As I would later share with that audience of people who worked in family courts, I thought that I'd protected my girls from the violence in our home by getting out, that because they hadn't been hit, they hadn't been harmed. But children exposed to intimate partner violence, like mine, aren't equipped to understand the roots of the violence they're seeing. They don't know why one parent reacts with violence, as the other slides into despair and depression. A child doesn't have the cognitive capacity to look at their parents and say, "My mother is struggling with normalized patriarchy and intergenerational trauma and so doesn't recognize she's being abused, doesn't know how to protect herself. My dad is conditioned by false definitions of manhood, toxic masculinity and unhealed trauma of his own and so doesn't know how to deal with it except through rage and anger." They think they're the cause: that their parents fight because of them, that the violence is something they need to control by being good or by distracting or cajoling a violent parent and that the aftermath is something they need to help heal by comforting the victim. They blame themselves, find unhealthy outlets for the emotions they don't learn to manage and become hypervigilant, living in constant readiness to fight, flee or freeze at the first sign of violence. Even if they aren't victims of physical violence, witnessing violence is a form of abuse with impacts that, if ignored, will stunt emotional and physical health.

There was so much my girls and I needed to unlearn.

"Your job isn't to make your kids successful, it's to keep them safe and happy," my friend and mentor John told me when he met me for a quick coffee during Kinza's struggle. He'd seen me trying to mask her problems at school, pushing her to stay in classes she didn't enjoy. He'd once done the same thing with one of his children, he confessed, putting them at loggerheads until he finally realized his child needed to follow their own path.

Maybe he was right, I thought. Clearly, pushing Kinza to follow a road I imagined for her wasn't working.

Weeks later, Kinza and I sat side by side in a group therapy session in an office building in a quiet business park. I don't remember now what was being said, just that suddenly Kinza bolted, a panic attack overtaking her. When I found her outside, she was sitting in the middle of the empty road, crying. What was she doing? What if someone saw her? What would they think of me, her mother? How could I make her better? The questions tumbled over each other in my head, old impulses bumping into new insights. And in that moment, I realized all I couldn't do. I couldn't control what others thought. I couldn't make my daughter better. I couldn't take away her pain.

All I could do was be with her. And so I stepped into the road and sat down with her.

"What are you doing?" she said through her tears. "You're wearing a skirt and heels."

"What I'm wearing doesn't matter," I said. "I just want to hold your hand. Can I please do that? We can sit here for as long as you want to. You don't have to go back inside. We don't have to do anything." She broke down and sobbed. I held her.

As her tears slowed down, she drew away. "Okay," she said after a few minutes. "I'm ready to go back inside."

It wasn't a solution: it was a step. But that's what solutions are made of—one step after another. In that moment, I realized my children didn't need me to solve their problems, they needed me to create space so they could process their emotions and begin to solve their own problems—figure out their own steps—for themselves. Kinza's emotional role models—her angry dad and her tearful mother—had taught her two ways to handle powerful emotions: to shout or to shut down. She hadn't learned to safely experience and understand her emotions. And having me swoop in to solve her problems and maintain appearances hadn't helped, as those actions increased the pressure on her while telling her that I didn't trust her to solve her own problems, that she couldn't figure things out for herself—which further undermined her confidence.

There were other bumps along the way. One day, I noticed a couple hundred dollars missing from my bank account. When I looked at my withdrawals, I saw one made in the middle of the night and realized she had taken my card from my wallet and snuck out to make the withdrawal. I was furious, about both the money she'd taken and the danger of the late-night trip to the ATM on her own. But when I confronted Kinza, her response stunned me.

"If I'm so horrible, why don't you just leave me as well, like Dad did?"

I felt as if someone had thrown a bucket of cold water in my face, extinguishing my anger and replacing it with sadness for the pain I could see she was in. I drew a breath, trying to figure out what to say.

"I hate that you took that money. But I love you. And that will never change. I'm not going to abandon you. I'm not going to leave you. And I'm not going to stop loving you," I said.

Our fight had started with us both inflated with anger. Her pain had deflated mine, my reassurance deflated hers. It was a breakthrough for both of us.

In the months that followed, I did my best to stop hovering, helicoptering. I told Kinza she could make her own decisions about school and did my best to deal with my fear and shame when she struggled to find her way. At school, she didn't feel supported by teachers in coping with her mental health challenges, and I worried she might end up leaving altogether. Education had saved me, and holding back my urge to step in and help "solve" things to keep her in school wasn't easy. I spent hours talking it through in therapy. But as I unlearned my habits of parental control, Kinza was learning new, healthier patterns that empowered her to make her own decisions and embrace her independence. She earned the rest of her diploma at an alternative school centred on independent learning and is now excelling in a top journalism program. I held back my need to control and created room for her to explore. She took one step after another and found her solutions, knowing I was there for support if she needed it.

Watering the Seeds

I grew up in a family and culture that believed children were born to serve: to become who their parents wanted them to be, to care for their elders and to contribute to their communities within rigidly drawn boundaries. A good daughter looked after her parents and eventually her parents-in-law. A good mother shaped her children, fighting to contain her children's interests and desires, pushing them into roles and onto paths approved by religious leaders and the larger community. If children were seeds, mothers were gardeners. Yes, we were supposed to water and weed so our children could grow—but as they grew, it was handy to have a good set of sharp clippers nearby so we could prune and shape their growth to fit perfectly within the garden in which they'd been planted.

Here's the thing about seeds, though. They come into the world containing all of themselves within themselves. Within the case that surrounds them, they carry the essence of who they will be: this one a tomato plant, this one an apple tree, both beautiful and necessary and wonderful in and of themselves, but each truly unique and complete.

So what happens if the gardener wants a tomato plant but gets an apple tree? No amount of gardening is going to make that tree give you ruby red tomatoes. You might be able to stunt the tree's growth by clipping and trimming it, but it will be a constant battle, and eventually that tree is going to push its way beyond the limits of your garden bed—or you're going to trim it until it withers.

But what if you simply want apples from a nicer-looking apple tree? Have you ever seen espaliered apple trees? These beautifully shaped specimens are fixtures in the fanciest gardens, their limbs trained in straight, horizontal lines that sometimes then bend into ninety-degree elbows before reaching neatly for the sky. They look perfect—but their artificial structure means they need to be sheltered from wind and constantly cared for. They may look lovely, but it turns out the seemingly unruly apple tree that grows as it was meant to is better suited for surviving what the weather throws at it.

So what's a gardener to do? It's about striking a healthy balance: let the apple trees be apple trees, the tomato plants be tomato plants. Feed the soil. Water as needed. Yes, keep an eye out for pests, do your best to prepare for—and clean up after—storms. But mostly, let them grow!

What Was That About Guilt?

It sounds great on paper, right? Just let them grow! They carry the seeds of happiness inside them! Strike a healthy balance!

But what if you were a twenty-one-year-old who thought a scary clown mask was a good way to stop tantrums? A twenty-nine-year-old who encouraged your five-year-old to put on a happy face and your ten-year-old to be a mini-adult? A thirty-five-year-old yelling, "If you hate me so much, go live with your father."

Yup. I said that. I told my teenager she could either appreciate me—translation: do what I wanted her to do—or go live with her father.

"Mom, you can't say that to me." Kinza's words stopped me in my tracks. "I live here. This is my home. You can't threaten to take my home away from me."

She was right. I shouldn't have said it. But I had.

I am not a perfect parent. My ex-husband certainly thought I was a terrible mother, as did his parents. When my own mother visited, she endlessly criticized my parental inadequacies. By adopting more Western ways of dress and behaviour, I was leading my daughters to hell. Wearing a dress that showed my legs meant I would spend eternity having the skin burned from my limbs. I'd leave my apartment wearing long-sleeved tops and pants, then change into a skirt in the washroom of a nearby coffee shop, reversing the process on the way home to avoid my mother's displeasure at my skin-baring Western garb. When I did something she didn't agree with, she'd tell me Allah was testing me, and would soon take my successes away from me if I failed to do as she wanted me to.

My mother told me I was a terrible mother, and shame whispered in my ear that she was right.

"You can't change what happened in the past." My therapist's words were obviously right: as much as I might wish for it, time travel wasn't a realistic option. So how was I—how were we—supposed to move forward? Did I need to spend the rest of my daughters' lives apologizing for how they'd lived up until now? That didn't seem a healthy choice either.

"Accept what happened. Commit to change. Move forward."

My therapist was laying out the essential steps of Acceptance and Commitment Therapy (ACT). I needed to honestly face what had happened, accepting the impact my fear-based parenting had had on my girls. Were there explanations for why I behaved as I had? Of course there were—and over time, understanding that larger context would be helpful to us all. But right now, what mattered most immediately was saying, "I see how what I did affected you and I accept responsibility for it." Key here: responsibility—not blame, not shame. I still wasn't sure how exactly to untangle those three, but as my therapist and I worked through it together, I came to see that understanding the context for how I'd behaved was crucial for being able to separate responsibility from blame and shame—even if I didn't burden my daughters with all the "whys" and "hows." Responsibility allowed for clarity, while blame and shame created a toxic fog of paralyzing guilt.

And clarity was essential for the next step: commitment to change. Apologizing for what had happened in the past was meaningless if I didn't commit to changing the behaviour I was apologizing for. While there was little likelihood I'd use a scary clown mask to control my now-teenaged daughters' expressions of emotion, the root of that behaviour—communicating to my girls that they had to pretend not to be angry or scared or upset—was what needed to change. They could feel what they felt, express those feelings and I would be there for them. My love wasn't dependent on them performing in a way that made me look good.

This approach allowed us to break two patterns: I was disconnecting their behaviour from my ego. And they no longer had to worry that their access to my love and affection was dependent on them hiding what they felt or who they were. As Dr. Gabor Maté puts it in *The Myth of Normal*, I was no longer asking my children to choose between my love—attachment—and their authenticity: the "quality of being true to oneself, and the capacity to shape one's own life from a deep knowledge of that self . . . knowing our gut feelings when they arise and honoring them."[4] They could be themselves, and know I'd love them no matter what.

This is the part of the story where I'd like to be able to say that the healthier bonds I was creating with my daughters spilled over into our other family relationships. But they didn't. My mother remained locked in her religious judgmentalism. My ex-husband continued to demand his daughters conform to his views of how "good" girls behaved and believed. One evening, Kinza confronted me: she didn't want to spend time with her father anymore, and I'd been telling her she had to. "Mom, if he was just some random misogynist man in the community, would you want him to have any influence on me at all?" she challenged. "No, I wouldn't want a random misogynist man in your life. But he's your father," I replied.

"So why does he get a free pass?" she replied. "He's not good for me." Yes, she agreed, he was her father: a father who required her to hide her thoughts, her beliefs and her dreams, who wanted her to twist herself into the shape of a daughter acceptable to him and who accepted no responsibility for the trauma she'd been exposed to as a child. In her eyes, the price attached to their connection was too high to pay—and she was entitled to make her own choice about whether to have him in her life.

There are those who might argue that children need to forgive their parents for their failings. And it's true no relationship survives without forgiveness—my own relationship with my girls is grounded in that soil. But the key is that their forgiveness of my past parenting mistakes is matched by my commitment to change. Forgiveness without change is simply permission to continue harmful patterns. My girls don't deserve that. Neither do I.

And so, as my daughters drew boundaries with their father, I drew them with my mother.

But What About My Gut?

Scene 1

"You're going to be a doctor someday, Saarah!"

I was still working in banking when I offered these words of encouragement to my science-loving daughter. The look on her face suggested it might not be what she had in mind for her future.

"Ah, I don't think I want to be a doctor, Mom."

"But you're great at science, and you love making people feel better! You'd be amazing, healing people, helping them." I cajoled, convinced, pushed, my gut telling me my daughter *would* be a great doctor.

"Hmm . . . I guess?" Saarah's voice lifted the words to form a question, trying to please me, and the smile I gifted her with confirmed she'd made me happy.

"Dr. Saarah Zafar—it sounds nice, doesn't it?" I said. If I noticed Saarah's nod was half-hearted, I ignored that knowledge.

Scene 2

I'm letting my daughter ruin her life. That was the thought running through my mind each time I was reminded of Kinza's new boyfriend. She'd let me know she was dating, and we'd agreed she should go on birth control. But despite my belief that women should control their own bodies and are entitled to explore and experience healthy sex, when it came to my own daughters, echoes from my past rang in my ears: my husband telling me my daughters would end up whores like me; the early messages within my family and religion that said a woman who was not a virgin on her wedding day was ruined. *Am I letting my daughter ruin her life?*

Of course, these weren't thoughts I shared with Kinza. But as I wrestled with these internalized messages from my early life, I avoided talking to Kinza about her boyfriend at all, and that avoidance sent a clear though unintended message. Kinza, in return, retreated from her initial openness about her relationship, not mentioning if she was meeting him, where they went or what they did. Our mother-daughter relationship reshaped itself around a boyfriend-shaped no-go zone.

But if I'm uncomfortable, shouldn't I listen to my gut? I wondered. *Don't I want my girls to learn to trust their guts, to connect with their authentic selves?*

The problem, I came to realize, was the disconnect between my gut and my authentic beliefs. Those gut feelings originate in our primal unconscious brain, which is wired to protect us from the unknown and unfamiliar. Because of my upbringing, healthy teenaged dating was a complete unknown to me: I subconsciously associated it with sin. And while the cognitive part of my brain believed that dating was okay, that a woman's sexual pleasure was her right, my gut registered all of it as uncomfortably unfamiliar.

When you spend the first decades of your life trying to be what your parents, community or partner want you to be, your gut gets reprogrammed, tuned to signals others are broadcasting rather than to the song your soul is singing. Your gut becomes an indicator of what others expect rather than what is genuinely true to you and your values, and what seems comfortable isn't necessarily what is healthy. That gut feeling that Saarah would be a great doctor? That was my own doctor dream bubbling to the surface at a time when I thought I'd missed my chance. Sure, Dr. Zafar sounded nice—it's just that, really, I wanted it to be Dr. Samra Zafar, though I was ready to settle for Dr. Saarah Zafar if my dream for myself couldn't come true. And that gut feeling that Kinza would be ruined by having a boyfriend? That was the lingering toxicity of the messages from my family and ex-husband, judgments I'd already rejected when applied to me but still feared when applied to my children. It wasn't healthy intuition speaking, it was unhealthy conditioning.

So how do we, as parents, as adults, connect with our authentic selves if our gut feelings are so screwed up? And how do we know what to say, what to do, in the moment with our children if we can't trust those gut feelings? The good news is that our gut feelings can be rewired as we do the work to recognize old patterns and create new blueprints: we can set a new normal.

"Observe. Don't react." My therapist offered these three words of advice. He might as well have said "$E = mc^2$" because the instructions were as incomprehensible to me as Einstein's equation. I was supposed to do . . . nothing?

Not exactly. The key was to create space by shifting to neutral responses, parking the part of me that wanted to judge or solve or shape and just . . . notice. What does noticing do? It creates distance between our emotions and actions, so how we feel no longer equates with who we are. It allows space for us to say "I feel sad," rather than "I am sad"—we can acknowledge the emotion without it defining or labelling us.

If I was in the middle of a conversation with Kinza or Saarah, I'd notice my discomfort, label it in my head and put it aside to come back to on my own later. I'd continue the conversation, resisting the urge to make a decision or offer an opinion, opting instead to open the door to what they thought by asking neutral questions: "What did you think when that happened?" instead of "Didn't you think that was a bad idea?" Then, I'd listen to what they had to say. Later, on my own or in conversation with my therapist or a trusted friend, I could return to the discomfort that had bubbled up. What was I actually feeling? Where did those feelings originate? What did I need to do to address them? I didn't blame myself for what I was feeling: I tried to extend the same compassion to myself I'd offer a friend trying to sort out confusing feelings. Kindness, it turns out, is more conducive to emotional detective work than shame is.

And I checked in. In a perfect world, my daughters would feel comfortable letting me know when they needed me to step back, step up or step in. But our shared history meant we'd all crossed wires and sent confusing signals, and since I'm the mom, I needed to be the one to open the conversation about what was working or not.

This isn't:

- apologizing excessively
- burdening my children with my guilt about my past parenting mistakes
- seeking endless reassurance that they think I'm a good mom

This is:

- offering a clear, sincere apology when I do screw up (and trust me, I do screw up)
- asking directly when I'm not sure how my daughters feel about something I've said or done

Bit by bit, I'm retuning my gut, gradually turning the dial away from the frequencies of my upbringing and marriage, and towards the values I hold and the person I am today. I'm acting with compassion for myself and with accountability to my children. And as I do, I'm helping my daughters learn to trust their guts, too, secure in the knowledge that we can all be our authentic selves with each other— and be loved for who we are.

Scene 3

Kinza and I are doing the dishes together. She's in her early twenties, excited about the journalism courses she's taking at university. A few months ago, she broke up with her long-time boyfriend, and now she's wondering whether a friendship with a non-binary classmate might turn into something more. I had done the work to combat the voices of homophobia I'd grown up with, educating myself and working hard to be an ally. Still, my stomach does a little flip when Kinza tells me this, not out of fear about her potential relationship, but because I worried I'd say the wrong thing, even with good intentions based in strong, supportive beliefs. I had no models for how this conversation might unfold.

Observe, don't react, I tell myself.

And so we talk.

"I'm worried that getting into a relationship will ruin a good friendship," Kinza says.

"But maybe a good friendship might be the basis for a stronger relationship?" I say, trying to walk the neutral path. We talk some more. Kinza tells me her friend has to hide who they are from their family, and how lucky she feels to be able to talk to me about this. As she puts away the last dishes, she turns and says, "Good job, Mom! A few years ago, you'd have been freaking out."

We laugh, both grateful for the progress we've made together, aware of how precious the ease we've found in our relationship is.

"Thanks," I say. "I'm working at it."

Family Inheritance

I am convinced that the most important work I can do is to break the pattern of intergenerational trauma that has been my family's legacy. With support, honesty and effort, we can reject a family inheritance of emotional manipulation, unhealthy entanglements and even violence. Many of us have struggled as parents ourselves, but we can take steps to repair relationships with our own children by recognizing the damage we've caused and committing to behave differently in the future. Unhealthy family patterns can be interrupted: we don't have to pass on the pain we've experienced. There is a saying that "hurt people hurt people." Hurt people may not have had the opportunity, support or willingness to heal and change. But hurt people who have done the work don't have to be trapped in passing on that harm. What I believe is that healed people heal people. Once healed, these healed people go on to help others heal. You can be the one to interrupt the cycle. Some lessons to keep in mind:

- **Reject hand-me-down parenting:** You don't have to define parenting by how you were parented. Instead, focus on how you wish you'd been parented. I'm conscious about the moments when I hear my mother's voice of judgment and religious damnation whispering—okay, sometimes shouting—in my ear. I grew up hearing a girl's worth is tied to her virginity, her future determined by whether her hymen is intact. I was surrounded by rampant homophobia. I was praised for my achievements and yet told not to let myself outshine the boys. Today, I strive to be an LGBTQ2S+ ally who believes in a woman's right to express her sexuality and be successful on her own terms. Still, discomfort can bubble up when my daughters assert values my family of origin rejects, and I have to give my brain a moment to turn down the volume on the echoes from my childhood, making room for me to respond in a way that reflects my current beliefs rather than those of my parents.

- **Family is what you define it to be:** I've felt guilty because my kids don't have a big extended family in their lives. "It sucks to be pattern breakers," Kinza has joked. And she's right: it *can* suck to be pattern breakers, when choosing to step outside of unhealthy family patterns means you may no longer be welcome at—or want to join—family gatherings and events. I feel sad that we don't have those bigger family connections, and my kids sometimes envy friends with lots of aunts, uncles, grandparents and cousins. We don't pretend those feelings don't exist: we talk openly about them and acknowledge the loss, while also recognizing that those connections aren't healthy ones in our family situation. Traditional family structures aren't always nurturing or safe: creating a family where you're able to be your authentic self is what matters, and the family you create is more important than the one you were born into. And we've embraced what we do have: unconditional love and deep bonds with each other. "Castaways" from *The Backyardigans* is our theme song, with its lyrics about jumping off a sinking ship, finding our own island and creating a safe happy world. When my daughter Saarah said to me, "Mom, I'm an ex-Muslim brown queer teenager. I don't even know what that looks like," I wasn't sure how to respond. But as I thought about it, I realized it was simple. "Just be you," I told her. "It's okay to create your own template."

- **Create your own normal:** My girls and I have a group chat. Its title? "Perfectly unorthodox family." We don't eat supper at the same time every night. Our schedules are complicated. But my children know I love them. They know they have a safe place to turn if they fall or fail—and someplace that will celebrate their successes with the exuberance of New Year's Eve fireworks. Our normal might not look like yours, or yours like ours—and that's okay.

- **Your children do not need you to be perfect, they need you to be human:** My girls need me to model how to fall down and get back up again, how to screw up and start over again and how we can be responsible *to* each other rather than *for* each other.

- **Bubble wrap is an over-protection trap:** That part about not being responsible *for* each other? That means not stepping in to take responsibility for someone else's actions and the fallout from those actions. It's so tempting to try to solve our children's problems for them (see "Samra does Kinza's homework" elsewhere in this chapter), but that simply teaches our children that they're not capable of solving things on their own. Our brains are wired for struggle—it's one of the ways we build problem-solving neural pathways. Don't let your discomfort steal your child's opportunities to create success out of failure. Trust them to make their mistakes, learn from their experiences and become their own unconditional selves. Yes, be there as a safety net for situations that are dangerous or beyond your child's current skills—but leave room for them to reach within and work it out for themselves.

- **Be an "ask for help" role model:** Let your children see you asking others for advice—including them. And if they ask for your help? Assist them in finding their own solution by asking open-ended questions. If they ask what you'd do, walk them through your thought process rather than simply delivering a solution.

- **Focus on steps, not solutions:** You don't have to have all the answers to start making positive changes in your life or your relationship with your children. We don't start at perfect and neither will your kids! Take a step. Adjust as you go. Your children will learn from your example and create their own positive momentum in their lives as well.

- **Let go of the need to be right:** It's tempting—and ego-boosting— to try to create an image of yourself as the parent who always has the answers, the solutions. But our children don't need us to be right, they need us to be there. Letting them see us as imperfect and our decision-making as sometimes messy allows them to embrace their own imperfections.

- **You can't raise strong children and expect them not to push back:** My goal has been to raise bold daughters. And guess what: bold daughters aren't afraid to tell you when they think you're wrong! But I've learned so much from their wisdom, their push-back, lessons that have made me bolder too.

- **You can start working to heal damaged relationships with your children at any age:** Counsellor Nedra Tawwab recently posted a list of things adult children want to hear, many of which are useful even with younger children.[5] Try these:

- I didn't know what you needed. What can I do now?
- I didn't handle that well. Let me try again.
- You're right.

Some of the phrases on her list sound similar to ones I've used with my own daughters: when my girls share a problem with me, I often ask, "Do you want listening Mom or problem-solving Mom?" And while the phrase "I'm proud of you" is something all children long to hear, I've come to believe that "You should be proud of yourself" is even more powerful, placing the authority to determine the value of their actions into their own hands—and hearts.

Portrait of a Family

The plate in front of me featured three desserts—cheesecake, a brownie and a slice of cake—topped with a sparkler, next to it spoons for my daughters and me.

It was my birthday. I'd had mixed emotions leading up to the day. While I was filled with gratitude for my life and the loved ones in it, I also felt some sadness and loss for the years that had been stolen from me by people who were supposed to have loved and protected me. I hadn't known healthy love in my childhood or marriage, and without good role models, I'd struggled to be the mother—a good mother, a healthy and loving mother—I so wanted to be. It had taken work to change how I parented, commitment to build healthy, happy relationships with my daughters.

And together, we have built those healthier relationships, making happier memories that overshadow the traumatic ones. We travel together. We love spending time with each other. We have weekly family nights, and the girls have their own regular sister nights. Today, my relationships with both Kinza and Saarah are based on healthy love as we work at growing our relationship together diligently.

On my birthday, as the girls handed me a bowl filled with paper hearts, tears filled my eyes. The number of hearts matched my age, each one featuring a handwritten reason why they loved me. My favourite one? "You teach us to love ourselves."

It's a lesson we're learning together.

Whispered Wisdom

"It's not your fault. You didn't cause this. Nothing you could have done would have changed it."

I don't know if you needed to hear this, but I did, and so do countless parents of children who struggle with mental illness.

We've taken strides to combat stigma around parenting children with mental illness, but whenever you hear someone proclaim, "That kid would be fine if I were their parent," or "That mom just needs to lay down the law!" you're witnessing this stigma in action.

But children with the same genetic inheritance, raised in the same household, given the same opportunities, can be completely different. Why do we insist on assigning the blame for someone's "bad" kid on their parenting, when that same parent has raised a "good" kid with the same set of parenting skills?

I believe there are very few "bad" people, parents or children on this earth. We're all here navigating the hazards of human life as best we can with the equipment we've been given. Judgment makes us smug; only compassion can help us to understand and heal the hurt we see around us.

Blaming parents closes that parent and their child off from the support you could be offering. Cast judgment aside and look with loving kindness on both parent and child as fellow travellers who need your understanding more, not less, than others to whom you grant it most easily.

DR. MARGARET MACSWEEN, MSc, MD,

CHILD & ADOLESCENT PSYCHIATRIST, MOM OF THREE BOYS

Unconditioning Workbook

- According to attachment theory, how we connect with our primary caregiver as infants and young children can set the course for how we later engage with the world and the people in it. Children whose needs for food, connection, warmth and other life necessities are met develop secure attachment and come to understand they are protected, which allows them to cope with fear and explore their worlds, knowing they can return to the safe base of the person looking after them. Children whose emotional and physical needs are not met or whose needs are inconsistently met may develop insecure attachment patterns, which affect their ability to cope with fear and stress, to manage emotions, to connect with others and to feel able—or not—to explore the world around them. These patterns are not immutable. Later life experiences and insights might mean that those who experience insecure attachment can lead emotionally healthy lives. But children who benefit from secure attachment as youngsters have an emotional head start.

- Family of origin, community and the larger culture all influence our parenting approaches, but we are not destined to parent as others expect us to. We can make active, informed choices, especially when we take the steps to reflect on the lessons we learned from how we ourselves were parented.

- For those of us who are immigrant or first-generation parents trying to bridge cultures, the push and pull of how we were raised with "how it's done here" can present its own challenges.

- Children exposed to intimate partner violence aren't equipped to understand the roots of the violence they're seeing. They think they're the cause: that their parents fight because of them, that the violence is something they need to try to control by being good or distracting the violent parent and that the aftermath is something they need to help heal. They blame themselves, finding unhealthy outlets for the emotions they don't know how to manage. Even if they aren't victims of physical violence, witnessing violence is a form of abuse with impacts that, if ignored, will stunt emotional and physical health.

- Your children don't need you to solve all of their problems. They need you to create space so they can process their emotions and learn to solve their problems for themselves, one step at a time.

- We all make mistakes. The key to moving on is to separate responsibility from blame and shame. Responsibility allows for clarity, while blame and shame create a toxic fog of paralyzing guilt. Responsibility requires commitment to change; apologizing for a mistake is largely meaningless if you don't commit to changing the behaviour for which you are apologizing.

- Trusting your gut may be your goal but might not reflect your current reality. When you spend the first decades of your life trying to be what your parents, community or partner want you to be, your gut gets tuned to the signals others are broadcasting rather than to the song your soul is singing. Your gut becomes an indicator of what others expect rather than what is true to you and your values. As a result, what seems comfortable isn't always what is healthy.

- When we are retuning our gut, we need to create a pause between taking information in and responding. Observe, don't react. Create time to examine what you are actually feeling so you can assess whether you are reacting to the current situation or to unresolved echoes from your past.

- There is a saying that "hurt people hurt people." But hurt people who do the work of examining and addressing their emotional issues don't have to be trapped in replicating familial patterns. You don't have to have all the answers to start making positive changes. You can be the one to interrupt the cycle.

Reflection: Is That My Gut or My Ghosts?

When you've grown up trading authenticity for attachment, your gut gets confused—it's hard to differentiate when you're acting from your true values and beliefs, and when you're simply falling into old patterns, being pushed around by the ghosts of your past. The good news is that as you stop performing and behave in ways that align with your true self, your gut-check skills will improve. But it takes time—and self-examination.

As you interact with your children, pay attention to the moments when your gut is speaking to you—but don't necessarily trust every word it says. Pause. Observe. Reflect. You may need to park the feeling and come back to it later, working to figure out its origin and authenticity. Some things to consider:

- Watch for parentification, which means expecting support from your child instead of giving it. Are you reacting as a parent, or placing yourself in the child's role and expecting your child to parent you and put your needs and desires first?

- Does the response bubbling up match the scale of the situation you're dealing with? Catastrophizing can be a signal that you've tapped into deeper trauma and fear from your past. Downplaying might signal you're shutting down out of fear or fatigue.

- Write it down: Patterns can take time to see. Jot your reactions down and reflect on them over time.

This exercise may help.

Observe:

When _____ *happened, I felt* _____

_____

_____

_____.

My first instinct was to _____

_____

_____

_____.

Reflect:

In similar situations in the past, I _____

_____

_____

_____.

Often, this resulted in _____

_____

_____

_____.

As I reflect on the situation, in my feelings and my response, I hear echoes of the past, such as _____

_____

_____

_____.

As I consider how to respond, I think I need to _____

_____

_____

_____.

Whispered Wisdom

Journey from hard work to heart work.
Abandon the old adage that we must toil
and suffer in our quest for excellence. There is a
gentler way accessible to us when we integrate
and accept all aspects of ourselves and
embrace our authenticity. Herein lies our
unique genius. It is what the world needs.

**AYESHA SHAH, HUMAN RESOURCES
EXECUTIVE, TEDx SPEAKER &
AUTHOR, TORONTO**

CHAPTER THREE:

Superwoman in a Box

The lyrics of "The Champion" blasted from my car stereo
as I drove along the roadway hugging the St. Lawrence
coastline. My voice rose to meet Carrie Underwood's as she
belted out her anthem to survival and triumph over life's challenges,
joined by Ludacris to spell out the attributes represented by the song
title—courage, perseverance and more.

There were moments at work, at home and at the speaker's podium
when I felt like a champion. But while Underwood's song gave me a
jolt of energy, somewhere inside me, another voice whispered, *You're
no champion. You're not a champion* at all.

I've worn many labels over the course of my life. My first was as
the big sister in my family, when I labelled myself the peacekeeper.
I scurried between my mother and father, trying to coax and cajole,
distract and divert whenever I felt the tensions between them starting
to rise. If I could just keep them happy, I could keep my sisters and
me safe. And if I failed? Then I'd round up my younger siblings and
hide, trying to shut out the sights and sounds of the violence that
inevitably erupted.

Later, I was the black sheep, the girl with weird dreams, the one who launched a girls' cricket team when we were forbidden to play with the boys. Though surrounded by cultural messages of feminine subservience and obedience, I couldn't understand why women were supposed to dream only of marriage and children—I was sure the world offered more than that. But others labelled me unmarriageable as a result, a label I now see contributed to the erosion of my resistance to marriage. While I never believed a woman's only purpose was to be married, as a teen I wanted the approval of the adults around me, and being told I was unmarriageable turned up the volume on that need, drowning out my will to protect myself: attachment to those around me won out over my ability to be true to my authentic self.

And once married? I tried to live up to the label of good wife, certain that if only I could figure out what made my husband happy, I'd be able to earn his love and my community's respect. University opened up the possibility of other labels: student and nerd. And while I tried to hang on to the label of good Muslim girl even as my marriage ended, some in my community wouldn't allow it: "I can't be friends with you anymore," one woman told me in the aftermath of my divorce. "My family says you cause other women to divorce as well." I was a bad influence, back to being a black sheep.

Some labels we attach to ourselves as we take on roles in our family and community, such as peacekeeper or good wife. Some labels others affix to us in judgment or approval, like unmarriageable or good girl. Others we tailor to suit ourselves as they are handed to us, pulling them on like costumes or armour—black sheep or nerd. And the labels can vary widely, depending on the positions we occupy in the society around us. Men and women can end up with different labels for similar behaviours, for instance: he's assertive, she's aggressive; he's driven, she's feisty; he has leadership potential, she's pushy. Layer in racial biases, and the labels shift again: women of colour are often criticized for being loud or too expressive, while men of colour are often judged to be threatening for behaving in ways that aren't even taken note of in white men.

Why do we label? As a shortcut, to sort the world—and the people in it—into quick categories so we can save ourselves microseconds in how we respond to them—who's a threat, who needs attention, who's on our side, who isn't. *She's the shy one—as long as she's quiet, I don't have to pay attention.* Or, *That one's the pushy one, always wants more than she deserves—I'm digging in my heels when she asks for something.* In families and communities, we do it to slot people into the roles we're comfortable with—or that confirm our biases about "that type" of person. The shy one's quietness might be signalling hurt feelings, illness or nothing at all. The pushy one's request might be for something she's entitled to, maybe even less than she deserves—but we categorize it as "too much." And we label others to understand our own role in their lives and their role in ours: *She's the one who needs saving, so I have to be the saviour. He's the sad one, so I don't want to be in his company because he brings me down.* And when they change or grow? Discomfort can bloom because we no longer know who *we're* supposed to be. Is a saviour still a saviour when no one needs saving?

In each case, the label we use reduces people to a single word, a single story, and erases their complexity, the nuances in their behaviour.

Why do we label ourselves? To conform and confirm. To push back and push forward. To armour and announce. When some part of us knows that all parts of us aren't welcomed, we present a single version of ourselves, one that makes us feel powerful, that will gain us acceptance—or that we know others will label us as anyway. We're the fuck-up. Or the good wife. Or the champion.

But the real us is hidden away, tucked deep inside the label's costume.

Whispered Wisdom

When we concentrate our focus we achieve better outcomes, in all areas of our life. Simplify to amplify.

ANN GOMEZ, SPEAKER, BESTSELLING AUTHOR, & FOUNDER OF CLEAR CONCEPT INC.

Living Up to a Label

The email I'd just clicked open stung: a message from a woman who'd asked me to speak at an event chastising me for requesting a speaking fee. I was in my first year of medical school; I supported myself and my girls with income from the speaking engagements I did for corporations, community groups and associations. Still, I did some appearances for low or no fee, allotting a certain number as a way of giving back while still being able to support my family. When the request from a women's community agency came in, I was overloaded and had already filled my "free" speaking slots, but still I offered to speak for half my normal fee.

Her reply was scorching: she had no budget for speakers, suggesting that I was not truly an advocate like the others who'd said they'd speak without payment. Her words echoed another exchange I'd had recently, this one with a young woman who'd reached out to interview me on short notice for a school journalism assignment. I had no way to fit her in. Her disappointment left me feeling guilty and overwhelmed.

Why did their reactions cut so close to the bone? As I shared the exchanges later with a new therapist I was seeing, she asked me a question: "Have you heard of superwoman syndrome?"

Of course, I'd heard of Superwoman: she's a female superhero, and I'd been labelled as her more than once. I'd been happy to wear the moniker, imagining myself in her cape, ready to take on the world. But I hadn't heard of the syndrome before. As of January 2024, the American Psychological Association defines *superwoman syndrome* as "a set of characteristics found in a woman who performs or attempts to perform all the duties typically associated with several different full-time roles, such as wage earner, mother, homemaker, and wife." The syndrome itself appears to have been coined by Marjorie Hansen Shaevitz in her book *The Superwoman Syndrome* in the early 1980s.[1] Since then, the term—and the reality it reflects—has been both embraced as a celebration of female empowerment and rejected as a trap that pushes women to work double or triple time to meet the multiple demands placed on them. And it's worth noting that the idea that we have to be hyper-independent, doing it all on our own, can be a holdover from trauma. I know I often felt that way, ignoring the reality that as humans, we're built to be connected, and not meant to cope with all that life throws at us alone.

For women of colour, those demands can be even more extreme, as we are praised for our strength in the face of racial and gender bias, lauded for our determination to succeed despite limited resources and expected to support others within our community, all while appearing strong, suppressing our own emotions and hiding our vulnerability.[2] One recent study of African American women's views on the superwoman role by Dr. Cheryl Woods-Giscombé at the University of North Carolina at Chapel Hill found the women participating in the study viewed being "superwomen" as both positive and negative. A benefit of being a superwoman was simply surviving "despite personal obstacles, perceived inadequacy of resources, and unique life experiences attributed to the double jeopardy of being African

American and female . . . [especially] being able to survive while maintaining their self-worth and dignity." As well, the women saw their strength as important to preserving their families and strengthening their communities. The downside was more directly personal: the strain on romantic relationships caused in part by resisting vulnerability and stress-related health behaviours and symptoms—or as one participant put it, "[W]hat doesn't kill you makes you sick."[3]

And all those negatives can be exacerbated in situations where you're an "only"—situations often faced by women and particularly women of colour. A North American study of more than 64,000 employees in 279 companies conducted by management consultants McKinsey & Company and LeanIn.org found that 20 percent of women reported that they were "commonly the only person of their gender in the room or one of very few."[4] In tech and engineering, the percentage was much higher. For women of colour, it rose to 45 percent. (Just 7 percent of men had the experience of being "onlys.")

What happens when you're an only? An earlier study by McKinsey & Company and LeanIn.org in 2018 found onlys were more likely to have their judgment questioned, to be mistaken for someone more junior and to be subjected to unprofessional and demeaning remarks.[5] And the frequency of these microaggressions was much higher for female onlys than for men, with male onlys most often saying they felt included rather than excluded.

As my therapist and I talked about superwoman syndrome, I was struck by how strongly I'd identified with that label, with the image of myself as someone who had the strength to save myself—and others. Later, as I read more, I realized, too, how frequently I'd been an only: the only woman, the only Muslim woman, the only woman of colour, and once in medical school, the only person over thirty-five among the students. Each "only" episode compounded my impulse to hide any vulnerability, to put on Superwoman's cape and show the world I could not only keep up but excel. Adopting that label was my reaction to feeling excluded, an effort to be included in another way, to turn being an "only" into being "exceptional." Turning down a request—like the one from the community agency or the student seeking an interview—felt like failure, especially when it was met with the response that I was selfish for saying no.

For women especially, the pressure to do it all is immense. When I was a child, complaints about the load one carried or the troubles one faced were often met with an Urdu saying that translated to "The strongest steel is forged by the hottest fires." Motivational quotes of a similar flavour show up today in my Instagram feed: "The greater the pressure, the brighter the diamond." "A diamond is a chunk of coal that did well under pressure." Then there are the ones that praise women specifically for the load they carry: "Single moms: You are a doctor, a teacher, a nurse, a maid, a cook, a referee, a heroine, a provider, a defender, a protector, a true superwoman. Wear your cape proudly." And this one, attributed to Eleanor Roosevelt: "A woman is like a tea bag—you can't tell how strong she is until you put her in hot water."

While the impulse to offer encouragement in the face of adversity is understandable, the underlying messages can be toxic: that we've just got to carry on and do it all, or that we've got to actively seek out "hot water" to prove how strong we are, subconsciously seeking problems that allow us to prove to ourselves and others that we really are superheroes. After all, who wants to be a piece of steel that breaks or a lump of coal that cracks or a weak tea bag? Yet not every challenge is worth taking on; not every request should be met with a yes, especially when the cost of doing it all is often unsustainably steep. (We might even blame ourselves for being "lazy" when we need recovery time after traumatic events or in response to being overloaded.)

But when we label ourselves superwomen—or take on any other single label—we allow the world to view us narrowly and limit our own range of options. Superwoman doesn't get to say no: she's supposed to simply do it all.

At least, the superwoman label has some positive connotations. At times, we adopt labels that are more negative. Not long after I left my marriage, I met another South Asian woman who had left her husband as well. Where I was still focused on being the "good Pakistani girl"—dating a Pakistani man whom I knew wasn't right for me in an effort to fit into the community I'd been raised in—my new acquaintance was almost aggressive in her adoption of a more negative mantle. "I'm a whore," she told me bluntly, as she shared the details of the various sexual encounters she'd had. She wasn't claiming to be a sex worker, but instead waved the label as a defense against others in the community who had no doubt already applied it to her—telling herself, *If I call myself this, your words can't hurt me.* I was reminded of her again years later as I read Dr. Bessel Van Der Kolk's book *The Body Keeps the Score*. In it, he shares the story of a fourteen-year-old boy who had been arrested on Christmas Eve for breaking into a neighbour's house. Dr. Van Der Kolk was called in to assess him and began by asking the boy who would visit him in jail over Christmas. He had no one, the boy admitted—but the police knew him well, since he'd been caught during other break-ins in the past. In fact, this time, when he'd been found inside the home, one officer had said, "Oh my God, it's Jack again, that little motherfucker." As Dr. Van Der Kolk wrote, "A little while later Jack confessed, 'You know, that is what makes it worthwhile.' Kids will go to almost any length to feel seen and connected."[6]

Kids aren't the only ones. And if the choice is between being invisible and being called a whore or a motherfucker or some other hurtful label, often we'll take the label rather than be ignored.

"No" Is a Complete Sentence

We owe ourselves the same compassion and kindness we give to others. When I reflect now on the response of the community organization's executive director to my no, I can have compassion for her because I know she was likely acting from a place of conditioning common to many in the non-profit sector, pouring her heart and soul into good work while being underpaid herself, and expecting others to do the same. Similarly, I can have empathy for my former mother-in-law, even in the aftermath of her criticism and abuse. She was married at fourteen, endured abuse herself. Her treatment of me was in part a fulfillment of the belief that it was "her turn" to be in charge, the only time in her life she could have agency and power.

But while we can recognize the barriers others face, empathize with their suffering and feel compassion towards them, that doesn't mean we are obliged to ignore our own needs in order to make them happy. Empathy for others needn't come at the expense of empathy for ourselves.

Without boundaries, kindness towards others is a form of self-sabotage. Learning to say no to others is a critical tool in expressing our empathy for ourselves. And rewiring our brains to say no takes practise. If you're a "no novice," build up your "no muscles" the same way you would build any other muscle: start small and gain strength through repetition. Keeping a "no diary" can help:

- Write down your no: what and who you said no to.
- What feelings did saying no provoke? Guilt, shame, remorse, FOMO?
- Replace the word *am* with *feel* in your feelings list: "I *am* so selfish!" becomes "I *feel* selfish when I say no."
- Explore the feelings your no provoked in you. "I feel selfish when I say no because . . ."

- Talk kindly to yourself, extending the same empathy and understanding that you might extend to a friend.
- Stay firm in your decision to say no as long as the reasons to say no remain valid.

Labels and Gender-Based Violence

Recently, a woman I know shared this story with me (note that the following includes a description of sexual assault):

On a trip out of town, I spent the evening reconnecting with a man I'd met online a few years earlier. When we'd first met, we seemed to have much in common, though we lived in different cities. We enjoyed each other's company and conversation, but agreed we weren't couple material for each other, and though we stayed friends on social media, we weren't in touch regularly.

He'd noticed from my Instagram account that I was in his city and reached out. "Supper?" he asked. "Sure!" I replied. It was a beautiful August evening, and after dinner, he asked if I wanted to go for a walk. I'd spent the day in heels, and so I wanted to pop up to my room to change into more comfortable footwear.

"I'll come up with you," he said. At the door of my room, he grabbed me and kissed me, and yes, I kissed him back. Within moments he was in my room. Earlier in the evening, he'd asked why I wasn't dating anyone. "I'm going through some personal trauma and I just don't want to be sexual right now," I'd told him. Now, in my room, I repeated "no" more than once. "Please, please," I said. "This is going to mess me up. Can you just stop?" Still, he persisted, pushing me onto the bed.

And I just stopped resisting.

I felt myself floating out of my body, up to the ceiling.

Afterwards, when it was all over, I remember him laughing.

The next day, I went to the police station. I spent six hours being interviewed by them. At the end, the officer said there weren't grounds to pursue a charge. "Maybe the guy didn't know you were saying no," said the officer I spoke to.

I felt filled with shame, blaming myself for every point in the evening where I imagined I could have stopped it from happening.

My noes were clear and should have been respected. And there's no certainty that more physical resistance on my part would have worked: I might have ended up in even more danger. But still I blame myself for not seeing the risks ahead, for not having the skills I needed to end the evening earlier.

This woman's story gave me goosebumps. We live in a society where the labels we attach to victims of gender-based violence place the responsibility for the harm on the victims themselves. Was your no loud enough? Did you say it often enough? Why did you let yourself get put in this position in the first place?

The questions we rarely ask men: Was there an enthusiastic yes? Did you clearly ask for consent? Why did you let yourself get into a position where there was any confusion about whether she said yes?

Even the terms "violence against women" and "gender-based violence" can be problematic, since they erase the offender. Overwhelmingly, that violence is committed by men, and yet they are invisible in the labels we use, making these crimes a women's issue rather than recognizing the responsibility men have for addressing and preventing it.

Victims of gender-based violence are routinely doubted. But the reality is that false accusations are rare. The more common situation? In an estimated seven out of ten cases, victims of sexual assault *don't report* at all. Of those that are reported, an estimated 2 to 10 percent are false accusations, according to US-based group RAINN (Rape, Abuse and Incest National Network). That's not 2 to 10 percent of cases that are false—it's 2 to 10 percent of *reported* cases—a tiny fraction of the already small number of assaults that are actually reported (and about the same percentage of false reports that are found in other crimes—though we don't generally doubt men who say they've been robbed or beaten).

Why don't victims of sexual assault report? Because they are labelled as liars, as sluts, as asking for it.

And what happens when they do report? Across Canada and the United States, in an astonishing number of cases, police fail to move forward with cases because they judge them "unfounded"—often based on bias and faulty understandings of the law of consent. RAINN points out that in the US, out of one thousand sexual assaults, 975 perpetrators will remain free. Why? Only 310 of those assaults will be reported, only fifty will lead to arrests, and of those, only twenty-five perpetrators will be incarcerated.[7]

So much needs to change—starting with the blame we place on victims and the blame we place on ourselves when we are victims. The absence of a no is not a yes. The clothes you wear—or don't wear—are not a yes. Your smile is not a yes. Having a few drinks is not a yes. A marriage certificate is not a yes. Being on a street alone, in a hallway, in a hotel room—none of those are yeses. Yeses obtained through threat, manipulation and grooming are not yeses.

We blame ourselves when others don't hear our no, when the blame should rest with those who don't listen for our yes.

Integration, not Rejection

Labelling others can limit them to a single, simplistic version of themselves. Labelling ourselves can leave us struggling to live up, or down, to the image we created. With all the harm that can come with labelling, is the answer to reject them completely? I don't think it is. Sometimes labels help us manage through challenging times—there were certainly moments when singing along with Carrie Underwood and calling myself a champion got me through a difficult interaction with my ex-husband, or when wrapping myself in Superwoman's cape helped me make it through a week packed with family, work and school obligations. And even taking on a less positive label can help you navigate through troubling times: sometimes calling yourself a badass or even a bitch can add a bit of steel to your spine when dealing with situations that require you to stand up for yourself. The danger in those situations, though, is boxing yourself into a single label, seeing yourself through a single lens, rather than allowing the full complexity of your personality—and your range of possible choices, reactions and pathways—to be available to you.

That's where Parts Work Therapy can be profoundly helpful. As I wrote in the sidebar called Therapy's Alphabet Soup on page 11, Parts Work Therapy—which encompasses therapeutic approaches such as Internal Family Systems (IFS) and others—suggests that our personalities are made up of a number of sub-personalities. In his book *Introduction to Internal Family Systems*, Dr. Richard Schwartz puts it this way: "We have ongoing, complex relationships with many different inner voices, thought patterns, and emotions that are similar to relationships we have with other people. What we call 'thinking' is often our inner dialogue with different parts of us."[8]

One aspect of my personality might be Superwoman, but other aspects might be labelled rebel, good girl, black sheep and peacekeeper, with all of them contributing to make up "Samra." Perhaps not surprisingly, the parts of ourselves we work hardest to reject or distance ourselves from are most often the sources of ongoing pain.

Why? Because they're frequently linked to shame we experience attached to those roles. For me, for instance, rejecting the label "good wife" was essential to escape my marriage. But rejecting that label completely left me with unresolved feelings of anger towards my teen-aged self, the girl who had tried so desperately to earn her husband's love and to live up to her community's standards of female behaviour by trying to be that "good wife." And while I often extended empathy and understanding towards other women who had been similarly trapped in abusive marriages, deep inside, part of me still blamed that teenage good wife version of myself for not escaping sooner.

But we can't heal what we hate. Reacting to that aspect of myself with irritation, frustration or anger didn't get rid of her. It simply made me impatient with her—and unforgiving of myself.

Even the parts of ourselves we prize—like Superwoman—can be troublesome. As Dr. Schwartz puts it, perhaps one of your inner voices is great at keeping you organized and on track, creating and tracking the to-do list for your life, a "valued assistant" who helps you get things done. But what about when you want to relax, and that "valued assistant" starts criticizing you for being lazy or falling behind, triggering a fight in your head between the you who needs a break and the you who worries that if you stop, you won't start again. "The part of you that wants you to achieve makes for a wonderful servant but a terrible master, so you have a love/hate relationship with it," writes Dr. Schwartz.[9] In reality, we should be able both to work through our to-do lists and to enjoy some restorative time off. But when we allow one part of ourselves to dominate at the expense of others—the "doer" taking over and chasing the "relaxer" out of the house—we lock ourselves in a smaller box of behaviours. It's as if we've convinced ourselves that strength training at the gym means only exercising our right arm: we end up with a heck of a right biceps, as the rest of our muscles atrophy.

Sometimes it's easier to see and recognize the impact of labels when we shift from thinking about our own "internal family" of personality parts and look to our actual real life families. As a parent, the way labels narrow the range of possibilities became clearest to me in conversations with my daughters. Early in her teens, Saarah adopted the label empath, taking great pride in her ability to understand the feelings of others and being a sounding board and advisor to friends in need. But being the "understanding one" came to mean some friends expected her to be constantly available to hear their troubles. As we talked one afternoon, Saarah confessed that as much as she'd been proud of her empathic skills, she also felt pressured by the label. "It's like I'm expected to be empathetic to everybody but myself," she said. "I want to help people, but not at the cost of who I am."

The label had come to overshadow her, robbing her of the right to look after herself. She worried her friends would call her out as not really being empathetic, of being fake, if she stepped back from being always available to hear their emotional troubles—echoes of the feelings I'd had of being a fake champion when criticized for not saying yes to every request for my time.

"You know, when I call myself an empath, that's all I become," said Saarah. "But I can be an empathetic person without erasing all the rest of myself."

It was a nuanced and profound distinction, one I'd only recently begun to unravel in applying it to myself: that I could champion others without having to be a twenty-four-hour-a-day superwoman, that I—and Saarah—were both permitted to put boundaries around what we offered to others in our lives.

With my eldest daughter, Kinza, mature was the label applied to her from her earliest years—even as an eight-year-old. When I left my husband, I'd started calling her my partner, with others referring to her as

Saarah's "little Mom." All were labels attached out of love and admiration, but I came to see how limiting they were for the daughter I'd started thinking of as a tiny adult. She *wasn't* an adult, and thinking of her in these terms communicated in subtle ways that she wasn't allowed to be a child. In her late teens, when people praised her maturity, Kinza would retort with, "You can thank childhood trauma for that!"—and she was spot-on. Children exposed to chaotic and violent households often seem mature for their age, because their survival instincts have pushed them to act like adults when the grown-ups around them don't. The flip side to that, though, was an undercurrent of anger at being pushed to grow up too soon. When that anger bubbled up, I made the mistake more than once of failing to make room to hear it, trying to shut it down by blaming Kinza for her feelings. "Why are you always so angry?" I yelled in the middle of an argument with her.

With, yes, maturity beyond her years, she called me on it. "I'm allowed to be mad, Mom," she said. "That doesn't mean I'm 'always angry' and it's not fair to label me that way." She was right. Being angry didn't make her "always angry" or an "angry person." We're all allowed to be mad sometimes. And I, as her mother, needed to make space to hear it.

Putting the Parts Together

How does the work of balancing our inner selves, our many labels, happen? The first step is to acknowledge that we are more than any one label can capture, that we have many parts or many sub-personalities within us—and we have the capacity to rise above those parts or sub-personalities and observe them as they push to be heard. In Internal Family Systems (IFS) therapy, that listener is referred to as the capital-S Self, the internal leader of the team of your sub-personalities or parts. You might find it helpful to think of that internal leader as your name or simply as "me," recognizing that it is your fullest, most complex and complete self, the you who can stand back and observe your sub-personalities. It's you, the listener; you, the centre.

IFS categorizes our various parts under three distinct headings. The "exiles" are the parts of us that have been hurt, abused or shamed. Because they embody difficult or scary emotions, we often shun them, doing our best to keep them locked up or locked out. Unfortunately, these exiles might also embody desirable characteristics—like vulnerability, childlike wonder, enthusiasm, playfulness—that also get locked out with them, as our minds view our hurt parts as potentially dangerous to our overall internal system. The other two categories of parts both work to protect us from the scariness or toxicity we fear in our damaged exiles: "managers," who are the critical, perfectionist parts of ourselves, and "firefighters," who rush in whenever an exile lights an emotional fire. Our managers keep us on track, though they may also drive us in unforgiving and harsh ways, while our firefighters unleash numbing behaviours like addictions or self-harm to distract us from acknowledging the pain our exiles carry with them.[10]

Dr. Schwartz points out that all our parts or sub-personalities start out as expressing or possessing "naturally valuable talents and resources,"[11] but they get pushed into extreme and sometimes damaging roles as a result of trauma or other hurts and harms we experience. So, the part of us that starts out expressing our creative impulses and joy might get "burdened" with the role of chronic self-doubt when a primary school teacher accuses seven-year-old you of plagiarizing a poem or tracing a drawing. Twenty years later, that creative part of you is frozen at age seven, afraid to express herself for fear of being accused again of stealing someone else's art, and her response is to endlessly doubt your every creative impulse, whispering that you shouldn't bother, shouldn't try, shouldn't put your creative self out there for others to see. The key to healing is not to lock your inner creative seven-year-old away, but to let her know that you believe in her skills, that she can stop hiding them because the adult you—the Self—is now strong enough to protect her from unfair accusations and other harmful critiques.

The challenge is that when a part of us—especially an exiled part—is triggered, we may find it difficult to separate the current situation from the past emotions bubbling up around it. It's as if, in the moment, we lose our anchor in time: yesterday's emotions wash over us and we respond to them now as if the current situation warrants them, snapping at someone we love over what seems to them to be a harmless remark (our "fight" reaction is triggered), shutting down in a work meeting because we're experiencing the emotional echo of a childhood situation (our "freeze" reaction is triggered) or ending a relationship because we're overwhelmed with feelings from a past romantic failure (our "flee" reaction is triggered). Learning to recognize that a labelled part of us is acting up is the first step. The next step is to hit pause: to try to create a gap between the past emotions that have been triggered and our impulse to act, so we can assess what action is warranted in the here and now rather than sabotaging ourselves in the present due to a past hurt.

Then? It can help to speak directly to the part of ourselves that has been triggered. It can be as straightforward as saying, "I see your shame [fear, anger]. You're safe now. I'm here. I'm holding you. You can relax and rest. You don't need to protect us anymore. I've got this."

The goal of IFS is to integrate the exiles, managers and firefighters into a healthier whole, so the Self—the compassionate, creative, confident, curious person we are at our core—shines through. Key to the process is welcoming each sub-personality as it pushes itself forward, observing and listening to it nonjudgmentally, recognizing that even our destructive, critical selves are trying to protect us. This doesn't mean acting as each sub-personality wants us to, but rather working to understand the underlying impulses, emotions and fears driving those sub-personalities and meeting them with compassionate understanding. Especially for those of us who have experienced trauma, working with a mental health professional trained in these approaches can help, and Dr. Schwartz's books also contain valuable exercises and insights.

A House Shaped Like Armour

Whispered Wisdom

Learn who you are, and then be them more,
instead of thinking, always, that you are meant to be less.

ALEXANDRA GILLESPIE, VICE-PRESIDENT, UNIVERSITY OF TORONTO

& PRINCIPAL, UNIVERSITY OF TORONTO MISSISSAUGA

October's crisp autumn sunlight filtered through the red maple leaves as I sat in my car outside the house I'd once lived in. The two-storey, three-bedroom home backed onto a golf course, the residential street in front of it quiet and calm. I remembered the excitement I'd felt as my husband and I had bought the house, the joy I'd taken in selecting paint colours and window coverings, decorating it with love as I tried to paper over the chaos that our married life had become. Twinned images clashed in my head: the beautiful kitchen where he spit in my face, the cozy family room where he broke my laptop, the walk-in closet where he slapped me hard, the generous basement where he choked me.

It was a beautiful house, but a terrifying home.

Still, I had wrapped it around me like armour, trying to make it perfect in the hope that others might see it as perfect, too, that my efforts might transform my marriage into something safer, more loving.

More than a decade had passed since I'd left that home for the last time, and now I was on the verge of purchasing a new home for my daughters and me after years of renting. That morning, I had an appointment in this neighbourhood and found myself pointing the car back towards this house, this past life. I'd never felt safe there. And yet, part of me had been whispering in my ear about it ever since I'd started house hunting: *If only you'd found a way to keep this house,* that part of me said, *you'd be so much further ahead now, with a mortgage almost paid off rather than taking a new one on. Why did I let him sell it out from under us?*

That "why" had a simple answer: when our marriage ended, I didn't know what my rights were. I didn't have a job. I didn't know the court could mandate him to pay the mortgage. He'd told me he'd sell the house and pay the rent elsewhere for the girls and me. And I didn't know our daughters and I were entitled to stay in that marital home. I just assumed we had to move because he said so.

What part of me was it that was whispering in my ear, berating me for a bad decision I'd had no choice in more than a decade earlier? *Who are you?* I asked myself. *What are you trying to tell me?* As I listened closely, I could hear the fear tucked under the blame in her voice. *Are you really strong enough to carry a house on your own?* she whispered. *Is it safe to pour your savings into a down payment? That money is your safety net! What will happen if it all goes wrong? You've messed it up before!*

As I let her speak, I could feel her fears rippling through me, even as I knew I was strong enough, informed enough to carry the risk of home ownership on my own—and resilient enough to recover if something did go wrong.

It's okay, I whispered back to twenty-five-year-old me crying in the kitchen. *We've got this. You're going to be okay.*

Talking to Ourselves

We talk to ourselves all the time—that's what thinking is. But how can we begin to talk productively to the parts of ourselves we might otherwise turn away from, the parts we associate with shame, blame, criticism, self-doubt, recklessness and other negative emotional burdens?

- **Recognize:** Notice when negative self-talk whispers in your ear.
- **Reflect:** Rather than getting locked into fighting with yourself—or selves—step back and take time to reflect, not ruminate. What's the difference? Rumination is repetitive, negative thinking about past and present events that causes emotional distress.[12] Reflection steps outside of the negative thought loop and allows us to view what is going on in our heads with some emotional distance. Try to detach from the emotions swirling in your mind and ask what feelings are surfacing and where they are coming from. Which "part" or sub-personality is attached to the specific emotions? Which "you" is trying to be heard? One tactic: Replace *am* with *feel*—I *feel* depressed rather than I *am* depressed, or I *feel* dumb rather than I *am* dumb.
- **Acknowledge:** See the emotions this part of you is expressing, then look beyond to see what else this part of you embodies. *I see the worry you are carrying, but that worry isn't all of who you are.* As you listen to your fears, meet them with compassion and kindness. What value can you find in their concerns? What perspective can you bring that might reassure them?
- **Release:** Express gratitude. Thank the part of you that is carrying these difficult emotions into the situation. Recognize that their impulse, though it may be misguided, is grounded in protecting you. Let them know it is okay for them to relinquish the emotional burden they bear.

At the beginning, this type of reflection might happen over hours or even days. As you become more practised at it, you will find yourself able to more easily shift into Self mode, seeing more quickly where negative or damaging thoughts are coming from. You'll be less likely to be stuck in rumination or blown off course by disruptive emotions as you develop the skills to help the many yous inside of you put down their negative emotional burdens and let their natural strengths and talents shine through.

Whispered Wisdom

I was ambitious for as long as I could remember. I was always excited to "reach the next level." I couldn't wait to conquer my goals and set new ones. I loved being really busy, really productive and really successful. As I crossed off items from my many to-do lists, I felt victorious, and the word "Superwoman" was often on my mind. I felt proud and invincible. And then I got sick. I had breast cancer, chronic migraines, and I periodically wore a heart monitor.

I was forced to slow down and re-evaluate. What was important? My health, certainly. I wasn't invincible after all. I needed to take the time to learn how to sleep, eat and move properly. I realized that spending time with girlfriends was crucial. And I recently came to understand that one thing is often overlooked: the importance of having fun. Take the time to figure out what fun is for you, and make sure you do it. I used to feel guilty if I took time out of my day to focus on myself, but now I realize it isn't something to feel guilty about, it's the true meaning of being successful.

FARAH PERELMUTER, CEO, CO-FOUNDER, SPEAKERS SPOTLIGHT

Unconditioning Workbook

- When we label others, we reduce them to a single word, a single story, erasing their complexity.
- We label ourselves to conform to the expectations of others, to push back against those expectations or to armour ourselves against judgments.
- When some part of us knows that all parts of us aren't welcomed, we may present a single version of ourselves—one that might make us feel powerful—to gain acceptance or as a defense because we know others will label us anyway.
- If the choice is between being invisible or carrying a negative or hurtful label, often we'll take the label rather than be ignored.
- Sometimes labels can help us manage challenging times, but they can also box us into a single way of being, stunting us from developing our full complexity and exploring our full range of choices.
- The parts of ourselves we work hardest to reject or distance ourselves from are often sources of ongoing pain because they are linked to shame we experience attached to those roles.
- We are more than one label can capture. Each of us has many parts or sub-personalities within us, and we have the capacity to rise above those parts and observe them as they push to be heard.
- Internal Family Systems (IFS) therapy is one approach to

understanding and integrating our sub-personalities. It emphasizes that all our parts or sub-personalities start out expressing or possessing valuable skills and resources, but some get pushed into unhealthy and perhaps damaging roles as a result of trauma or other harms. The goal of therapies such as IFS is to integrate our sub-personalities into a healthier whole by resolving internal conflicts, so that our compassion, creativity, confidence and curiosity can shine through.

Reflection: What's Under That Label?

Think about the labels you've attached to yourself over time. How did those labels help or harm you? What aspects of yourself did they emphasize or hide? Are you carrying remnants of those past labels with you still?

As you go through your day, which yous bubble up and whisper in your ear? What strengths does each embody? What weakness is each protecting?

The next time you find yourself dealing with a troubling emotional situation, unsure of which route to take, try this exercise.

1. Describe the situation.

   _____

   _____

   _____

   _____.

2. Label: When I think about this situation, the voices I hear might include people from my past or aspects of myself. These are some of the voices I hear.

Name/Label:

What they say:

_____

_____

_____

_____ .

3. Ask: What emotion(s) is each feeling?

   Name/Label:

   What they feel:

_____

_____

_____

_____ .

4. Probe: What is each hiding, protecting or shielding?

   Name/Label:

   What they are hiding, protecting or shielding:

_____

_____

_____

_____ .

5. Reflect: How does what you've uncovered help you see your situation with more clarity?

_____

_____

_____

_____ .

CHAPTER FOUR:

Braveheart

I'll admit it: when my phone alarm jolted me awake at 3:00 a.m., I was tempted to hit snooze and go back to sleep. *Don't you dare,* whispered a voice in my head. The online trip sites all agreed: the sunrise at Land's End in Forillon National Park wasn't to be missed. And so I pulled on my clothes, pointed the car towards Cap-Bon-Ami and set off. The beach was dark as I descended the wooden steps from the parking lot, stars still twinkling in the dome overhead. I settled onto the stony beach, a blanket wrapped around my shoulders, to wait for morning's first rays.

I've always loved sunsets and sunrises. No matter how bad my day has been, a sunset reminds me it can end in beauty. And no matter how challenging life seems, a sunrise reminds me that each day can start with joy. Still, even for a sunrise collector like me, the view at Cap-Bon-Ami took my breath away: orange danced at the horizon and the sun's rays turned the Appalachian cliffs at the water's edge the colour of marmalade. A deep peace settled over me.

I hadn't fully realized it, but as I'd driven along the Gaspé coast these past days, I'd carried within me a chorus of voices. I'd been fighting in my head with my ex-husband as I considered whether to pursue him for his overdue support. I'd been carrying on conversations with bosses past and present as I tried to figure out what to do about work. I'd been trying to ignore the persistent voice of my mother, whispering that I'd failed as a wife, daughter and mother.

As the sun's rays touched me, the voices stilled.

Complications of Courage

"You're useless. Do you think you're some kind of hotshot who can make it without me? Because you won't: you're worthless."

Throughout my marriage, my husband said things like this to me. His words were like toxic seeds, and the soil they grew in had already been prepared by messages from the culture around me. Across cultures, women are still told we're "less than," that our dreams should be smaller, our ambitions more realistic—and that courage is for men.

But then, when we do find models to inspire us to dream big, we're told to be fearless, to bring our courage to work, to be authentically ourselves. And yet, especially for racialized women, LGBTQ2S+ people or anyone who is marginalized, being authentically ourselves can be dangerous, speaking up can make us targets and ignoring our fears can blind us to real risks in the workplace, our communities, even our homes.

Courage isn't simple.

If you search for definitions of the word, you'll find lots of lists, such as the four types of everyday courage (moral, intellectual, disciplined, empathetic).[1] Or maybe there are six types (physical, emotional, intellectual, social, moral, and spiritual).[2] Brené Brown describes courageous leadership as a collection of four skill sets (vulnerability, clarity of values, trust and rising skills).[3] According to Merriam-Webster's online dictionary, the definition of *courage* is "mental or moral strength to venture, persevere, and withstand danger, fear, or difficulty."

All those things are true. But when I think of courage in my own life and the courage in others that has inspired me, I see courage as circular, a kind of process where it looks like we're returning again and again to the same lessons, when in fact we're gradually—and sometimes dramatically—building our skills. As Angela Duckworth, author of *Grit: The Power of Passion and Perseverance*, points out, grit—or courage—is learned as we cultivate tenacity and figure out how to pick ourselves up after we fall down.[4]

Not long ago, I was in Prince George, a small city in British Columbia's interior that sits where the Fraser and Nechako Rivers meet, to give a speech to women entrepreneurs on the gift of adversity and the challenges of unlearning limiting beliefs. My core message: we can't control what happens to us, but we can control our response to what happens—and those responses determine the trajectory of our life. After, as I stood chatting with the event organizer and some of the attendees, a young woman edged into the circle. As the other women drifted away, I noticed her drawing a breath as if readying herself to speak. I gave her a smile of encouragement. "I guess, well, I wanted to ask . . . I mean, my question is, what is it inside you that gave you the guts to conquer the odds?" Her last words tumbled out in a rush. "I mean, how did you do that?"

I'd been asked similar questions in the past. "It's not a secret ingredient I have or a superpower," I said. I could tell it had taken some bravery on her part to approach the circle of strangers, and I put a hand on her arm to reassure her that her question was welcomed. "It's a muscle you build over time," I said. I told her that when I'd first arrived in Canada, I was completely isolated, my every move monitored by my husband and mother-in-law. After Kinza was born, they allowed me to sign up for a baby playgroup at a community centre, a fifteen-minute walk from our home. Over time, I realized I could push that fifteen-minute walk to twenty, and have five minutes that were my own to do with as I wished. Sometimes I had spare change I'd managed to squirrel away, and so I could buy myself a coffee or an ice cream for the walk back, carefully discarding the telltale garbage in a can around the corner from home. The library was on the way, and before long, I started telling my mother-in-law that the playgroup leader had suggested I get some books for Kinza, extending my time without supervision by thirty minutes or more. I'd grab books for Kinza but also snatch some precious time to read a few pages of a book that interested me, or even just sit and enjoy being able to simply be.

"Since leaving my husband, I've travelled to more than thirty-five countries in the world," I told her. "But it started with small steps, of finding ways to be on my own for five minutes and thirty minutes and more."

"But weren't you scared they'd catch you?" she asked.

"I was scared all the time," I told her. "Being brave isn't about being fearless: I was afraid, and I had good reason to be. But being afraid helped me figure out what steps I needed to take to protect myself. Being afraid helped me be smart about being brave."

Courage can be instilled in these small ways, I told her, but so can fear. It's what my husband was trying to do with put-downs designed to erode my confidence, by scaring me with a look or a raised voice. We build our courage with small acts that accumulate over time—and those who would keep us afraid try to erode our courage in the same way. Their threats, undermining messages and actions are like threads, each one tying us in place. One loop doesn't have the strength to hold us, but repeated loops cut our skin and bind us in place.

"What kept you going?" she asked.

At first, I just wanted to get an education, I told her, something my husband had promised I could pursue when our marriage was arranged. But as he became more violent towards me, I realized I needed to escape. I wanted to be free to be myself—and I wanted my daughters to be free as well.

"Your girls are lucky to have you," she said.

"I'm lucky to have them," I replied, as we parted.

In the days that followed, my mind returned to our discussion. Her questions weren't new ones, but I found myself thinking about courage and its components, the enduring idea that courage is something you have or you don't, like a perfect trophy in a silk-lined presentation case. My courage didn't feel like that. It felt scrappy and bruised and imperfect, bearing the marks of my stumbles as well as my successes.

When I tell the story of leaving my marriage, it looks like a natural series of steps: I dream of getting an education. Slowly, I take a series of steps to gain more and more freedom, support and control. I leave my marriage. And in the years following, I build a life with my daughters. Step 1, step 2, step 3, step 4.

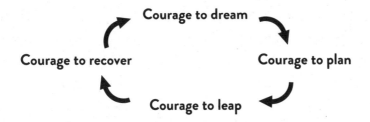

Many stories of courage focus on the courage to dream and the courage to leap, perhaps because they seem like the logical beginning and ending: the moment we start to imagine a situation could be different from how it currently is, and the moment we actually take the steps to change it. And those steps are essential: research shows that being able to imagine a future "possible self"—a term coined in 1986 by social psychologists Hazel Markus and Paula Nurius[5]—can be a powerful motivator, fuelling us to take the steps to achieve our vision of who we might become. Interestingly, even a negative future vision—for instance, picturing your future self as an alcoholic—can prompt behaviour that sets you on a positive path (perhaps to being a non-drinker).[6] And perceiving ourselves as having a purpose in life can literally be life-saving: one study of almost seven thousand American adults found that those who scored higher on tests to measure life purpose lived longer, with lower mortality rates particularly for heart disease and circulatory and blood conditions.[7] But to me, the two far more interesting and less understood parts of the circle—and the parts where the internal shifts occur allowing us to change our external circumstances—are the courage to plan and the courage to recover.

The Courage to Plan

When I finally completed my high school credits through distance learning, I applied to university and was accepted to both York University and the University of Toronto. But my elation quickly evaporated. My parents-in-law believed I should focus only on my roles as wife, mother and daughter-in-law. Faced with their opposition, my husband, who had initially agreed I could apply to university, refused to use our household income to pay for my tuition—income that was high enough to disqualify me for student loans. I could feel my dream slipping away.

In order to go to university, I needed income of my own. But how? I'd had a retail job in the past, but my husband's jealousy and suspicion made it impossible for me to keep it. I tried googling "work from home," but the jobs that popped up seemed to fall into two categories: scams and internet sex work. Then, one day, as my mother-in-law and I shopped for groceries, I saw a sign on the community bulletin board advertising in-home daycare. People did that—looked after other people's children in their home? I turned the idea over in my head, wondered if this might be something I could do in the home my husband and I shared with his parents.

I knew I would need to get my mother-in-law's approval, and slowly, I broached the subject. Perhaps we could do this together? I ventured. I would do all the work. She wouldn't have to do a thing. And we could split the money!

At each step, I appealed to my mother-in-law's self-interest. As my independence grew, I wanted my own phone, so I convinced my mother-in-law to support my request by pointing out that if I had one, she wouldn't have to worry about her calls to friends on the house phone being interrupted by calls related to the daycare. I wanted to learn to drive and made the case based on how much more convenient it would be for us to go shopping—for daycare supplies, groceries and her own needs—if we didn't have to rely on my husband or father-in-law.

From a distance, it may look like I had a master plan, with each step moving logically from one to the next, but the truth is that it was much less methodical. My main goal—to get an education—remained my North Star, but there on the ground, my journey involved one small step after another, each one chosen based on what then stood in my way. It was a bit like carving a path through the woods: sometimes boulders blocked my way, sometimes rivers appeared before me, sometimes the climb seemed impossibly steep and other times the route flat and clear, until it wasn't again. I did what I had to so I could get past the limits others placed on me—that a good mother didn't need to seek an education, that a good wife's sole focus was serving her family. I had to be flexible, changing my route when it made sense to do so.

Sometimes I had to have the courage to break the rules. When I finally enrolled at university, there were times when I skipped my classes so I could attend appointments with a mental health counsellor. My husband wouldn't allow me to see a counsellor; neither would he let me stay on campus outside of my class time. And so I lied to him, letting him believe I was in class when I was in counselling.

I lived in a state of constant discomfort, but the source of that discomfort shifted over time. I went from living with the discomfort (too mild a word) of being controlled, isolated and abused, to living with the discomfort of trying to change my circumstances. As that shift happened, I went from making approval-seeking decisions to making empowered decisions: decisions based not on the wishes of those around me, but rather on finding a way to be true to myself.

That shift is significant because the approval of others is important to us all. Our health and safety often depend on our connections to each other. But when our decisions are driven by gaining that approval—doing whatever we have to in order to maintain those connections—we place the power to determine whether our decisions are good or bad, welcomed or rejected, in the hands of others. Approval becomes the goal, and our happiness and authenticity become secondary. When we build the strength to shift to empowered decision-making, we flip those priorities: being true to ourselves becomes primary, and the approval of others becomes secondary. This isn't simple, especially when we are in circumstances where we depend on others for our income, housing or other necessities.

And so we have to build our paths and our skills, taking steps in the direction we wish to go while also developing the attributes we need to stop relying on the support of others that we may lose along the way. What does this mean in real terms? When I started taking my first steps, I thought I could find a way to meet my goal—of getting an education and doing work I enjoyed—within my marriage, being true to my dreams while also keeping the approval of my husband, family and community. But as I took the steps to gain that education, I came to realize that wasn't the case. Choosing education would eventually mean either drastic changes in my marriage—which I realized over time wasn't going to happen—or I would have to leave.

What would leaving mean? I knew that my standard of living would drop, that I'd have to find a way to support myself and my daughters financially. I knew I would lose connections within the community, face the judgment of others and be shamed by my own family. And so my plan grew as I tried to carve a path towards a career that would provide an income and forge connections with others outside my husband and his family's circle.

But here's the thing about the planning part of the cycle of courage: you have to plan enough—and you can never plan enough. There is no crystal ball to tell you it will all work out fine. There is no perfect moment when you can be certain that if you act now, all will be well. You step. And you plan. And you step. And you plan.

And then you leap. Sometimes, literally.

What Does It Feel Like to Fly?

Let me tell you a secret: I'm afraid of heights. But I've always dreamed of skydiving. After I left my marriage, I visited family in Dubai. Jumeirah Beach is one of the world's top destinations for skydiving, and for weeks before I left Canada, I'd go on the Skydive Dubai website. I'd book a skydiving appointment, put it in my online cart . . . and then abandon it. The next day, I'd go back and do it again, over and over, never completing the booking. Eventually, the spots filled up.

Once in Dubai, I spent days on Jumeirah Beach, watching the parachutes in the sky above me, dreaming of being in one of them. Still, I put it off. It was so beautiful. But I was terrified.

Finally, two days before I was scheduled to fly back to Toronto, I called. Booked solid, they told me, but the good news was if I came first thing in the morning, I could go on a waitlist. The bad news? Not a single waitlist spot had opened up in the past two weeks.

Okay, I thought, *but I'm still going to try*. The next day, I showed up at 8:00 a.m. Four people were already in line in front of me. Still, I signed up and sat down to wait.

I'd already looked at the safety statistics: I was more likely to die in a plane crash flying back to Toronto than jumping out of a plane over this beach. Now, I stopped people as they exited. "What was it like?" I asked. "Weren't you afraid?" Many said yes, they'd been scared. All said it had been amazing.

By then it was late afternoon. Just one more round of jumps to go. I was getting ready to pack up when I heard my name called. A spot had opened up for a tandem jump with an instructor! Before I could change my mind, I paid my fee and signed the release. As I suited up with the instructor, I quizzed him on how many jumps he'd done: more than ten thousand. I was in good hands.

Minutes later, we were in the air. The door opened—and all the research I'd done seemed to fly out into the wind. The fears kicked in. Was I going to be Skydive Dubai's first accident? What if my harness broke? Was I being unfair to my children by taking this risk? The questions whirled through my brain. In that moment, the choice was mine. I could succumb to those fears and watch with envy as others jumped and landed safely. Or I could trust that I'd done enough homework to just let go—as I'd done at other times in my life, with going to school, leaving my marriage, sharing my story. I had been afraid. And then I'd let go.

We can never know for sure. And if we wait to be sure, we'll be frozen in place.

I let go and jumped. I will never forget the moment I began to fly. It was like nothing I'd ever experienced before. There was no stomach drop, no sense of direction or gravity. Just the sheer force of the clear, crisp wind. I was flying, free and fabulous!

To the west, the sun was low in the sky. Thirteen thousand feet below me was the white sand of Jumeirah Beach and the sapphire waters of the Persian Gulf. For sixty seconds, we were in freefall. And then our chutes deployed. For six more minutes, we floated down, watching the setting sun.

It was magical.

The girl who was denied the most basic freedoms is flying like a free, courageous badass, I whispered back in time to the girl who had been afraid she wouldn't survive leaving her marriage. *That girl is me.*

Ride Your Own Ride

There is a woman I know whose early life was much like mine: an arranged marriage, an abusive husband, children she loved. Like me, she took steps to get an education. But for all kinds of reasons, she did not leave her marriage. Her husband is powerful, and it's possible he'd have been able to keep her from her children. Her community and religious connections are important to her, and it's possible she couldn't imagine her way to a future where she could withstand the judgment and exclusion that might have come with divorce. Still, even as she has stayed in her marriage, she has made sure her daughters are educated and empowered to make their own choices about their marriages and futures. And each year, she uses her status within her community to fundraise substantial contributions for local women's shelters, so those who do leave have a safe place to land.

Does she lack courage? No. Her courage—or perhaps her leap—simply looks different from mine.

A friend of mine is an avid motorcyclist, and she shared a saying from the motorcycle world with me: Each of us has to ride our own ride. What does that mean? Whether travelling alone or with a group of other motorcyclists, our circumstances are unique. My motorcycle might have more horsepower than yours—or less. Your tires might be in better shape. You might be a more experienced rider I may have had a better night's sleep and be more physically and mentally alert. We might be riding the same road—but there's a patch of gravel in my path and a pothole in yours. What does it all add up to? You don't have to match anyone else's speed. If you need a break, take one. And on some days, you may be ready to ride, and I should stay parked in the driveway.

Being courageous can be life-threatening. Some women—the women fighting for their rights in Iran and Afghanistan, women everywhere who try to leave abusive situations—still choose to speak up, to act, despite that danger. Others choose to fight silently, perhaps by working to instill different values in their children.

We each have to ride our own ride.

The Courage to Recover

So, we ride or we don't ride, we leap or we don't leap. Both are decisions that can change our paths. In the aftermath, maybe everything changes. Or nothing changes at all. Or you land somewhere in between. And then you have to recover.

We think of "recovery" as a phase that follows injury, failure or some other kind of negative change. But in the aftermath of any change, we need time to figure out our new normal—even if it's a better normal than the one we left behind. In the case of positive change, new options might open up to us. We might have developed or discovered new skills or made new allies or connections. The possibilities we now see ahead of us may have shifted substantially enough to make us rethink our direction: our North Star might be a little north-northwest instead.

Or our jump may have been more of a stumble, and we need to regroup. We might need to take steps to ensure our safety. We might need to hold ourselves accountable for a mistake or misstep. We might need to grieve our losses and rebuild our strength, reorient ourselves as we check our direction and take another step.

We may feel as if we're walking in circles, repeating the same lessons over and over again. And in a way, we are, but our journey isn't flat and two-dimensional. It stretches like a coiled spring as we both circle and climb.

Whispered Wisdom

You know that "little voice" in your head? Get curious about what it's trying to tell you. Make some space to explore it. So many people are searching for their purpose in life, but more often than not, it's your little voice that holds the key to the answers that you seek.

JULIE FRY, ACC CERTIFIED

CAREER REINVENTION COACH

All That Glitters

"How did these ever fit you?" Saarah's words hit me with unexpected power.

The two of us were sitting in the bedroom of our new home at the end of a long week. I'd been worried about money, as interest rates had started to rise just after we'd moved in and embarked on a kitchen renovation that, inevitably, was costing more than planned. Earlier in the week, as I unpacked some boxes in my bedroom, I'd found one containing my wedding jewellery: gold bracelets, necklaces, earrings and more, all items I'd never wear again, their beauty tarnished by their association with those unhappy years. Maybe they'd look better as a new kitchen, I thought, as I put them aside, planning to get them valued in case I needed the cash to top up the renovation fund.

Now, Saarah examined the baubles she'd spread on the bed. "Mom, the bracelets are so small—they look like children's jewellery!" she said. And it struck me: Saarah was sixteen, just a few months younger than I'd been when I was forced into marriage. And she was right, these jewels had been made for the skinny teenager I was then. "Yes," I said. "And that child was me."

Later, I went to the park nearby. Alone there, I shed some tears. In the days that followed, grief clung to me. At other times, I might have ignored it, tried to push it away. But this time, I knew I needed to sit with it, feel it.

I am grateful for the life I have built. My daughters are gifts. But I grieve for the girl I was, the girl who lost years that can never be recovered. I missed out on relationships and experiences that are the norm for teenagers and young adults—first dates and friendships, time to explore and develop dreams. My earliest experiences of sex were coerced. They involved little pleasure and complicated negative emotions. I was pregnant twice—and never experienced the support and care of a loving partner. As a young mother, time with my daughters that should have been about learning and loving them was instead complicated by fear and insecurity.

Those difficult times, those losses, are not erased by today's happier times. Trauma, for all of us, doesn't simply disappear, though if we face and reckon with it, unravel its emotional impact so its echoes don't dictate how we respond in this moment, its effects can be diluted. In simplest terms, in the immediate aftermath of trauma, our lives might be described as nine-tenths trauma—but each day we reclaim as our own shifts that proportion. Our lives will never be trauma free. But they can become less trauma full.

We will still have moments when we notice what we've lost, even as we value who we have become. Pushing away that sadness is as misguided as scolding a tired child when what they need is a hug and a safe place to rest. But neither should we live in sadness, our eyes focused always over our shoulders on what we've lost or left behind. We need to rest, restore, rebuild. And when we are ready, we need to take another step.

Catalogue Your Courage

Believing in ourselves is a powerful force, one that can literally change our lives. For instance, researchers studying resiliency in children have found that a belief in our own abilities—what the researchers called "self-efficacy"—helps protect children from the otherwise damaging impacts of poverty. In one study of four thousand Danish schoolchildren, Charlotte Meilstrup and her colleagues found that kids who had greater self-efficacy had better mental health than kids with low self-efficacy despite coming from lower income backgrounds.[8] Canadian researcher Dr. Michael Unger's work at the Resilience Research Centre at Dalhousie University points to factors such as self-confidence, optimism and problem-solving as among eight personal "ruggedness" attributes that contribute to our ability to survive and thrive despite adversity.[9] All of these factors can also be viewed as contributing to self-efficacy and, I would argue, courageousness.

Courage is a funny thing, though. Ask people if they've got it, and in many cases, they'll say no. Sometimes we simply don't see when something we've done has required courage. At other times, we undercut our efforts, focusing on what we failed to do, what we didn't do enough of or how we otherwise fell short of some imagined perfect version of courage. Like soldiers reluctant to accept a medal of bravery, we tuck our moments of courage in a box and put them aside, when we should say "Yup, I did that" and let it boost our belief in ourselves.

If you believe you're brave, that's great. But if you're having trouble seeing yourself as courageous, it can help to keep a "brave book," a place where you jot down moments, whether small or more significant, when you've taken steps to face your fears, make a change or stand up for something you believe in.

Whispered Wisdom

Fear-filled thoughts are the collection of voices that have tried to control, shape, and teach you but may no longer serve you. The voice you hear that is kind, loving and compassionate, that is the real you. Trust that voice. That voice originates from your highest self, the depths of your soul, and the breadth of the greatest good. Listen to that voice. It is your truest voice, your wisest self.

DR. ROBYNE HANLEY-DAFOE,

RESILIENCY SCHOLAR & AUTHOR

Unconditioning Workbook

- Being brave isn't about being fearless. Listen to your fear: it can help you figure out what steps you need to take to protect yourself. Being afraid can help you be smart about being brave.
- Courage is complicated. Especially for racialized women, LGBTQ2S+ people or anyone who is marginalized, being authentically ourselves can be dangerous, speaking up can make us targets and ignoring our fears can blind us to real risks in the workplace, our communities and even our homes.
- Embrace the courage to plan, but know that while you have to plan enough, you can never plan enough. There will be no perfect moment when you can be certain that if you act now, all will be well. At a certain point, you must transition from the courage to plan to the courage to leap.
- We may feel as if we are walking in circles, repeating the same life lessons over and over again. And in a way, we are. But our journey isn't flat and two-dimensional. It stretches like a coiled spring, as we both circle and climb.
- Trauma doesn't simply disappear. But if we reckon with it, unravelling its emotional impact so its echoes no longer dictate how we respond in the moment, its effects can become diluted. Our lives will never be trauma free. But they can become less trauma full.

Reflection: What Do You Already Know?

Envisioning our future selves is worthwhile, even essential, as the "possible selves" research confirms. But fixating on one image of that possible self can blind us to the real gifts of our life's journey. We might not get what we set out to find and we might end up at a destination we never imagined, but we can build skills, gain knowledge and equip ourselves to continue our travels if we remain open to the possibilities of inner transformation and keep sight of our key values along the way.

Try this exercise. Think back to a simple example of "possible self" transformation that you have already achieved. Maybe it was a wish to learn to skate—to *become* a skater. Or to bake a perfect loaf of bread. Or build a deck.

My goal was to _____
_____
_____.

I took these steps _____
_____
_____.

The hardest part was _____
_____
_____.

The easiest part was _____
_____
_____.

What I expected to learn was _____

_____

_____.

What I really learned was _____

_____

_____.

Now, as you think about your current vision for your future "possible self," what lessons can you take from your past experiences of self-transformation? Perhaps you can flip through your "brave book." What have you already learned that will help you on the next leg of your journey?

Consider your next goal. Using what you discovered above, fill in these blanks.

My goal is to _____

_____.

Some steps I can take include _____

_____

_____

_____.

As you move forward, pause to reflect.

What I've found hard is _____

_____

_____

_____.

What's been easy is _____
_____
_____.

What I expected to learn was _____
_____
_____.

What I've really learned is _____
_____
_____.

The next steps I can take include _____
_____
_____.

Whispered Wisdom

There is a power that comes from knowing yourself, bringing a clarity and focus that will neither let you be diminished nor denied. Simply by being, you are worthy of all good things, unconditionally. Knowing that truth is the beginning of joy and the end of living a life that does not serve you.

ELISABETH BURKS,

CEO OF KNOWN ENTITY

CHAPTER FIVE:

Love Lessons

There's nothing like being on a solo trip to make you aware of the couples around you, walking together through the Jardins de Métis, sitting side by side watching the sun rise at Cap-Bon-Ami. Early in my trip, I'd wandered through the cobbled streets of old Quebec City on my own, stopping to watch a guitarist play in Place Royale as a crowd gathered around him. I swayed to the music as one couple and then another started to dance. I watched them with a touch of envy as the musician played on. *Why am I stopping myself?* I wondered. Dancing didn't require a partner. And so I let my feet move as the music moved through me. I felt a subtle shift in my thinking: I wasn't *by* myself. I was *with* myself.

The Girl at the Bedside

In my earliest memory, I am four or five years old. We are in an apartment in Pakistan and my mother is telling a story. In it, a pious woman, a mother, is getting ready to go to bed, and she asks her young daughter to fetch her a glass of water. The daughter goes to the kitchen, and when she returns, her mother has fallen asleep. The girl doesn't want to disturb her mother's slumber, so she stands next to her mother's bed with the glass of water, waiting for her to wake. Hours pass. The night darkens, and as the moon moves across the sky, the blackness fades and slowly lightens to morning. The mother's eyes flutter open. Her young daughter stands next to her bed, holding a glass of water. The mother's heart fills with love, her affection spilling over as she sits up and hugs her daughter tightly, kissing her head and face.

"This is what a mother deserves, what you should strive for," said my mother as she finished the story. "The obedience and love of a daughter who would stand at her bedside all night, waiting for her to wake up and take a sip of water. This is how you earn a mother's love."

Oh, how I wanted my mother to shower me with hugs and kisses like the obedient girl in that story! I had seen other mothers cuddle their children this way, but mine had never been very affectionate, especially with me. My parents' relationship was volatile, filled with yelling and fighting, their marriage a series of battles waged over years. As my siblings and I grew up, we were recruited as foot soldiers, perceived to be on one side or the other. My mother saw me as being on my father's side, though I don't remember ever choosing. "Mujhe tang mat karo," she would say in Urdu when I asked for a hug. "Don't bother me. What have you done for me that you deserve a hug right now?"

Now, with the story of the bedside daughter, she had shared a secret to earning her love, and so, not long afterward, I snuck into her room after she had gone to sleep. In my small hands I held a glass of water. I stood at her bedside, watching as she slept, imagining the love I would see blossom on her face when she opened her eyes to see me there.

I could barely conceal my excitement. The minutes passed as my mother breathed the slow breaths of someone deeply asleep and I shifted from foot to foot as I struggled to stay awake. Surely it would be all right for me to put the glass on the bedside table? Perhaps she wouldn't mind if I curled up on the floor. After all, the floor was hard, and wouldn't that be a test of love as well? I would still be here when she awoke, and then she'd see how I had waited to serve her. I set down the glass, settled onto the floor and fell asleep.

When I woke up hours later, my mother was already up and going about her day. If she had noticed me or the glass of water, she hadn't remarked on it. *Why did you fall asleep?* I thought. *Why weren't you strong enough to stay up all night like the girl in the story?* Guilt and shame filled me as I realized I hadn't done enough to earn my mother's love.

It seems silly, doesn't it? A four-year-old tries to re-enact a story of devotion. It's so simple in the parable: Just stand there all night. Hold one small glass of water for eight hours and you will prove you deserve to be loved.

Simple. And impossible.

Like so many love tests, the underlying message was this: love must be earned. I am not loveable simply because I am. I am not loveable when I am in pain or afraid or upset. I am loveable when I do what you want me to do. I am loved when I am obedient, compliant, sub-servient. It was a common theme in my mother's stories: the obedience children owed their mothers. After all, hadn't she carried me in her tummy, tucked under her heart for nine months, and endured unimaginable pain in giving birth to me and my siblings?

There were ways to earn a hug or kiss: my mother liked to have her feet massaged at the end of a long day and sometimes to have her back scratched before bedtime. Whichever child was lucky enough to be close at hand to perform these tasks might be rewarded with a quick hug or kiss. As the eldest daughter, I tried to make sure I was first in line. But these simple tasks repaid only a little of what my mother believed we owed her.

"Even if you worship me your entire life, you will not be able to pay back even a fraction of your debt to me," she declared. "Heaven lies beneath a mother's feet, and the more you serve your mother, the more you will earn your way into heaven." Yes, you should obey your father. But a mother's pedestal was seventy times higher, and those who proved their devotion to their mothers would go straight to heaven—like the son who carried his frail mother on his back to do the pilgrimage to Mecca, only to die of fatigue as they arrived. "Straight to heaven his soul had gone!" my mother claimed.

The stories my mother told me may be new to you. But many of us the world over—girls especially—are told stories with similar messages, grow up in families that demand similar subservience. And what we learn about earning love from our families gets carried forward, tucked in our hearts as we offer love to others: What must I do to earn your love? How would you like me to act—not *be*, but *act*—to be rewarded with your affection?

Love's Blueprint

How do we figure out what it means to love and be loved? From the time we're born, we seek connection. We need that connection and protection to survive, but it's also how we learn about love. We watch. And we learn. How do our parents treat us? How do they treat each other? What stories are we told about love?

In my home, love was confusing. In public, my parents looked like the picture of marital harmony. My mother took great pride in her appearance, using the most expensive skin creams, makeup and luxurious perfumes as she readied herself for dinners out on her husband's arm, her jewellery perfectly matched to her clothing. My father, with his thick, dark hair, moustache and wide smile, was outgoing and charming, the kind of man who could walk into a room of strangers, and an hour later, leave behind a roomful of new friends. He loved to have the latest "thing"—the first in our circle to own a mobile phone, always driving a new car—and, in truth, looking successful mattered to both of my parents, so much so that we teetered on the edge financially as my parents racked up debts to maintain their image.

Behind closed doors, our life was chaotic. Sometimes it was as it looked from the outside and my parents were pleasant with each other. But things could shift in an instant, with my father's mood swinging to violence at the smallest perceived slight from my mother. Then, the fights were loud and scary, and later my mother used her expensive makeup to hide bruises.

The lesson? Love could be unpredictable, violent.

As the eldest of four daughters, I would scurry to keep my sisters and me out of sight and sound when the fighting started, often hiding in closets until things settled down. I wouldn't recognize it until later, but my parents used us against each other as well: my father treated me and my youngest sister as his favourites; my mother chose her two middle daughters for her "side" in this protracted family war.

I never knew what version of love I would see when I came home from school. Would my parents be happy? Would my father bring my mother a gift? Or would he be shouting and throwing dishes across the room? As one of his favourites, could I coax him back to a good mood, make him laugh? Because if I could, the tension might ease—though then my mother might be irritated with me for taking his side.

The lesson? Love took coaxing, meant choosing sides.

The chatter around us offered no clarity on love, with marriage matches described as successful in terms of appearances and family connections. And as I grew up, my appearance became part of that conversation. "Her skin is so light—she'll have many suitors!" my aunties would exclaim. "She's getting so tall—you'll have to find her a tall husband as well!" they would say, some even suggesting my mother take me to a doctor for medication that would stop my growth.

The lesson? As long as you looked good in the photos, what went on behind closed doors didn't matter.

And while we were encouraged to do well in school, there were also messages about not doing *too* well. My father's own sister blamed her multiple degrees for her late and unhappy marriage. "Don't make my mistake," she warned me as I celebrated my high marks and school prizes.

The lesson? Men wanted intelligent wives—but not wives who would outshine them.

The tricky part? We may not be conscious of the lessons we learn about love growing up, even as they influence our choices and behaviour.

Settling

My marriage ended one January night when my husband picked a fight with me, accusing me of not doing enough housework. His fist tightened. I grabbed my telephone. "If you touch me, I'm going to call 911," I yelled. And then he shouted the word divorce, in Urdu, three times: "Talaq, talaq, talaq."

It would take more than those three words to end our marriage under Canadian law, and in truth, I had been taking steps to escape for some time, pursuing an education and secretly saving money. But his utterance signalled the beginning of our official ending. He sold our family home, giving me and our two daughters three weeks to pack up and leave. I scrambled to find someplace for us to live, eventually ending up in University of Toronto graduate student housing.

As news of our separation and eventual divorce found its way through the Toronto Pakistani community we were both still part of, those around me found ways—some subtle, some not so—to let me know my value as a woman on her own with two children. A butcher at the halal grocery store where I shopped got my phone number from my grocery order and started texting me lewd comments. Others I thought cared for me let me know I was now considered damaged goods: the mother of a good friend told me she had a marriage proposal for me— from a sixty-year-old man. "Auntie, he has children older than I am!" I told her, surprised she would think I would entertain such an offer. "Do you think you're going to find someone close to your own age?" she said. "You're divorced. You should be grateful for the offer. Men can easily find eighteen-year-old virgins instead of a divorced woman like you."

And then a member of my extended family propositioned me. During a visit with him and his wife, he had sat quietly listening as I told my female relative about the success I'd had at school and the position in corporate finance I'd accepted. (In truth, I was hoping my example would inspire her to end her marriage as well.) Later, he asked to speak privately with me and suggested that he could divorce my relative and marry me instead, continuing that he would allow me to do all that I was doing as long as I stopped wearing revealing clothing. Clearly, I was supposed to fall at his feet, grateful that a man would accept a damaged woman like me with only ONE condition. How lucky was I? When I turned down his disgusting offer, his anger was clear, as if a woman's only purpose was to revolve around a man.

I still hoped for a loving relationship. Once we had housing, my girls were safe and our lives felt more stable, dating became a possibility. It had taken strength to leave my marriage, but each of these judgments chipped away at my resolve. Was this what I had to look forward to—perverts, old men and losers? Was I supposed to simply settle for whatever I was offered, rather than expect to have a healthy relationship? And did I even know what a healthy relationship was?

And then I met Faisal. My romance with Faisal didn't start as a romance at all, it started with food. My marriage had ended and I was at school full-time while juggling multiple jobs to keep my girls and me financially afloat: as a teaching assistant in economics, a student mentor, a researcher with the City of Mississauga and doing night shifts at the campus student information centre. Because I was a good cook, I also sold Pakistani meals I made from home. That's how Faisal and I met, when he showed up at my door to buy some of my biryani.

He was Pakistani, charming and funny. While English was the language of my life at school and work, Faisal and I shared the ease of speaking Urdu, the language I'd grown up with. My daughters loved playing with him. We liked watching Bollywood movies together. Then one evening, he bumped his head as we got ready to turn on the television. I joked about kissing it better. And I did. "What about here?" he said, pointing to his chin. "I think that hurts too." A kiss. "And my cheek," he said. A kiss. "And my forehead," he said. And another.

If it sounds like puppy love, it's because, in retrospect, that's what it was, the kind of immature love teenagers have, the kind I'd never had as a teenager myself. And if, at first, he didn't want to tell anyone about us, that was okay, even a little bit exciting because it meant our love was our secret. When his parents came to visit and he introduced me as a friend—not a girlfriend—that was okay, too, I told myself.

But in truth, it wasn't. Hiding our relationship made me feel like the "damaged goods" I'd been told by others I was. When, after a short breakup, he agreed to publicly acknowledge me as his girlfriend, I felt vindicated. *See, Auntie,* I said to myself, *I can have someone my own age!*

While I was happy, his family wasn't. Oddly, he couldn't resist sharing every unkind thing they said about me. "The only thing she has going for her is that she's smart and she'll make money," he told me his father had said. "If that's why you're with her, leave and I'll give you more money." With each unkindness he passed on to me, it was as if he was waiting for me to thank him for staying.

I shrugged off my discomfort. Things didn't feel right, but I had so little romantic experience. Perhaps this was the trade-off you made for love, the small slights nowhere near as bad as what I'd endured in my marriage. As well, I worried about what might happen if I ended our relationship. What would people say about me? People in the community told me I was lucky to have him—and they told him that Allah would reward him for taking on someone like me. They didn't seem to care that I was the one earning more. The end of our relationship wouldn't be his failure—it would be mine.

With each of my successes, his insecurity grew. When I told him the University of Toronto had invited me to join the Governing Council, jealousy rather than happiness flashed across his face. "It's not that big a deal," he said. "You know, you've become too full of yourself. Don't forget that I accepted you when you were nothing, and now that you've gotten some success, you think you're all that."

"I was never nothing," I shot back.

And still I stayed. Then he falsely accused me of cheating on him. "Any other man would kick you to the curb," he told me.

The worried voice asking *What will they think?* evaporated in that moment. I wouldn't beg for forgiveness when I'd done nothing wrong. "You don't have to kick me out," I said. "I'm walking out on my own." I didn't see him again.

I'd been a good wife and a beaming girlfriend. Now, as neither of those things, I didn't feel comfortable within the Pakistani community, though I still longed for connection with someone who understood where I came from, who liked the food I liked and the music I enjoyed.

I told myself I just needed to accept that I was a misfit. And so when I saw a Pakistani man on Bumble who described himself as feminist, progressive and atheist, I thought, *Well, maybe he's a misfit like me.*

His name was Hamza. In our first phone conversations, he was charming and funny, though he asked few questions about me. At our first coffee date, I told him I'd left an abusive marriage. "Did he hit you?" he asked. "Yes," I said. "What did you do to cause that?" he replied, and when I told him no woman causes her abuse, he scrambled. "I just meant what were the reasons he hit you," he said. Later, I told a girlfriend I thought his remark was insensitive, that he wasn't right for me. But then his campaign began. He called me every day. Within five days, he told me he loved me. Flower delivery guys soon knew my address by heart. Reservations awaited at the best restaurants in town. He sent love notes filled with praise.

It felt romantic, like what you see in movies. My initial doubts were erased by the avalanche of affection, with constant activities and affirmations that left little time for reflection. For my birthday, he arranged a surprise trip to Calgary and Banff. He'd placed me on a pedestal, and his adoration was addictive. *Finally*, I thought, *a man who treats me right!* I felt like a fairy princess in a bed of roses.

But then the thorns started to appear. The shift came slowly, subtly. I'd started doing some public speaking about the power of education in helping women escape abuse, and when I shared the good news about a weekend speaking engagement, there was a pause before he spoke. "I just wish you'd checked with me first, before accepting," he said. "You know I like to spend my Saturdays with you, and it's just a bit disappointing." He paused again. "I mean, it's okay, I guess. I still love you, but I'm just . . . disappointed."

The combination of flattery, woundedness and slight withdrawal was compelling. *He loves me so much he doesn't want to lose even an afternoon with me!* I thought. If my solo decision to accept the speaking invitation had caused me to slip just a bit off the pedestal he had me on, I'd work extra hard to prove how much I loved him in return, to earn my way back onto that plinth. I wanted his adoration back, not the disappointment I now saw in his eyes.

Still, doubts bubbled below the surface. He texted me first thing in the morning, sent me emojis, voice messages and texts throughout the day. At first, it had seemed flattering, but as time went on, it became annoying and distracting, interrupting my workday and my time with my daughters because I felt obliged to respond to his constant stream of messages. He had shared his online calendar with me within days of our first date, expecting me to share mine as well. "It will just make it so much easier to plan our time together," he said. But to me, it felt intrusive and controlling, echoing the way my ex-husband had tried to monitor where I was and who I saw. Still, Hamza was so much more loving than my ex: Was I letting memories of my marriage poison this relationship?

And then came Hamza's confession. We'd been together for a few months and were on our way back from one of my speaking engagements, the first one Hamza had attended. "I have something to tell you," he began. "The reason I'm telling you this is because I love you and I really want to be honest with you. It's about something I'm not proud of." His words came slowly. In his marriage, he had struck his wife, he said, though he now deeply regretted it. She was emotionally unstable. She'd been throwing things at him, had struck him. He'd acted only in self-defence. "I didn't really hurt her. But I should never have done it," he said. "Being with you, hearing you speak, it's made me realize that no matter what, I shouldn't have hit her. You've helped me see that."

I was stunned. How could this man who was so demonstrative in his love for me have also abused a woman? If he'd told me this at the beginning of our relationship, I would never have continued seeing him. Still, I'd never have known if he hadn't told me—and he didn't have to tell me. Wasn't that a good sign, his confession and regret? With so much already invested in this relationship, I felt I should give him the benefit of the doubt.

While the compliments continued, they now sometimes had an edge. "Oh, you're wearing the red dress. I mean, it looks good. You look good. Just a bit like a fire engine." When I mentioned seeking a friend's advice on something at work, he was wounded. "You don't need to lean on friends for that kind of thing," he said. "Now that I'm here, you should just lean on me."

And then I told him I'd signed a book contract.

Just before we'd met, *Toronto Life* magazine had published a story I wrote about my escape from my marriage, and it had become the magazine's most shared story online. Then I got a call at work telling me that a publisher had offered me a contract to write a book based on the story. My first impulse was to call Hamza with the news, but I paused. Some part of me wondered if he'd be happy for me. Surely he would be, wouldn't he? I dialled and shared the news. His reaction was grudging.

"Oh." He paused. "Congratulations. I mean, that's a great thing. It's just, I have to say, it makes me feel a bit intimidated. I mean, I'm happy for your success, but I also feel like I'm going to get lost and small in all of this. I worry you'll leave me if you get too success-ful. You might become arrogant." And so instead of celebrating my happy news, I spent the rest of the call trying to make him feel better, important.

A few weeks later, as I came into my bedroom where he'd gone for a nap, I caught a glimpse over his shoulder of a photo on his phone, a woman, and I watched the motion of his thumb swipe the image. As he sensed me behind him, he slid the phone under the pillow and pretended to snore.

"What's going on?" I blurted, still surprised by what I'd seen. He stretched and yawned, pretending to awaken from sleep. "Is it raining?" he asked. "I was just dreaming it was raining."

"Were you on a dating app?" I asked. "You were just on your phone and I saw you swiping."

"What are you talking about?" he said, his denial firm and direct. "Are you crazy? Why would I be on a dating app?" He held my eyes with his, not a hint of guilt in them. "I can't believe you're this kind of suspicious woman. Why would I do that? I thought you were more secure than to imagine such things." He continued, recasting my observation as evidence of some character flaw of my own, so convincing in his denial that I began to doubt what I'd seen. Had I been wrong? Maybe I'd imagined it?

I hadn't heard of the term gaslighting. I'd never read about love bombing, and it wouldn't be until later that I understood how it works: how the constant communication, flattery and attention encourages dependence and prompts the dopamine rush of feeling special, and then the flat-out lies keep the relationship off balance.

Around this time, my daughter Kinza was admitted to hospital. As I waited to hear from the doctors about what needed to happen next, I dialled his number. I didn't want to have to cope with this on my own, wanted the support of the man I now considered my partner by my side. "Look, I can't just drop everything and come down there," he told me. "Pull yourself together. Your daughter is sick and you're making this all about you—what a selfish mother you are!"

I wasn't trying to put myself ahead of my daughter; I was doing my best to support her. I simply wanted my partner to help support me at the same time. "I'm just asking for you to come and hold my hand for a bit," I managed to reply.

"I'm disappointed that you're being so selfish," he said. "You always just think of yourself."

The line went dead. My daughter's health concerns were first and foremost, but worry over my boyfriend's reaction buzzed like static in the background. The next day, when it was safe to leave her side, I headed to his home.

He wouldn't answer the door.

I texted that I just wanted to talk to him. His reply was blunt: if I didn't leave, he'd call the police. Humiliation washed over me as tears filled my eyes. *If anyone who knows me could see me now,* I thought . . . I was a successful career woman who gave speeches about female empowerment. I'd just signed a book deal to tell the story of my escape from my abusive marriage. And yet here I was, begging a man to love me, being threatened with arrest if I didn't leave.

What the fuck am I doing? I thought as I wiped my tears and walked away.

In the days after I stood on his doorstep, Hamza gave me the silent treatment. He thought he was punishing me. When he'd pulled back before, signalling his disappointment and disapproval, I'd leaned forward, trying to win back his attention, his love. But this time, I realized I was better off adjusting my life to his absence than adjusting my boundaries to his disrespect. As this lengthier silence stretched on, it allowed me to hear a small voice, *my* small voice: *I'm so tired of standing here in the dark trying to prove I love you enough to deserve your love in return.*

It was the voice of the four-year-old deep inside me who had once stood at the side of her mother's bed, just wanting a hug. I didn't need to find my way back to *him*; I needed to find my way back to *her,* that child-me, to tell her it was okay to put the glass of water down and go back to bed. She was loved. Just as she was, for just who she was.

I blocked Hamza's number and started looking for a therapist.

Unsettling

I didn't want to talk about my childhood. "What's done is done," I said to the psychologist sitting across from me. It was our first appointment, the one where you say why you're there and give the thumbnail sketch of your life story: Born in Pakistan. Raised mostly in Abu Dhabi. Mom and Dad never really loved me but I was over it. Arranged marriage at age sixteen. Two daughters. Abuse. Escape. Dad died. Divorce. Back to school to rebuild my life. A successful career in finance. And relationship troubles because I didn't really think I'd healed from my marriage.

"Wait," he said. "Let's go back to your childhood."

It wasn't what I wanted to hear. I didn't want to revisit painful family memories; I wanted to figure out why I kept settling for men who weren't right for me, to learn how to have a healthy relationship and move forward instead. "Can't you give me some kind of checklist?" I asked. "I just need a way to make sure I'm picking good men to date." A checklist wasn't the answer, he said. We needed to look back before looking ahead. Soon our hour was up, and I left his office not sure if I'd return. But as the week passed, the thought that maybe the cause of my relationship issues ran deeper than my failed marriage persisted.

A week later, I sat in his office again. "You might be onto something," I said. "Let's talk about my childhood." In the months that followed, I worked hard at understanding the patterns of my romantic relationships. My psychologist specialized in childhood trauma, and together we explored what I'd seen growing up and what I'd experienced in both my parents' home and my marriage, working to replace the idea that love was unpredictable and violent with the idea that relationships should be built on mutual respect and care. As we peeled back the lessons I'd learned from my family and culture, I realized I'd carried some of these same lessons into my relationships with my daughters. I wanted my daughters to have choices that I hadn't. I'd left my abusive relationship as much for them as for myself, drawing strength from the fact I was protecting them by leaving their father. But there were moments—especially as they became teenagers with minds and views of their own—when I'd waved my sacrifices in their faces, like my own mother had, berating them for not doing what I wanted them to. "If I'd stayed with your father, you'd be married with two babies by now and you wouldn't be able to go to school!" I heard myself saying to my daughter Kinza in the heat of an argument.

I cringed at the memory, at the echo of my mother's voice in mine. I hadn't demanded they worship me—but I had clearly conveyed they were in my debt.

I'd escaped the physical abuse of my marriage, but as I read and talked, journaled and reflected on the relationships I'd been in since, I could see the patterns of emotional abuse I'd been trained to ignore: from name-calling and insults and jokes at my expense to gaslighting, isolation and control. Developing new instincts—and learning to listen to them—was the challenge. "When you notice something that seems off, you can act on it right away, or you can note it and park it for later," my therapist told me. "Just don't ignore it."

The Test

It had been two years since my relationship with Hamza had ended, two years I'd spent unravelling the love lessons I'd learned from my culture, my family, my marriage and my post-divorce relationships. I'd rejected the beliefs I grew up with, that I was less-than because I'd left an abusive marriage—and in the process, severed many of my ties to the Pakistani community.

In other aspects of my life, this was a big year for me: my book had been published and a production company had purchased the film rights. I was giving speeches across the country and beyond on women and education, diversity in the workplace and resiliency. I continued my full-time work in corporate finance and serving on the U of T Governing Council. I'd even begun setting up my own charity, Brave Beginnings, to match mentors with women who had escaped oppression.

Then I met Rahul. A friend had told me about a dating app for high-achieving professionals, and I signed on, reasoning that perhaps someone successful in his own field might be more secure with my success. Rahul was divorced, like me, but without children. He was Indian, close enough culturally to share common ground with me but perhaps different enough to be reading from cultural scripts other than those my other relationships had adhered to. His parents were professionals, educated in North America, and so that, I reasoned, might also mean he was more liberal.

Our first conversations had . . . hiccups. He told me he didn't like that I described myself as a feminist. "Would it be okay if I called myself a chauvinist in my profile?" he asked. When I pushed back, he retreated. "Hey, hey, I'm just joking," he said.

I recalibrated my expectations: *He'll be more liberal because of his North American upbringing* became *I just need to educate him about what feminism really is.* But I didn't completely brush away my concerns.

After our first date, Rahul admitted he was intimidated by my success. "But that's not a *you* problem," he said. "That's a *me* problem. I'll work on it. You just keep kicking ass." And as we continued to date, Rahul showed a nurturing side. When I'd had a tough day at work, he showed up with flowers and hot chocolate to cheer me up. When

I shared the details of my past and its ongoing impact on me, he held me and cried with me. When I shed tears after an argument with my daughter, he countered my parenting insecurities with praise for my mothering.

Some of his behaviour was over the top—like driving an hour from his home to mine to "drop in" for a thirty-minute visit followed by another hour-long drive home. It was nice but also a bit . . . much. And so I noted it.

He was charming and funny and confident. Until he wasn't.

"You are so successful that I don't feel like a man with you," he said one evening over dinner. "Everything you have going on: it just makes me feel inadequate." It seemed that the "it's a *me* problem" work he'd said he was going to do wasn't progressing so well. In the past, I'd have moved directly into soothing and reassuring. This time I paused. I didn't dismiss his concerns. I did have a lot on the go. "Is this a 'we don't spend enough time together' thing, or is it a 'I don't feel comfortable with your success' thing?" I asked.

"No, no, I love you," he said. "I just want more time together." Days later, he changed his mind: he couldn't be with me, he said. Days after that, he begged me to take him back. "Look, I realize this is my problem, and I'm going to work on it myself," he said.

We'd only been back together for a few days when I received news I'd been named one of Canada's Top 100 Most Powerful Women by Women's Executive Network. I was on my way to see him and excitedly dialled his number from the car to share the news. His congratulations were perfunctory, and in the next breath he picked a fight about something I'd said when we'd seen each other a week earlier. "Okay, I'm going to turn around," I said. "I'm not going to let you ruin my good news." Later, when I posted a photo to Instagram of a congratulatory drink with a girlfriend, he texted to complain: "I can't believe you posted that photo—like rubbing your success in my face to make me feel like a douchebag."

How had this man who had been so supportive become so insecure? As I reflected on the things that had seemed off, the little flags along the way, I saw the pattern. Rahul was at his best when I was at my weakest. My bad days brought out his best behaviour. My weak moments were opportunities for his strength to shine through. *Oh, dude,* I thought. *You want a damsel in distress. And you are with the wrong woman.*

Days later, he called to apologize. He'd been wrong, he said, inviting me out to supper at Scaramouche, an upscale French restaurant, to celebrate. *One more try,* I thought. I'd had another piece of good news in the interim: an invitation to speak at an event in Singapore. *Okay, this will be a good test.*

I waited until we'd had our dessert. "I've been invited to speak in Singapore," I said. His face went white. "Oh," he said, taking a moment. "That's great." A few minutes passed. "You know, you're just travelling all the time," he said. "How are we ever going to build a future together, have a family, if you're always travelling? Why can't you have a normal career?"

"You're doing it again," I said. "I've shared good news with you, and you're not happy for me. Shouldn't you be proud of a partner who's making a difference in people's lives? Instead, you're picking a fight. I don't think this will ever change."

"Why should I care about those people? I'm not the one who abused them. I'm not the one who married all these child brides. So why should I care?" He paused. "You have no right to talk about kindness in your speeches. You're this powerful, full-of-yourself bitch. You're unkind to *me,*" he said, swinging the spotlight back firmly to him.

"So why are you with me, then?" I said as I got up from the table and left. *That's it, I'm done,* I thought.

An hour later, he was at my apartment building door. "Please come down and speak with me," he said. "Please just talk to me." Fatigue washed over me. I did not want to continue this conversation, a conversation that felt all too familiar. I needed to put an end to this. So I pulled a sweater over my pyjamas and went down to his car.

"Look, can you just meet me halfway?" he said as I sat in the passenger seat. "Like, be as successful as you are now, but no more. You've written a book, but no more books. Don't let it become a movie. Just make it a bit easier for me."

It was laughable. I couldn't imagine a woman anywhere in the world asking her partner to try to be less successful. "Just tone it down a bit," he said into my silence.

"No," I said. "No. I'm not going to. No."

"So you're not going to meet me halfway? Not even ten percent?"

It was absurd. What would being 10 percent less successful look like?

"I have so much love for you," he said. "I just need you to do this for me."

As I sat there, I could see the faces of the others in my life who had tried to control me, limit me, tell me what I could do or should do. The four-year-old inside me wanted so badly to be loved. But the woman I'd become knew his request was toxic—and it would not be the last one. Don't let it be a movie. Don't go to Singapore. Don't be too successful. Don't shine too brightly.

He was upset with me for saying no. But that didn't mean I should say yes.

But he held you when you cried, my four-year-old self whispered. She was right: he had. But he only *ever* supported me when I was sad. *He only loves me when I'm broken,* I thought.

"This is not love," I said to him. "This is control. And I don't want it."

As I stepped out of the car and turned back to my building, I wrapped my arms around myself, rubbing my hands along my shoulders. I didn't realize it until I felt my body relax, but I was hugging myself. Hugging four-year-old me. *It's okay*, I thought. *We're going to be okay.*

The Stuff They Should Teach Us at School

Few of us learned about healthy relationships in school. The good news is that it's changing: today, more educational systems recognize the importance of teaching young people about healthy dating and the warning signs of even more nefarious risks like human trafficking. I've been privileged to speak with young people about this, both in person and on-screen, to share the lessons I've learned and the red flags they—and all of us—should be alert to. At a recent presentation to hundreds of students in Ontario's Durham Region, I shared my stories of marriage and dating, along with these relationship red flags.

- **Love bombing:** It can be addictive to be showered with affection, promises of love, gifts and praise—and the love bomber knows this. Contrary to what the movies tell us, if someone says they love you without taking the time to know and understand you, it's not romantic, it's a red flag. If it's moving too fast, it's not love—it's manipulation.

- **Isolation:** "Do you really need to see your friend? I just miss you so much when you're not here." It might sound like affection, but if your partner demands that your world revolve around time spent together, it's another form of control. Other warning signs: wanting to know where you are at all times, accessing your calendar, tracking your spending and showing up unannounced when you're out with others.

- **Guilt tripping:** Phrases that suggest you are indebted to your partner for the care they give you or the money they spend on you—"How could you do this after all I've done for you?"—could be a sign of controlling behaviour.
- **Cutting remarks:** Undermining jokes and cruel comments about you and the people you care about aren't funny, they're an attempt to diminish your power and support.
- **Blame and shame:** "I love you so much that I can't control myself." That's how my husband blamed me after he hit me—that his love was so overpowering, he couldn't help it when he got mad at me. It sounds crazy. And it is. But abusers often blame their actions on emotions so powerful they can't control them, making their loss of control somehow your fault for causing those powerful emotions in the first place. You're not responsible for someone else's actions. They are. Always.

It can be tough to recognize these signs and patterns in the moment. What can help?

- **Journal:** Keep notes. You might choose to jot them in a notebook, on your phone or in a file on your computer. It doesn't have to be pages long—even just a few words to remind you of what happened and when, noting things that seem off. Pay attention to your feelings and intuition. Having notes could help you spot a pattern if there is one and give you the confidence and certainty to trust those instincts.
- **Double-check:** Ask trusted friends or family how they see you acting around this person. The people who love you will have your back. My daughters always knew when I was behaving in a relationship in a way that wasn't true to my authentic self.

- **Read up:** I didn't know I'd dated a love-bombing manipulator until I started reading up on gaslighting and love bombing, and the patterns became clear.
- **Be your own bestie:** Think of what advice you'd give your best friend in your situation, what standards you'd hope she would set for what she deserves. My benchmark for love used to be how I was loved by others. Today, my benchmark is how I love myself—unconditionally and unapologetically.

Healthy relationships respect our boundaries. Healthy relationships make room for friends and family. Healthy relationships don't cut us down, they lift us up. Healthy relationships don't rush us, they walk with us, valuing our growth and autonomy.

What the Universe Sends You

In the days and weeks that followed, my mind returned to that evening. Each of my three post-divorce relationships had featured versions of the same man: charming, like my father. Good on paper, in pictures—like my parents had been. Full of showy declarations of devotion—dinners, flowers, trips—designed to impress others as much as me. Successful in the eyes of my community. The universe had kept sending me what my childhood and community had taught me to think of as love—and what I now realized was simply a kind of love candy that had no relationship nutrients in it, leaving me heartsick and empty at the end.

Later, as I sat in my therapist's office, running through what had gone wrong, he stopped me with a question. "Would you have been friends with any of these men?"

I turned the question over in my head. "I don't think so," I said. "No."

"So why are your standards for friendship different from your standards for a partner?"

With each, I'd had some intuition that the relationship wouldn't work out. But with the first two, I'd ignored it, blamed myself when things started to go wrong, thinking if I just worked harder, I could earn the love I wanted. It wasn't until Rahul that I'd really paid attention to my inner voice.

Why? The four-year-old inside me had a natural desire: to be accepted, seen and loved for who she was. But she'd learned that love came with conditions, that in order to "earn" love, she needed to contort herself to what others wanted her to do and be. As Dr. Gabor Maté says in *The Myth of Normal*, when faced with a choice between attachment and authenticity, survival forces children to choose attachment—and the adults they become continue to conform to that early trade-off.[1] Is it any wonder that what we accept in romantic adult relationships often mirrors the toxic love patterns we grew up with?

I'd been taught as a child to ignore what my heart knew. When I'd seen violence at home and watched my parents call it love, I'd learned not to believe what my child's eyes had seen. When I saw that image was prized over safety and mutual respect in relationships in the community around me, I learned not to want what my child's heart knew was healthy. And when I saw knights in shining armour paraded through pop culture as the romantic ideal in a partner, I learned that being broken, not strong, was the way to win love—to be saved by someone else's love rather than saving myself.

As I thought back to the end of my marriage, though, I realized no knight in armour had saved me. I had taken the steps to save myself: finding a way to finish high school; secretly saving money to pay for university; excelling in my courses. And despite the messages from those around me telling me to settle, to put up with, to be grateful for, in my bones, in my soul, I knew I deserved more. And so, late at night, in my basement bedroom of the home we lived in, I would stand in front of the mirror with a rolled-up document in my hand, pretending to give a valedictorian's speech, imagining a time when my accomplishments would be acknowledged and my choices would be my own. Imagining my way into my future.

Along the way, I was helped by the kindness of those around me: a university professor who noticed my struggle and offered me work as a teaching assistant, a university counsellor who cautiously broached the subject of spousal abuse when I told her my husband didn't want me at school, departmental staff who helped me scramble to find housing when my husband sold the house, friends who helped with babysitting while I attended class and worked. I took the steps to escape. And then with the kindness and support of my community of friends and colleagues, I built a new life.

"If I told you my boyfriend was asking me to change myself, what would you tell me?" my daughter Kinza had asked me in the days after I broke up with Rahul. "You'd tell me to drop him like a hot potato," she said, answering her own question. Rahul had tried to convince me that it was difficult to be with me because my life wasn't "normal." Kinza's response? "You're not normal—you're extraordinary. And he should have been counting his lucky stars that he got to be within ten feet of your light!"

It wasn't my desire for love that needed to change. It was my benchmark for the love I was willing to accept. No longer was "better than my marriage" or "better than my family" enough. I was learning to love and accept myself wholeheartedly and unconditionally. That was the kind of love I was willing to give others. And it was the kind of love I deserved in return.

Rewriting the Script

So what's the right ending for a chapter on relationships? Happily ever after is what we're trained to expect.

But what about happily now? Happily with ourselves, making room for the possibility of happiness with someone else?

I've continued to date. I've met men who are lovely—but not right for me. I've walked away from men I wouldn't be friends with. I've met men who turned out to be good friends but not romantic partners.

And then I met Michael: kind, funny, supportive. No pedestals here, no over-the-top gestures, just two people standing side by side. Learning about each other. Learning to be—authentically be—with each other.

Example #1: It was a blustery evening. I had a med school exam in the morning, but I was having trouble focusing. I'd just gotten off a call with my sister in Abu Dhabi. She was in the middle of a messy divorce and I was worried about her, though there was little I could do for her at this distance, in that moment.

My phone rang. It was Michael. We video chatted. Just talking to him helped dampen my anxiety. I told him what was up, how worried I was about my sister. The wind howled outside my windows: I knew a weather warning had been issued, that the drive from his home to my condo would be miserable. "Listen, babe, I'm here for you if you want to talk, vent, whatever. Call me," he said as our conversation wound down.

"Okay, maybe I'll talk to you later," I said as we hung up, a hint of irritation creeping into my voice. I turned my attention back to my books, cramming for the next day's test.

In the moments that followed, my irritation at Michael . . . irritated me. I knew something was off in our conversation but was having trouble figuring out just what. *What did you expect him to do?* I asked myself.

And the answer dawned on me: I expected him to hop in his car and rescue me. From what, I'm not sure. But in my moment of unhappiness about my sister's situation, part of me wanted my knight to climb onto his steed, wind warnings be damned, and head to my castle to comfort me. I know it wouldn't have made a bit of difference if he had. I'd still have had an exam to study for. My sister's situation wouldn't have changed. And he'd have been travelling on a dark highway in high winds so he could arrive here to sit watching me study.

I poked at my answer a bit more. Why did I expect him to rescue me? Because in the past, I'd always been with men who claimed they were doing what was necessary to look after me. And once I depended on them, I was dependent on them, vulnerable to their manipulation and abuse.

But Michael wasn't like that. I recalled a trip we'd taken to Quebec for a speaking engagement I had there. As we stood at the rental car counter, I noticed the bill had some extra unwarranted charges. I asked to speak to the manager to get them sorted out. Michael stood next to me, saying nothing. As I argued to have the bill reduced, I felt Michael's hand on the small of my back, a gesture of support. He didn't try to take over, didn't step in to "save" me: he just literally had my back. *I'm here if you need me, but you're doing fine*, his touch said. Other men I've been with—and my parents as well—would have pushed me out of the way to take care of it for me, in the process making me feel like I wasn't capable of solving anything, even a simple billing error.

Michael trusted me to look after myself. He had my back—but he didn't hold me back.

Example #2: It was a few months into my relationship with Michael. My med school classes had become progressively more intense—and so had my emotional response to them. It wasn't just the work that heightened my emotions. It was the fact that I was a decade or more older than most of my classmates. I didn't think it would bother me, but as we progressed, I found myself dealing with what I realized was grief, mourning the years I'd lost trapped in a marriage that interrupted my life and my education. I couldn't help wondering what my life, my career, would have been like if I'd had the opportunities these younger students with a head start on me had.

As I grappled with these emotions and the intensity of my classes, I was stretched thin. Then, Michael called with news of an upsetting situation in his family—not an emergency, but an emotional mess he needed to unload about. And I. Just. Couldn't.

For a moment, I felt like the world's shittiest girlfriend, worrying that I should bottle up my emotional fatigue and find a way, *any* way, to offer Michael the support he wanted. But I just couldn't. I didn't have the emotional reserves. And so I drew a breath, and drew a boundary. "I'm really sorry," I told him. "But I have nothing left in my emotional tank right now. I can't give you the support I'd like to. Can you find support from somewhere else? For the next little while, can we make our time together about just having fun?" I was afraid for a moment my boundary-setting might be a relationship deal-breaker. But I would have wanted him to say the same to me if our situations were reversed, and I also knew if I couldn't be honest with Michael in that moment, it was a bad sign for the long-term health of our relationship.

He didn't hesitate. "Sure," he said, the best four-letter word I could have hoped for. "How about a picnic this weekend?"

Part of me wants to stop here, to leave you with the impression that we continued on the path to happy togetherness. It didn't work out that way. Michael and I both grew up in difficult families, and part of our initial bond was forged in the understanding we shared about the impact our families had had on us. But as our relationship continued, our conversations looked more and more like therapy, a connection based in our pasts rather than built on a shared vision of a loving and joyful future. And I came to realize that while he understood my trauma, I am more than my past.

Michael was a man who would never hurt me. I wasn't unhappy—but I wasn't happy either. It was a bit like being locked in a nice house: secure, safe, comfortable. But there wasn't a lot of joy. Michael was a good man and I was a good woman—but we weren't good together.

I struggled with our ending. We're taught that the only successful relationships are the ones that last forever, when in truth, we can learn and grow successfully even in relationships that end. I thought I knew how to leave a relationship, but it turned out, I'd only ever learned how to leave an unhealthy relationship. Ending things with Michael was a new love lesson: that wanting more is just as valid as not settling for less.

And so, for now, I'm dancing solo, holding space for a partner whose rhythm matches mine.

Whispered Wisdom

The best decision I ever made was to stop basing my worth on other people's perceptions of me and to instead set my own standards. This has been the key to my confidence and self-love, as I have learned to only give my energy to people that add to my life and leave me feeling whole and not lacking.

JENNIFER CLARK, CHEMIST,

SENIOR R&D LEADER

No Means No, Even in Marriage

In recent decades, legal systems around the world have begun to acknowledge that wives have the right to say no to sex with their husbands. (This change happened in the 1980s in Canada and in the 1990s in the US.) But even with these legal shifts, there's still misunderstanding about what the frequently used term *marital rape* means. I want to be as clear as possible: marital rape doesn't have to involve beatings or other physical violence. Marital rape is coerced sexual activity.

Let's break that down: What is coercion? Yes, coercion can include use of physical violence. But it can also include the threat of physical violence, threats of violence towards others, financial coercion, verbal abuse and manipulation. Sometimes it's subtle, with a partner using false promises and pressure: "If you really loved me, you'd do this" or "If you'll just do it this once, I promise . . ." The combination of grooming techniques and gaslighting often leaves victims questioning their own experiences. And what is coerced sexual activity? It includes "sexual acts without consent, threats of repercussions for refusing sexual activity, forcing someone to watch or participate in the making of pornography, sexually degrading language and belittling sexual comments."[2]

How prevalent is marital rape? Studies have indicated that as many as one in three women have had unwanted sex with their partner.[3] And the awful reality is that marital rape is often repeated.[4] The result is that the abuse can start to feel "normal," as women are taught that their bodies don't belong to them. They can feel a disconnection from themselves: a loss of autonomy, agency and sense of self. We're often told to "trust your gut" or "trust what your body is telling you," but this kind of disconnection affects our ability to even hear what our bodies are telling us. And when we don't have the right to our own bodies, the right to say no on such a fundamental level, our ability to set boundaries in other areas of our lives is also eroded.

Why is it important to name marital rape for what it is? Because its impact is traumatic and damaging. Women can experience physical effects, including injuries, unwanted pregnancies, sexually transmitted diseases, bladder infections and more. And they experience psychological effects as well: PTSD, anxiety, shock, depression, suicidal thoughts, disordered sleeping, disordered eating, intimacy problems, negative self-image, sexual dysfunction and more.[5]

No means no—even within marriage or other intimate partner situations. And it would be so much better if we taught women and men that only yes means yes—that healthy sexual consent requires not just the absence of no but the presence of an enthusiastic yes, that if it's not a "hell yes!" it's a "hell no!"

If you are experiencing or have experienced marital rape, seek help. Crisis lines and women's shelters can direct you to resources in your area. Search online using the terms "marital rape support." If you include your location, specific local supports should show up. For safety, you may wish to search on a library computer or another computer in a safe location.

Unconditioning Workbook

- Understanding the love lessons we carry within us can require excavation. We may not be conscious of the lessons we learned about love growing up, even as they influence our choices and behaviour.
- You are better off adjusting your life to someone's absence than adjusting your boundaries to their abuse.
- Just because someone is upset with you for saying no doesn't mean you should say yes.
- Of potential partners, ask yourself: Would I be friends with this person? If not, why are your standards for friendship different from your standards for a partner?
- Your benchmark for what you should expect in a loving relationship shouldn't be how others failed to love you in the past.
- Healthy relationships don't cut us down, they lift us up. Healthy relationships don't rush us, they walk with us, valuing our growth and autonomy.
- New relationships can be filled with hope and excitement, and problems may be hard to detect. Journaling can help you see patterns and recall past experiences you may have forgotten. Early on in a relationship, write things down. Journaling can be your mental bank.

Reflection: What Are Your Love Lessons?

My family, culture and experience taught me a series of lessons about love that I unconsciously carried forward into each of my relationships:

- Love is unpredictable, manipulative and even violent.
- Looking happy is more important than *being* happy.
- And perhaps most of all, I have to earn love by shape-shifting into what someone else wants me to be rather than being loved for who I am.

These lessons may sound familiar to you—and you may have others that emerge from your own life experience. We can't unlearn the love lessons we've been conditioned to accept as fact until we uncover and examine them. It's hard work, and a good therapist can help you dig deep, but you can work on it on your own as well.

Something I've learned is that we carry lessons in stories: the stories we tell about our family, about our relationships, about ourselves.

1. What one story about your parents' relationship stands out in your memory?

_____

_____

_____

_____.

2. What one story about your dating life stands out in your memory?

_____

_____

_____

_____.

3. What one story about your current or most recent relationship stands out in your memory? _____

_____

_____

_____

_____

_____.

4. What love lessons do your stories reveal?

_____

_____

_____

_____

_____.

5. How are these lessons affecting the way you give and receive love today? _____

_____

_____

_____

_____.

6. How can you reframe these lessons to reflect your new, healthier path to love? _____

_____

_____

_____.

CHAPTER SIX:

The Perfect Imposter

What the hell am I doing here?" I didn't mean "here-here"—the location on the map, a roadside café with wi-fi—but rather "virtual here-here," the online team meeting I was sitting through with the bank's marketing team. Figuring out my next steps at work had been a key impetus for my Gaspé trip, but the truth was, I didn't feel as if I'd made much progress sorting it out. As my journey continued, I worried I'd end up home with nothing resolved. I had begun negotiating my exit with my boss but still didn't have a sense of what I'd do next. While we waited for senior management to sign off on my exit agreement, my manager had me tracking and evaluating media mentions of the bank, a task that filled just a few hours a week, and showing up for online meetings where I had little to contribute. I was frustrated and irritated.

I'd talked to my mentor John at length about my possible next steps, but nothing I explored seemed like quite the right fit. Before setting out on my trip, I'd come across a book about the Japanese concept of ikigai, which refers to things that bring value and joy to one's life.[1] Co-authors Héctor García and Francesc Miralles had interviewed more than a hundred Japanese elders about what made their lives worth living and, in the process, refined the ikigai concept. They formulated it as a series of four overlapping circles: what you love, what needs doing, what you are good at, and what you can be paid for. The sweet spot—where all four overlap—is your ikigai. As I thought about my own passions and skills, it seemed as if my speaking engagements might logically fit the bill, and certainly some friends had encouraged me to strike out on my own, to set up a business as an inspirational speaker and focus on being an "influencer." But it felt like an *almost* fit, like a dress that looks good as long as you don't try to move. I had lots of life experience to draw on, but I wondered if that was enough.

I felt more and more like an imposter at work. I didn't want to feel like one onstage as well.

Faking It

I don't belong here. When they realize I don't know what I'm doing, they'll fire me. I was just lucky.

If those lines sound familiar, you're not alone. Many of us have moments of insecurity when we feel unsure of our abilities or our accomplishments. But for some of us, those feelings of phoniness can be persistent and damaging. The term *imposter phenomenon* was first coined in 1978 by Georgia State University psychology professor Pauline Clance and co-researcher Suzanne Imes in a study of high-achieving women. "Despite outstanding academic and professional accomplishments, women who experience the imposter phenomenon persist in believing that they are really not bright and have fooled anyone who thinks otherwise," they wrote almost five decades ago. "Numerous achievements, which one might expect to provide ample objective evidence of superior intellectual functioning do not appear to affect the imposter belief," they continued, with women in their study attributing their success to luck, accident or faulty evaluation by others.[2] In later research, Dr. Clance and co-researcher Maureen O'Toole went on to explore how fear of failure and the humiliation attached to it caused those who considered themselves imposters to avoid taking risks and turn down opportunities for advancement, fail to enjoy the success they did have and not realize their potential because of anxiety, self-doubt and guilt.[3]

Interestingly, in those early studies, the researchers hypothesized women were more likely than men to feel like imposters. Later research—their own and that of others—suggested something more nuanced: both men and women experienced feeling like imposters, but the impact of those feelings were felt more strongly by women. Why? Men were encouraged by mentors, teachers and society to strive for success despite their imposter feelings, "to override their fears and to go for success,"[4] while women were less likely to be encouraged or supported—and in fact were more likely to have their imposter feelings reinforced by societal and family messages telling them they didn't belong. As one *Harvard Business Review* author put it, "[W]hen women are successful, they're not the only ones who suspect imposture. Many of their competitive male colleagues likewise assume that chance or an affirmative action program—not talent or skill—was responsible for [the women's] success."[5]

Who else gets told they don't belong? Racialized people. LGBTQ2S+ people. Immigrants. To various degrees, pretty much anyone who is not a cisgender straight white man. I'd argue if you've ever had someone tell you that you have to be "twice as good to get half as far," you're at high risk of feeling like an imposter—because the society you're operating within is constantly telling you that you *are* an imposter!

And that feeling is enormously stressful. It can lead to depression and anxiety and result in low job satisfaction, emotional exhaustion and burnout.[6] The irony in all of this? People struggling with imposter syndrome are often viewed by the people around them as competent and successful.[7]

One way people dealing with feelings of being an imposter cope is by leaning into perfectionism, including overpreparing, ruminating and catastrophizing about possible mistakes or inadequacies. And while the classic job interview response to the question "What is your area of weakness?" is to answer, "I'm a perfectionist," it turns out that perfectionism isn't necessarily a great trait. In a landmark study, Canadian psychologists Paul Hewitt and Gordon Flett defined three different types of perfectionists: self-oriented perfectionists, who set high personal standards for themselves and are driven by internal motivation; socially prescribed perfectionists, whose perfectionist behaviours come in response to the pressures of others (parents, teachers, authority figures); and other-oriented perfectionists, who pressure others to achieve perfection.[8] They found that self-oriented perfectionists tended towards self-criticism and self-blame, while socially prescribed perfectionists were—not surprisingly—more likely to fear the negative evaluations of others, seek their approval and be more likely to feel helpless in the face of perceived or real judgment. Again, not surprisingly, other-oriented perfectionists—the ones pushing others to be perfect—were more likely to blame others and scored high on measures for authoritarianism and dominance.

While Hewitt and Flett—and many other researchers before and since—focused primarily on the negative impact of perfectionism on mental health, more recent research has explored whether perfectionism has a positive side, separating perfectionists into "adaptive" and "maladaptive" groups. Remember our discussion about attachment theory, where we talked about that early bond between baby and caregiver? It turns out that adaptive perfectionists are more likely to have secure attachments, meaning that they had early healthy bonds with their caregivers that allowed them to explore their worlds secure in the knowledge that they could return to the safety of their caregivers' embrace.[9] Adaptive perfectionists are more likely to be driven by internal motivation than external pressures,[10] and they also tend to score high for life satisfaction, life purpose and positive emotions: they set goals, work towards them and feel that the ability to reach those goals is within their power. Maladaptive perfectionists tended to be driven by "the fear of making mistakes, the fear of negative social judgments, the sense of disparity between expectations and performance, and the negative response to imperfection,"[11] and are more likely to suffer from depression, anxiety, obsessions, eating disorders and psychosomatic disorders.[12] And those differences can show up early in life. A study of children between the ages of seven and eleven found that children who tended towards adaptive perfectionism did fairly well in relation to their peers. Those who scored high for maladaptive self-criticism were more likely to develop emotional symptoms like depression and anxiety. Those who scored high for socially prescribed perfectionism, feeling pressure from others to do well, were more likely to have behavioural and peer problems.[13]

Why is it important to tease out the nuances in all of this? First, let's talk imposter phenomenon: if we ignore the context of society's messages to women, racialized people, LGBTQ2S+ people— basically anyone who is marginalized—we end up blaming people for feeling like imposters. And trust me, when you feel like a fake, it doesn't help to have other people say, "It's your own fault—just stop feeling like a fake!" But when we take into consideration the social messages we're getting—*you don't belong here, you're taking someone else's (read a white person's or white male's) spot, you have to be twice as good to get half as far*—it opens up room to step back and view our situations in a more emotionally detached way. And that room allows us to develop and employ coping mechanisms that are—to use a word borrowed from the psychological research—adaptive.

It also takes some of the pressure off us to fix the whole problem ourselves. Sometimes you feel like a fake *because the world is telling you you are a fake!* You're not going to change that with some positive self-talk, *but* stopping the negative self-talk can help you draw a breath—and draw up a better action plan for dealing with it. That action plan may have to take into account that some people will keep telling you that you don't belong here. You might need to address that bullshit head-on. Or you might need to simply notice it and work around it. But what you shouldn't do is pretend it isn't out there. Why? Think of it this way: Let's say your imposter phenomenon has a psychological weight of ten kilograms. And let's say, for the sake of argument, that its root causes are equally split between your unique psychological makeup and external messages. That means five kilos are internal and five kilos are external—and you are expending psychological, spiritual and, yes, physical energy and resources in carrying it. Sure, deal with your five kilos of internal factors. But put down that other five kilos of external nonsense!

A Perfect Dream

Along with feelings of imposture, perfectionism can also limit us. When we feel like fakes, we're less likely to take on challenges where we might be exposed. When we aim for perfection, we may avoid risks and opt for the safer path.

And if we belong to a marginalized group, we'll likely find ourselves in a double bind: we *will* face pressure to perform to a higher standard while also possibly being taken to task for having too high standards if we actually meet those performance goals. In the Tallest

Poppy 2023, a study of more than 4,700 people (most of whom identified as women) in over a hundred countries, Dr. Rumeet Billan and
Women of Influence+ found that almost nine out of ten said they
had experienced hostility or been penalized or ostracized *because of
their success or achievements.*[14] In the survey, Dr. Billan heard from women
who described being undermined or excluded, experienced microaggressions and belittling, had their achievements downplayed or were
gaslighted by bosses, clients, suppliers, professors, donors and others,
in response to their achievements at work.

Acknowledging and understanding the external components of
perfectionism can help us sort out what is ours to deal with, and what
is not. And it's important to recognize that even the positive aspects
of perfectionism can be wielded against us. Having goals, ambition,
standards, purpose: these positive perfectionist traits can be weapon-
ized against us as accusations that we are "striving," too exacting or
think we're more than others think we ought to be.

While we may need to address the markers of maladaptive perfectionism—self-criticism, self-blame, fear of judgment and the humiliation of failure—we can do so while acknowledging the reality of
social pressures to meet higher standards because of who we are as
women, racialized people, people with disabilities and so on. Doing
this means we can get real about the burden and negative impact of
those social pressures. If we belong to marginalized groups, our paths
may not be as barrier-free as they would be if we were cis white males.

And the complications of race, gender, orientation, ability, social
status, immigration status and other marginalizing factors also means
we may have been subjected to—and may be subjecting our loved
ones to—"other-oriented perfectionism." Our parents or caregivers,
recognizing the unfair standards to which we could be held, might
have pushed us towards perfectionism. We might be pushing *our* kids

towards perfectionism out of the same impulse to equip them for the inequities they will face. The troubling reality is those inequities aren't likely to disappear overnight, and so we are still faced with the challenge of how to equip ourselves, and the generations that follow, with the skills to achieve our dreams without hobbling ourselves with traits that sabotage us as well.

Perfectionism may lead us to carry unnecessary emotional baggage that weighs us down and burns us out. We may ruminate and over-prepare in ways that deplete our emotional and intellectual energy. In the middle of an exciting, exhilarating but scary new endeavour, we may find ourselves asking *What am I even doing here?* And we might even think about quitting.

Whispered Wisdom

Every mistake you've ever made is "tuition." We talk a lot about self-compassion as if it's a destination, a prize, a goal. Actually it's a constant curiosity about how we stumbled upon something we didn't know (or keep having to relearn) about ourselves and our life script and whether we're going to choose to grab the lesson. After all, that failure can *save* us time, money, hurt, energy, etc. Rather than get mad about it, acknowledging the "cost" it had, list this "tuition" under expenses like you would hydro: you don't have to like it, but living without electricity is worse than paying that bill. You may only need to pay that tuition once, or you'll keep having to relearn that lesson and have more tuition yet to pay. Regardless, see it as an investment rather than a cost.

SARAH McVANEL, CHIEF RECOGNITION OFFICER, GREATNESS MAGNIFIED, SPEAKER & AUTHOR

Reality Check, Please!

You might be tempted to think that my journey from the road-trip realization that becoming a doctor might be the sweet spot in my ikigai Venn diagram to studying medicine was smooth. I might even be tempted to let you think that. But it wasn't.

Eighteen months after I started medical school, I was thinking of quitting.

What the hell am I doing here? The question I'd asked myself while still in banking was back. I was at the halfway mark of my medical degree, on an internal medicine rotation. Along with other students, I was evaluating, diagnosing and treating hospital patients under the supervision of fully qualified doctors and medical residents—trainee doctors who had completed their MD degrees and were now doing specialist training. If you're wondering where I was in the pecking order, look all the way down to the bottom of that pile of people in lab coats. Way, way down there. Yup, that's me, at the bottom, along with my classmates.

While cardiologists focus on the heart, dermatologists on the skin and gastroenterologists on the digestive system, internists generally deal with patients with advanced illnesses often affecting more than one system. As students, we'd all taken internal medicine classes, but this was our first rotation alongside trained specialists in the hospital. Two of us rotated through each shift, taking patient histories and presenting our evaluations to the rest of the medical team under the supervision of the resident.

And I hated it. Or hated most of it, anyway. Gathering patient details to try to understand their situation was interesting. But then translating that information for presentation was challenging: it quickly became clear that the other student on my shift had more familiarity with medical acronyms and ease with diagnostic statistical analysis, and his jargon outshone my tendency to put medical issues into plain English. "You killed it, dude," whispered the resident to my colleague after he presented a case, his verbal praise accompanied with an approving nod. My case presentation didn't rate even the nod, let alone the "dude."

It didn't help that my colleague seemed to be giving me the cold shoulder as well. As students, we shared a small on-call office. When we were there together, he immediately popped in his headphones. When I went for coffee, asking if I could bring him back one, he ignored me. I wasn't convinced the headphones were to blame, but maybe the volume on my insecurity was dialling up as well.

From my earliest memories, I'd been successful in school. Shining in my correspondence high school courses and in class at university, as an undergraduate and then a graduate student, had helped sustain me during the darkest times of my marriage. My mother-in-law might have considered me a terrible mother, my husband might have berated me for being a terrible wife, but no one could say I was a terrible student. Doing well in school mattered to me—a lot.

But now, back at school in my late thirties, I was unsure of myself. Almost all the other students had come straight from other university programs and were a decade or more younger than me. Few—none?—had the family responsibilities I had. The program I was in explicitly welcomed students without a science background, but that gap in my education often made me feel like I was playing catch-up. During the classroom phase of our studies, I'd already accepted that there would be many areas where others would outshine me on tests and exams. It wasn't comfortable for me, but I'd adjusted to aiming for a solid passing mark rather than the perfect marks I'd often garnered while studying economics. (Though I can't stop myself from saying—there were times I got great marks in medical courses too!)

Still, it stung not to be acknowledged after presenting my patient's history and my diagnosis. I felt like an imposter. What was I doing here?

"Maybe I should go back to banking." I was on the phone with my former manager and best-boss-turned-good-friend, Justin. It was the weekend after my first internal medicine rotation, and my imposter feelings were still dialled up to eleven.

How bad was it? I'd spent the morning scrolling through finance industry job ads.

"Maybe I should just cut my losses," I continued. I'd studied sunk-cost fallacy in my first graduate degree in economics: the tendency to continue pouring resources into a bad bet because you'd already invested so much. Yes, I'd already invested eighteen months' worth of high-priced tuition and time in my medical degree. But better to get out now than to spend as much again to finish the degree—and then even more to complete my residency.

"I'm not saying you shouldn't quit," said Justin. "But should you be quitting *now*?" Justin listed the challenges I'd faced in the past few months: a protracted dispute with my landlord, the decision to buy a house in a record-hot real estate market, a breast cancer scare—and the intensity of my medical program, including the confidence-shaking challenge of being an almost-forty-year-old second-year med student in the first of her clinical rotations. "It's your decision to make, but make it from a place of strength, not from a place of emotional depletion," he advised. "Give yourself some time."

"Stop playing the comparison game," said my mentor John, when I told him I'd been scrolling through LinkedIn, comparing myself to my former colleagues in banking who were advancing up the executive ladder. "You're envying other people's planes while what you're building is a rocket ship."

"You're not the first one to feel this way," my friend Ron, a psychiatry resident four years ahead of me in his medical training, told me when I spoke with him later that weekend. Like me, he'd made a mid-life shift to medicine, in his case, after training as a lawyer. "Samra, I had moments in my first couple of years where I thought, why am I here? I don't want to study this stuff—I don't care enough about this. I should go back to law!" He laughed. And like many students, he'd failed his licensing exam the first time he took it. "When you get into the clinical training in the area you're interested in, you'll feel like you're learning more in a week than you've learned in the previous year because you'll be focused on your specialty," he said. "You don't need to be perfect. You just need to get through." Done is better than perfect and "okay" can be just fine, he continued: it wasn't necessary to hit the ball out of the park on every task and exam, and then feel like a failure when you didn't.

"Look, medicine needs science geeks like your colleague, but it needs people like you too—people who understand the emotional aspects of health," said my therapist. "Nobody excels at every aspect of an endeavour. You don't need to like every piece of this experience to make it through. So what can you do to get yourself through the next two years?"

If it sounds like I spoke to everyone I knew about what I was going through . . . well, I kind of did. And it was exactly the right thing to do. At other times in my life, I might have held back, been more cautious about sharing my fears of failure. But in that moment, I was so tired and so unsure, I felt as if I were drowning. I didn't need my friends to make the decision for me, but I was tired and burned out, and I worried I might be neglecting perspectives I'd normally be able to tease out and consider on my own under better circumstances. I needed my friends to help pull me back to shore. And one by one, they formed the chain that got me out of the waves and onto the sand.

I still hadn't figured out what I'd do next. But at least I could sit on the beach and draw a breath.

Self-Improvement or Self-Punishment?

How do we differentiate between a genuine desire for self-improvement and self-punishing perfectionism combined with feelings of imposture? It's a tough question, especially when we layer in the complexity of context.

Maybe this will help: Picture two people working out at the gym, on the treadmill, side by side. They're both running at about the same speed, with about the same level of exertion—enough to sweat but still be able to say hi to the gym manager as she walks by. They both look fit. And if you were asked to say who was healthiest, you'd probably have a hard time choosing.

So let's fill in some more details. Shaima, on the left, hates the treadmill, but she's planning a mountain hiking trip this summer and wants to be fit enough to handle the steep trails and the weight of her backpack. She's been playing around with the incline settings on the treadmill to vary the pitch of her workout, and next week, she's decided she'll try working out with a small, weighted pack on her back. What's she playing on her earpods? Not music—it's a mountain soundtrack, complete with birds, wind in the trees and the occasional babbling brook.

Natalia, on the right, has a "no pain, no gain" attitude to working out. Her high school track coach used to give out gold stars to runners who ran till they puked, and Natalia earned more than one. She's not sure she'd say she likes the treadmill, but she likes the sense of control she has while running on it. Her eyes flick to the mirrored wall throughout her workout, viewing herself and her gym mates with a critical eye. She's not sure why that one in the corner even bothers coming in, given the puny weights she's lifting. And she's not too happy about the hint of a jiggle she spots at the back of her thighs. She probably needs to skip lunch for a few days to get that under control.

Okay, so maybe that's a bit too broad of a stroke, but you see what I'm saying: Shaima may not love the treadmill, but she's got a goal in sight she's training towards. Natalia, well, the negative self-talk is the soundtrack of her life—sometimes it's her dad's voice she hears, sometimes her high school track coach, sometimes her own voice—and no matter how well she does with her workout, there's always some fault she'll find with it. They both look healthy, but Shaima's mental load is much lighter, her attitude more positive, while Natalia carries the weight of her negative self-judgment and criticism wherever she goes. Natalia's critical attitude gets in the way of relationships at work and in her personal life, and she's talked herself out of more than a few of life's pleasures, not wanting to risk looking silly or incompetent.

So what are some of the key differences?

- **PERFECTIONISTS FOCUS ON THE GAP, NOT THE GAIN:** Shaima uses her increased strength as a motivation while Natalia berates herself even as she improves because she's not meeting the unrealistic goal she set for herself.

- **PERFECTIONISTS LOOK OUTSIDE RATHER THAN INSIDE:** Natalia doesn't measure her fitness by how she feels, but rather by how she thinks others are judging her.

- **PERFECTIONISTS DON'T GIVE THEMSELVES A BREAK:** When Natalia is sick or injured, she powers through with her workout, not giving her body time to repair or restore itself, in part because she's afraid that if she stops, she won't start again.

- **PERFECTIONISTS DON'T LEARN FROM FAILURE, THEY PUNISH FAILURE:** It's hard to learn from your mistakes if you're busy beating yourself up for them.
- **BECAUSE THE STANDARD OF PERFECTIONISM IS IMPOSSIBLE, PERFECTIONISTS ALWAYS FEEL LIKE FAILURES:** Shaima's going to feel great on her mountain hike. Natalia will be in the gym, watching for thigh jiggle.

Okay, I'm going to stop beating up on Natalia, because (a) she's already beating herself up for both being a perfectionist and not perfect enough, and (b) only comic book villains get stronger by being made fun of. Natalia—like the rest of us—doesn't deserve to be blamed for being a perfectionist. She—and each of us who struggles with perfectionism—needs some strategies for learning to lean into *im*perfection, to get herself off the treadmill of self-blame and criticism, along with loads of self-compassion.

Step 1: Listen Up

As we talked about in Chapter Three: Superwoman in a Box, we've all got lots of voices in our heads. Rather than simply acting in response to the voices of perfection and feelings of imposture, stop to consider whose voices you're actually hearing. Is it your track coach? The neighbour who teased you when you got your first bra? The boss who made your life miserable?

Step 2: Hit Pause

No matter whose voice is buzzing in your head, telling it simply to "shut up" isn't likely to work. So try this instead: just hit the pause button. "Thanks for your input—I'll get back to you" works for cranky customers and for critical self-talk!

Step 3: Step Back

Write down the words of criticism or blame the voices are whispering in your ear. Now, take off your shoes and step into your best friend's: How would she rebut these critiques on your behalf? If the voices are telling you you're an imposter, write down some of the accomplishments that have gotten you where you are. If they're picking apart your actions or blaming you for a less-than-perfect outcome, flip the script and try to recast the critiques in the most positive, generous light.

Step 4: Seek Support

Check in with rationally supportive friends, colleagues and professionals. By "rationally supportive" I mean the people who genuinely care for you, whose perspective you trust and whose advice you value. These are people who aren't frenemies (seriously, ditch those ones) or toxic positivity cheerleaders. (People who say "Everything happens for a reason" or "It will all work out like it's supposed to" aren't helpful.)

Step 5: Make It a Mantra

Combine your best insights with the best rationally supportive advice, and boil them down to a mantra—or two or three. Jot them in your journal, make a motivating Post-it note or record a pick-me-up voice memo for yourself to turn to when your inner critics pipe up again.

What else can help? Perfectionists tend to be addicted to forward motion. Looking backward—or even pausing in the moment—feels risky because of the negative self-assessment and past failures that might flood in. But when forward motion is your default, you may not be deliberate in your choice of destination—Let's go over here! Let's go over there!—and you're more likely to keep moving even when you need a break, emotionally or physically. Perfectionists are often really *imperfect* when it comes to rest, relaxation and recharging, which is why burnout is common. And when we're run-down or worn out, our susceptibility to self-blame is even higher. So, taking a literal break, even a few hours where you focus on something that recharges and restores you, can help you think more clearly and rationally about your options rather than dancing to perfection's soundtrack.

What's My Why?

Two other things happened while I was busy hating my internal medicine rotation. First: a friend had let me know about a speaking opportunity with his company and told me he'd need me to send him a couple of speech ideas by early October. And I completely, 100 percent, totally forgot. Blanked on it. Blew past the date without even the hint of a memory of it. Totally effing forgot.

Around the same time, the speaker's agency that manages my speaking engagements asked me to put a hold on a date for a possible speech later in the fall. This is common: a group is looking for a speaker for a specific event, and while they make up their mind, they ask three or four different speakers to hold that date in their calendars. If they pick you, they confirm the date. If they pick someone else, they get back to you to release the hold. And in this case, a week later, they released my hold.

Normally, that would be no big deal. Like I said, it happens all the time. Sometimes you're not quite the right fit, or your speaking topics are too similar to something they've already heard, or they just like another speaker more. But this time, together with already feeling insecure about school, I felt like a fuck-up for forgetting my friend's deadline and a failure for not getting the speech booking.

My name was no longer spelled S-A-M-R-A. It was spelled L-O-S-E-R.

Or that's what it felt like inside my head.

Now I want to get outside my head and walk over to the other side of the room and tell you what it looked like from the point of view of someone else looking at me. What would they have seen? An in-demand speaker with more than a dozen speeches booked for the coming months. A student in a competitive medical program. A mom to two amazing young women. A woman whose philanthropic foundation had just been designated an official charity by the tax authorities. An author working on her second book.

But I was having a really hard time seeing any of that. I was so far down in the weeds of self-blame, I'd lost my connection with *why* I was doing any of it.

And without a *why*, it's hard to figure out a *how* when a big old pile of *what* lands in your way.

When I'd been trapped in my marriage, trying to imagine my way to a better future, the valedictory speech I practised in front of my bedroom mirror with that rolled-up piece of paper as my pretend diploma helped me stay connected to my why: a belief that education would give me options and allow me to be a role model for my daughters. I hoped it would open doors for me—figuratively and literally—even if I didn't know exactly where those doors would lead. And it had.

When I'd applied to medical school, I connected to a new why. I loved speaking to groups about mental health, diversity, gender-based violence and other topics that grew out of my lived experiences. And I was good at it. That's two of the four ikigai quadrants (what you love and what you are good at). While simply being a motivational speaker might have also fulfilled the other two quadrants—what the world needs and what you can be paid for—I realized that going that extra distance to become a doctor specializing in mental health would allow me to do so much more than stand on a stage. I'd be able to tap into a knowledge base far beyond my personal experience, treat patients, take part in psychiatric research and connect with others doing important work in this field. And, yes, as a medical doctor, I'd also have a secure income, something that, as a single mom who had experienced the economic instability of poverty, was vitally important to me. I could imagine a life where I could help people address the mental health challenges they faced, both through speaking and treatment. I especially wanted to help those who had been marginalized because of their race or ethnicity, their gender, their ability or other factors, and to do so in ways that acknowledged their unique challenges, strengths and needs.

That was my why—a why that didn't require me to "kill it, dude" on an internal medicine rotation. It needed me to survive it and move on.

And, with the support and advice of my friends, I did. In the months that followed, I did rotations through family medicine, paediatrics and more. But it was in child psychiatry and forensic psychiatry rotations that I felt the pieces really come together. I still wasn't perfect, still had lots to learn. But my why was clearer than it had ever been.

Eleven Ways to Embrace Imperfection

We can't ignore the fact that many of us are bombarded with the double whammy of messages telling us we don't belong and that we have to be "better than" just to have an equal shot at success. There are steps, though, that we can take to diminish the weight of our internally driven messages around imposter feelings and perfectionism. (And for those fortunate to be the recipients of the privilege that reduces those cultural messages, these steps will work for you as well.)

Start Small

1. **Accept a compliment:** Compliments are scary to both our imposter selves and our perfectionist selves. Neither wants the scrutiny a compliment might bring: *Don't look too close or you'll see I'm a fake! It's not as good as you think it is!* But from the outside, turning down a compliment—*Oh, it was nothing!*—can read as ungracious or disingenuous. A compliment is a gift: accept it with good grace. And when your internal voices try to diminish its value or validity, respond with a firm "thank you for your input" and mentally turn down the volume on their chatter.

2. **Take a (small) risk:** Both perfectionism and imposter feelings can rob us of the willingness to try new things, out of fear of looking incompetent. But if we don't stretch, we don't grow. If you're a risk avoider, build your bravery by trying something new in a part of your life where the stakes seem lower. Not ready for work-related risks? Try something new on the hobby front. Worried your extended family won't accept something new from you? Do a trial run with friends.

3. **Get smart about mistakes:** One of the ironies of perfectionism is that it can rob us of the chance to learn from our mistakes, which fill us with such shame that we avoid looking at them at all. And that *is* a shame, because the best way to avoid a mistake is to learn from one. Next time you think you've blown it, try telling your self-blaming voices to quiet down so that you can sit with your mistake for a while. Turn it over. Look at it from this side and that side. What is it ready to teach you?

Build Skills

4. **Discover the joy of delegation:** Look at the best leader you know. Watch how they handle a big project. Odds are they

aren't doing it all themselves—no effective leader can. The best leaders assemble a team and delegate effectively. Imposter-perfectionists, on the other hand, rarely loosen their grip, ending up burned out from trying to do too much all at once. Look at what's on your plate: What can you delegate? Maybe your teen with that freshly minted driver's license can do the grocery shopping this week. Perhaps there's some flex in your budget to allow you to hire someone to deal with lawn care this summer. Find one thing that's adding to your stress level that someone else can do, and hand it off to them.

5. **Choose compassion:** Would you talk to your best friend the way you talk to yourself? Do you berate your kids the way you beat yourself up in your head? When you find yourself slipping into mean self-talk, press pause. Draw a breath. Try to imagine you're talking to someone you love—and choose compassion, not criticism.

6. **Recognize that we can't change what we fight:** When we feel so-called negative emotions, we tend to fight, ignore or belittle them, even pretending they don't exist. Guess what happens? They come back, like a boomerang, often with more impact. Try this instead: notice, pause and create a shift in your internal script. "Hi, fear/shame/imposter syndrome. I see you. You are welcome to sit here, but I am the one in charge."

7. **Give yourself permission to feel proud:** *Don't brag. Don't get too high on yourself. Who do you think you are?* If these messages sound familiar to you, odds are you aren't comfortable taking pride in your accomplishments. But feeling justifiably pleased with the results of your effort isn't the same as being a braggart. You're allowed to be proud! Celebrate your successes. And use what you've learned from your successes to propel you on to your next challenge.

Think Big

8. **Ask yourself, "Is this a life crisis or is it just life?"** For imposter-perfectionists, catastrophe is just one tiny imperfection away. But life isn't perfect—and imperfection isn't an existential crisis. The next time you catch yourself catastrophizing, step back. If a friend were going through this, would it look like a crisis to you? Or would it look like one of life's bumps, the kind you've survived in the past and will survive this time as well?

9. **Discover the restorative value of low points:** "I'm beginning to think that unhappiness is one of the simple things in life: a pure, basic emotion to be respected, if not savoured," writes author Katherine May in her bestselling book *Wintering: The Power of Rest and Retreat in Difficult Times*. "I would never dream of suggesting that we should wallow in misery or shrink from doing everything we can to alleviate it, but I do think it's instructive. After all, unhappiness has a function: it tells us that something needs our attention. If we don't allow ourselves the fundamental honesty of our own sadness, then we miss an important cue to adapt."[15] Perfectionism often papers over unhappiness with more frantic activity, never allowing us the quiet time to consider what it is that's making us unhappy in the first place. And we can't change what we don't acknowledge.

10. **Even when your path is clear, it may be bumpy:** Something I learned from reading Oprah Winfrey's book *The Path Made Clear*[16]: even when you can see where you're heading, there may still be—in fact, likely *will* be—bumps along the way. Paths that haven't been travelled by hundreds of others *are* bumpier and less worn. Especially if you're blazing a new trail by doing something unique or uniquely you, there will be unexpected obstacles, twists and turns. Those are the

moments to remind yourself of your why. You can choose to continue on your path or shift to another, but make the choice from a place of clarity and power.

Give Yourself Permission to Finish

11. **Done is good enough:** Focusing on perfection stops us from finishing projects and tasks and robs others of the benefit of our work, as it blinds us to the value in what we have already contributed, created or accomplished. There will always be room for improvement, but if we aim for perfection, we never experience completion. Allow yourself to get things done, put them out into the world and move on to the next task. Confession: I was adding to this book right up until the last minute, always spotting things that could be clearer, ideas I wanted to expand upon. If I'd kept at it, the book would never have been published—and the value in all of the rest of the words would have been lost!

Whispered Wisdom

People have always told me, "You have to see it to believe it." I don't accept that. When you are the first—as I have been in so many places—you have to be courageous enough to be it and believe it before you ever see it.

JENNIFER BERNARD, PRESIDENT & CEO,

SICK KIDS HOSPITAL FOUNDATION

Unconditioning Workbook

- Perfectionism comes in a number of stripes. Self-oriented perfectionists set high personal standards for themselves, are driven by internal motivation and tend towards self-criticism and self-blame. The perfectionist behaviours of socially prescribed perfectionists come in response to the pressures of others, and they are more likely to fear the negative evaluation of others, seek the approval of others and feel helpless in the face of perceived or real judgment. Other-oriented perfectionists pressure others to achieve perfection, score high on measures for authoritarianism and dominance and are more likely to blame others.

- It's important to pay attention to context. Those of us from marginalized communities are often on the receiving end of social messages that tell us we don't belong or are not entitled to own our successes, and then we are blamed for feeling like imposters. Many times, we feel like a fake because the world is telling us we're a fake. Acknowledge those external messages, and then work on the part you can control, your internal self-talk.

- Feeling like an imposter and adopting perfectionist tendencies both limit us. When we feel like fakes, we're less likely to take on challenges where we might be exposed. When we aim for perfection, we may avoid risks and opt for a safer path. In both cases, we may carry unnecessary emotional baggage that burns us out, and we may ruminate and overprepare in ways that deplete our emotional and intellectual energy.

- One of my favourite quotes from former first lady Michelle Obama: "You can have it all, just not all at the same time."[17] Aim for satisfaction over time, rather than full-life perfection in any single moment.
- Finding your why can help you recover from feeling like an imposter or defaulting to perfectionism. And once you're clear on your *why*, you can focus on your *how*.

Reflection: Do a Deep Dive on What Success Means to You

What does success look like to you? It can be challenging to unravel our personal vision of success from the messages that society, family and pop culture bombard us with. Does success look like the richest man in the world? Before or after he bought Twitter? Does it look like the dream our parents had for us? The dream we had for ourselves at fourteen—or twenty-four? Or the online life of a social media influencer with four million followers?

You've likely heard the line "Nobody looks back and wishes they spent more time at the office," a prompt to encourage us to focus on spending time with the people we love. But it's also true that most of us have to spend at least some time at the office! Many of us also have professional goals, community contributions we'd like to make, passions for hobbies and other interests we want to spend time on—as well as relationships with family and friends we want to nurture.

Some suggest writing your imagined obituary as a way of figuring out what really matters to you. I find that a bit . . . depressing. An alternative? Researchers Johannes Bodo Heekerens and Kathrin Heinitz in Berlin have found that "best possible self" (BPS) intervention can boost your commitment to your goals and increase optimism and positive expectations.[18] What's involved? Block out twenty uninterrupted minutes on four consecutive days. On each day, spend that time imagining and writing about your best possible *and realistic* future. This isn't "If I won a million dollars, I would . . ." It's a picture of what your life could look like based on the skills you have or could realistically develop and in the context of the community, family and relationships you are likely to sustain into your future. If everything in your life were to go as well as possible, what would your life look like? What work would you be doing? What would your personal relationships look like? What contributions would you be making to your community? What passions would you pursue? Where would you live? How would you feel?

Simply doing this thought experiment is enough to make people feel more optimistic, according to the studies. (Tip: Doing the values exercise at the end of Chapter Nine: Questions of Faith will help you here as well: Do those values align with your imagined successful life? Tweak either or both to help you clarify what you stand for and what you're aiming for.)

And the next time you're tempted to berate yourself over a small failure or imperfection, go back to your vision of success. Does today's stumble really matter? What lesson can you take from it to help move you closer to your vision of success?

1. I commit to spending twenty minutes on imagining my best possible and realistic future on each of the four consecutive days starting on _____.

2. I can consider any and all of the following subject areas. (Check off each area as you cover it in your imagination sessions but know you aren't required to cover them all.)

_____ work life

_____ family life

_____ romantic relationships

_____ friendships

_____ community contributions and connections

_____ hobbies and passions

_____ spiritual life/religious life

_____ where I live (geographic location and type of home)

_____ emotional life

_____ financial life

_____ learning and education

_____ health

_____ physical activity

_____ other aspects, such as_____

3. My best possible life looks like this:

_____

_____

_____

_____

_____

_____

_____

_____

_____

_____

_____

_____.

CHAPTER SEVEN

Tokenized

M y latest office views," I typed, followed by #virtualwork-
places, as I posted photos of La Martre Lighthouse, Percé
Rock and other locations along my Gaspé road trip route.
I was away from home but not entirely away from work. My office was
still in remote-working mode, and I was checking in as needed.

Part of the prompt for my journey had been trying to figure out
what my next career step would be. The world of finance had seemed
a logical step as I'd completed my master's in economics, but seven
years into a banking career, I was finding it harder and harder to
imagine what the next seven might look like. And even from the
beginning, I hadn't quite fit banking's mould.

It had been 2013, and I was still at university, completing my economics degree. A senior finance executive had forwarded my résumé
to one of the human resources leaders in the financial company he
worked for, and the woman and I had booked an informational phone
conversation to see if I might be a good fit. With each question she
asked, I tried to make myself sound like I had what it took to compete
with the other candidates. But the truth is, I wasn't like them. They

were in their early twenties. I was in my early thirties. They were just starting their lives. I'd been married, divorced and had two young children. They'd had internships at other financial institutions. I'd worked five jobs while at school, including selling meals out of my kitchen, to make ends meet. They had MBAs. I had a master's in economics.

They were young and without family responsibilities. I wasn't.

A few days later, the hiring manager called me. "Most of the people we hire for these jobs, they're twenty-three-year-olds with business degrees. I don't think you'd fit in. You're amazing, but it just isn't the right job for you."

It wasn't the first time someone had tried to convince me they were doing me a favour by telling me I wouldn't fit in. When I'd been eighteen and pregnant, my husband had accompanied me to a high school near our home to see about enrolling to finish my diploma. The female principal had taken one look at me and told me I should consider distance education because it would be a better "fit" for me. And so, instead of finishing high school in a year and having the chance to connect with other people my age, to perhaps find supports in the guidance office, I'd been sent home. It took me six years to earn my high school diploma, as I worked in isolation, interrupted by my husband's whims, taking one or two courses at a time without support. The principal—like the HR manager—had said she didn't think I'd fit in, though later I'd wonder if it was my discomfort or her own she was most worried about.

The finance job hadn't been my dream job, but it was a good job. And that's what I needed: a good job. One of my professors was encouraging me to pursue my Ph.D. in economics. But that meant years more in university, subsisting on student loans and scholarships. I didn't need more debt, I needed financial stability, the means to look after my girls. My ex-husband paid some child support, but in a city as expensive as Mississauga, I was always scrambling to make ends meet. The financial industry seemed a good bet: well-paying positions with room to move up. And every company in the sector touted their commitment to diversity among their corporate values on their website, a practice that continues today, with claims to stand for diversity, equity and inclusion[1] and commitments to building a more sustainable future and an inclusive society.[2]

But that diversity didn't seem to embrace someone who was quite as diverse as me.

How Was I?

Oprah Winfrey has probably interviewed more people than just about anyone on the planet, from movie stars to athletes to presidents and everyday people. She's often shared that when the camera stops, her interviewees ask the same questions: "How was I? Was I okay? Do you think people will like me?"

They're questions that speak to our fundamental psychological needs as human beings: the desire to be seen, accepted and respected for who we are. But those are balanced against another set of some-times conflicting needs: the need to fit into the community around us. And as a result, we're constantly calibrating our inner and outer selves in order to establish and maintain connections in the community in which we find ourselves, as we seek to find friends and companions, to get work, to be successful.

Those dual pressures are present for everyone, but those of us out-side the dominant culture—especially, in North America, those of us who aren't white—face additional pressures to be anyone but who we are. We try to conform, be like everyone else—or everyone else who is white. Layered on top of that, we're also bombarded with messages within our own cultures about how we should be, conditioned by our religions, cultural norms and other social structures to represent our communities "well" out there in the world. It's hard to be yourself when you're carrying that many "shoulds" on your shoulders.

And each of those shoulds carries with it the message that who we are really isn't okay.

We're not "enough."

I grew up with those messages, was told explicitly and implicitly that I wasn't enough. I was a girl, so my dreams weren't valid. My gender made me less capable, less smart, less worthy. I was married off as a teenager to a man I hadn't met before and came to Canada feeling lost, alone and completely dependent on my husband. I tried to be a good wife and mother, to fit into the gender role prescribed to me, always falling short in the eyes of my husband, my mother-in-law and those around us. "You weren't trained properly," my mother-in-law told me more than once. "It's now my job to train you to be a proper woman." In her eyes, I wasn't "enough" as a wife, mother or daughter-in-law.

When I escaped my forced marriage and started to create a life on my own with my daughters, the biggest game changer was the relationships I built, the friends, professors and mentors who formed my new community at the university. They saw me and respected me, helping me to shine as my authentic self: someone who loved Bollywood movies and cooked a delicious biryani, who could also guide students through linear regression and game theory models and assist my professors with research on income inequality in developing countries, while raising my amazing daughters. Yes, I could think—as well as cook!

My girls and I were supported by friends who volunteered to babysit so I could work evening shifts at the university info desk, and I supported those friends in return, with a hot meal and an on-campus couch to crash on between classes or after late nights studying. Each interaction helped me cultivate the courage to be true to myself and start seeing my authenticity not as a barrier to being "enough" but as a source of strength to become "more."

Those authentic connections helped build my resiliency and, I think, helped build the resiliency of the people around me. How? Because authentic connections allow us to share the full range of our emotions, the full range of who we are. We're hard-wired for connection. When something good happens to us—or something bad—what's one of our first impulses? To call a friend, to share the load of the bad or the glow of the good. We feel happier when we feel connected, and we feel stronger when we know the people around us have our backs. We can take more risks—and bounce back from setbacks. And so can the people we're connected to, as our resiliency becomes an example for them to develop theirs. Our connections become a safety net as we feel held and free at the same time. It's an authenticity that allows us to find and unlock our true purposes and gifts.

Still, not every job welcomes our true, full selves.

Scenes from a Workplace
Scene 1

"Are you sitting down?" asked the woman on the phone, a senior leader with a national bank. I'd had coffee with her a few days ago over the Christmas break after one of my university professors introduced us. I'd sent her my résumé, but when we met, she'd pushed it aside. "I don't want to talk about your résumé," she said. "You're a stellar student. You don't have any corporate job experience but that's okay. We can teach job skills—I'm interested in your life experience.

I want to know about you." Her words and her warmth opened the door for a genuine conversation. Still, at the end of our talk, she was clear: she enjoyed our conversation but there were currently no openings in her department.

Author Maya Angelou once said, "If you're always trying to be normal, you will never know how amazing you can be."[3] Maybe, I thought, in job interviews I needed to stop trying to make myself look like everyone else and start letting myself stand out. I wasn't the same as the other candidates. But maybe being me was my strength.

A few days later, she called. "I'm offering you a job," she said. "We don't usually hire part-time people, but I've created a job you can start while completing your master's. Once you graduate, you can come on full time."

Scene 2

There weren't many people of colour in the department, and even fewer women. I am a quick study, but because my work schedule was unique and I came from a non-MBA background, I had to scramble to figure out how to compile reports for the portfolio manager I worked for in the bank's asset-based lending department. At university, if you had a question, you asked someone who might know: a prof or another student. But at the office, I quickly learned that asking a co-worker a question wasn't quite as straightforward.

"Samra, can you come into my office?" My boss, Ben, had been supportive throughout my training, but I could tell he was irritated. "Look," he said as I sat down, "there are complaints that you're asking too many questions. If you have questions about generating the reports, just come and ask me. Don't ask the other analysts."

His words caught me off guard. "What do you mean?" I asked.

"If you ask the others for help, people will say I haven't trained you properly," he replied.

"But I'm still in training," I said. "Shouldn't I ask questions?"

"This isn't university. This is real life. Just ask me. Don't bother the other analysts."

Scene 3

"You'll need to stay until 6:05 to clock your full day," said the receptionist as I hurried past her one morning, five minutes late. I worked ten to six so that I could drop my girls off at school (my neighbour or babysitters picked up the girls at the end of their day). Perhaps the office receptionist watched all the new hires, but I felt she watched me with particular attention. Never mind that from my desk near reception, I could hear her frequently talking on the phone with her family.

Scene 4

My later day gave me insight into co-workers' habits. I passed people who "worked late" playing solitaire on their computers and then strategically sent emails at 6:30 p.m. to show they were still at their desks. "It's not enough to do the work," a friendly colleague had advised me. "You have to make sure they *see* you're doing the work." *Okay*, I thought, *I can play that game. I'll stay late a couple of evenings each week and send off an email to a supervisor or portfolio manager as I leave.* The subject line might have said "Client update" but the real subject was "Hey, look at me, I'm at work at 8:45 p.m."

Scene 5

A white senior executive stopped me in the hallway not long after I started. It was one of the few conversations we ever had. "You're from Pakistan, right?" came the question. I replied that I was. "My

God," they replied, then mentioned the Peshawar school attack in which Taliban terrorists had killed 141 people, 132 of them children. "What a barbaric culture you come from!"

Let's Talk about Microaggressions

Here's the tricky thing about talking about the things said and done that end up "othering" us: the culture around us often insists that each of these individual comments and actions is . . . small. Not that big a deal. And when you tally them, you are accused of making a mountain out of a molehill, being hypersensitive. Though if you're on the receiving end, it feels more like death by a thousand cuts. "She didn't mean it in, like, a racist way," we're told when we point out racism. "He's not really sexist—he's a good guy," they say, when we point out sexism.

And so, we've started using a more comfortable word: *microaggression*.

The term was coined in the 1970s by Harvard professor of education and psychiatry Chester M. Pierce. Dr. Pierce was the first African American full professor at Massachusetts General Hospital and was also a senior consultant for the legendary children's television show *Sesame Street*. Before he was "Dr." Pierce, he was the first African American president of his high school and the first African American college football athlete to play in a major college game at an all-white university below the Mason-Dixon line in the United States.

It's a fair guess that Dr. Pierce had some real-life experience with racism. And in coining the term microaggression, he wasn't trying to avoid calling out racism, he was trying to find a new way to point out its subtleties. He put it this way:

> These assaults to black dignity and black hope are incessant and cumulative. Any single one may be gross. In fact, the major vehicle for racism in this country is offenses done to

blacks by whites in this sort of gratuitous never-ending way. These offenses are microaggressions. Almost all black-white racial interactions are characterized by white put-downs, done in automatic, preconscious, or unconscious fashion. These mini-disasters accumulate.[4]

Since Dr. Pierce's coining of the term, its use has been expanded, with psychologist Dr. Derald Wing Sue broadening it to include "brief, everyday exchanges that send denigrating messages to certain individuals because of their group membership (e.g., race, gender, culture, religion, social class, sexual orientation, etc.)."[5]

But while they may seem micro from the point of view of the person dispensing them, for those of us on the receiving end, micro-aggressions accumulate and eventually affect how we view our place in the classroom, the office, the community and the world, shifting our comfort level and sense of belonging. As author Ijeoma Oluo puts it in *So You Want to Talk About Race*, microaggressions are tough to address because of that smallness. Think of it this way: to the wasp, each one is a single sting, but to the person getting stung, the venom from a hive's worth of insects can be debilitating. Addressing microaggressions one by one is exhausting. Even more complicated, writes Oluo, "Many people do not consciously know that they are perpetrating a microaggression against someone,"[6] the offenses often committed out of ignorance or subconsciously. Examples: "Are you the first person in your family to graduate from college?" "Wow, you speak English really well." "Your name is too difficult for me. Do you have a nickname?" "You're so exotic." "Your accent is adorable." "Wow, you're so articulate." (I get that last one after almost every speech, said in a way that clearly suggests surprise that I can speak well.) And they can be non-verbal as well: A store clerk follows you.

A shop customer assumes you are an employee, not another shopper. You're chosen for a random security check—the kind that always seems to randomly select you. As a woman of colour who is a doctor, I am constantly mistaken for a nurse or a cleaner—something I know colleagues with similar backgrounds have also experienced.

"Microaggressions are constant reminders that you don't belong, that you are less than, that you are not worthy of the same respect . . . . They keep you off balance, keep you distracted, and keep you defensive,"[7] writes Oluo. And they have a bigger effect than simply making one individual at a time feel cumulatively crummy. They normalize exclusion.

There are those who argue that the impact of these actions is so significant we shouldn't call them microaggressions. "I detest its component parts—'micro' and 'aggression,'" writes educator Ibram X. Kendi in his *New York Times* bestselling book *How to Be an Antiracist*. "A persistent daily low hum of abuse is not minor. I use the term 'abuse' because aggression is not an exacting term. Abuse accurately describes the action and its effects on people: distress, anger, worry, depression, anxiety, pain, fatigue, and suicide." He goes on: "What other people call racial microaggressions, I call racist abuse. . . . Only racists shy away from the R-word—racism is steeped in denial."[8]

And when it's gender-based, I'd argue we don't like to label it sexism either, despite the fact that women still face real and significant barriers to workplace, pay and social equality. Just one example: Statistics Canada tells us women spend almost three hours a day on housework, compared to two for men.[9] The US Bureau of Labor's Time Use Study adds in caregiving and comes up with a higher tally: that women spend 5.7 hours daily doing housework and looking after children and elders, while men spend 3.6 hours on those same tasks.[10]

That's a two-hour-a-day imbalance, on average. Think about what your life would be like with fourteen "extra" hours each week.

That's a solid month's worth of twenty-four-hour days every year! But we still don't treat this workload imbalance as a societal issue: we blame individual women for not having figured out work-life balance—without acknowledging the scales we're using aren't balanced to begin with.

Whispered Wisdom

When I look around and I don't see anyone who looks like me or leads like me, instead of saying "Why me?" as if I don't fit in, I say "Why not me?!" The slight change in that question really shifts your mindset to what is possible.

SHERI GRIFFITHS (SHE/HER), SVP,

HEAD OF ONTARIO CORPORATE FINANCE

BMO COMMERCIAL BANK, CANADA

Authentic Leadership

My first years in banking passed in a blur. I'd been volunteering my time on some non-profit boards for organizations supporting refugee and assaulted women, and had found a placement working with some of the bank's non-profit clients that was a good fit. I'd also started doing some public speaking about my experiences as a child bride.

I'd felt vulnerable about sharing my story so publicly, and it did feel strange to have so many people I worked with—many whom I didn't know personally—know what I'd been through. I'd spent so much of my life hiding it, blaming myself, worrying about how my experiences made me different from those around me. But as people reached out to me, I realized my being vulnerable was creating new opportunities for me to connect authentically with the people around me. I felt stronger, and I think they did as well, as our shared experiences and understanding created a kind of shared resilience.

The bank seemed happy with my new visibility. I was asked to speak on behalf of the institution at an International Women's Day event, invited by various departments to give presentations to employees and clients, and eventually received a corporate global citizenship award.

But as things fell into place at work, they started to fall apart at home. My girls were now in their early teens, and my eldest daughter was struggling. On the day of my quarterly review meeting with my new boss, Justin, Kinza's school called: she'd been skipping classes and was in danger of losing her school year. As soon as I stepped into his office, Justin knew something was wrong.

"Are you okay?" he asked as I sat down at his meeting table. I started to cry, mortified he'd think I was a basket case. Justin reached across the table and slid the quarterly meeting reports to one side. "This can wait," he said. "What's up?"

I shared some of the details of my daughter's situation. "I'm not sure what to do," I said.

"How do you want to be supported?" he asked.

Some of the tension left my body. I'd been warned in past work situations about allowing my home life to affect my work life. I realized I'd been waiting for Justin to reprimand me as well. Instead, he not only offered support, but gave me the agency to decide what kind of support would help best. His question opened new possibilities. "My job gives me a lot of joy," I said. "I don't want to have to take time off. But I do need some extra support."

"Okay, let's figure that out," he said. By the time our meeting ended, he'd assigned someone on the team to be backup for me, so that if I needed to take a day off or work from home, I'd have help in meeting client obligations. And he got into the trenches with me, spending an hour helping me look for community supports online. Neither solved the challenges I was facing with my daughter, but both helped me know I wasn't alone and gave me the breathing space I needed to help Kinza get back on track.

Over the next year and a half of working under Justin, I learned what real leadership looks and feels like. He didn't manage from fear: he managed through support. First, he reassured me that I was valued by the organization and my career trajectory within the company was safe. Then, he gave me agency in determining what would best allow me to move forward successfully. And he let me know I had his ongoing support, sending me links to articles and resources he thought would help. While that was a difficult time, as the crisis period passed, I was able to soar at work, not only meeting but even surpassing those targets.

And Justin wasn't afraid to admit when he'd erred. In our early conversations, he had said more than once he was "colour-blind." I understood what he meant, but I didn't think he realized it also was a kind of erasure. Saying you're colour-blind suggests that someone's skin colour doesn't affect how they are treated in the world, when the reality is that people of colour are discriminated against. When that distinction was brought to his attention, he paused. His brow furrowed. I could tell he was turning it over in his mind. "Okay, yeah," he said. "I see what you mean. I'm sorry. " Where others might have been defensive, Justin saw a chance to learn. I never heard him use that term again.

Colour-Blind

I was running through my notes for the speech I was about to give to a group of human resources professionals when a middle-aged white woman approached me. "It's great to see you here," she said as she introduced herself as a senior executive with a financial institution and a member of the organizing committee for the conference. "It's a great group—lots of opportunities to get involved as a volunteer," she said as she offered to introduce me to others. It was clear from her manner that she assumed I was a newcomer looking for career connections. "And what do you do?"

"I'm the keynote speaker," I said. "I'm giving the talk today on inclusion, diversity and unconscious bias."

"Oh." I could see her recalibrating, shifting me from someone she needed to help to someone she should try to impress. "Well, I work for a great institution. Those issues aren't a problem for us—it's a colour-blind office, a really special place."

Now it was my turn to recalibrate. I was going onstage in minutes. I needed to focus and prepare. Was now the time to get into a one-to-one discussion about the myth of colour-blindness?

It wasn't. "If you'll excuse me, I need to prepare for my speech," I said, turning back to my notes and ending the conversation.

A few minutes later, as I spoke from the podium, I looked for the woman in the crowd, spotting her near the front. I'm not sure if she noticed my eyes on her, but still I aimed two key points in her direction. "When people say they're colour-blind, what they're saying is that they are blind to how colour affects people, that they're blind to racial discrimination," I said. "And when you say discrimination is not happening around you, it's because it's not happening to you, and as a leader, you haven't created a safe environment for your employees to tell you it's happening to them."

Did she hear my message? It's impossible to know. But it was my choice in how to respond to her in that moment: I wasn't obliged to redirect my energy and responsibility from my presentation to her education. I had my work to do. And she had hers.

The "I'm the Boss" Boss

Not all managers are as supportive as Justin was.

"Can I get your advice?" The text that popped up on my phone was from Shadia, a woman I'd been mentoring through a volunteer organization supporting women escaping domestic violence. Like me, she was a single mom originally from Saudi Arabia with two young children. She'd recently left her husband and had had to take time off work to move and get resettled, so some in her workplace—a big corporation—knew what she'd gone through.

"Sure. Lunch?" I texted back to her. We both worked downtown and were able to meet later that day. As we sat in the busy food court, she shared her dilemma.

She was still in her first year on the job and was in training for her role, so she worked four days in the office and one day from home on her coursework. Her manager, Jim, himself a first-generation Canadian from the Philippines, was a stickler for hierarchy and rules. On a recent morning, Shadia's son had awoken with a fever. Shadia scrambled to find a babysitter: no one was available. Maybe she could switch her day working from home, she thought, and called Jim to ask his permission. He wasn't happy. "Shadia, if you don't solve your personal problems, you won't succeed in this company," he told her, transforming her request for a single swapped day into a personal failing. "Other bosses aren't as flexible as I am. You're setting yourself up for failure. You can stay home today, but I suggest you get your shit together and show people you're serious about this job."

Shadia hung up the phone in tears—and then like so many of us single moms, she wiped her eyes and tried to make things work. Dialling through her list of friends, she eventually found someone to watch her sick son and headed into work. "What are you doing here?" Jim asked when he saw her. "I found someone to watch my son," she said. "I'm here because I'm serious about this job."

"Oh, so now you're just here to make me feel bad," he said as he walked away.

There had been other incidents as well, each communicating to Shadia that Jim didn't think she belonged, that she wasn't serious enough, that her parenting was potentially a barrier to her progression. When a team-building session was booked for a day when the local schools were closed for professional development, Shadia mentioned that some staff who were parents might find it difficult to attend. "If you care about your job, you'll sort it out," said Jim.

Another time, when she went to his office to ask a question, his response was dismissive: "You have to earn the right to come into my office—don't forget you're still a trainee." As the incidents piled up, Shadia discovered other women had had similar experiences with Jim, weeping in the women's washroom after unpleasant interactions with him while he invited male colleagues out for a beer after work. And while Shadia knew microaggressions happened within the BIPOC community, could in fact happen between women and within groups as people jockeyed for favour and advancement, being on the receiving end of such behaviour from another person of colour was disheartening.

Still, Shadia had kept her head down and tried to focus on demonstrating the quality of her work. Once her training period was up, she knew she'd be transferred to another department, since Jim's team was full. But then, just as she was wrapping up her training, a position opened in Jim's department, and despite his unpleasantness towards her, Jim told her he wanted her to apply for the position.

Shadia was stumped. She'd talked to the company's training supervisor informally, sharing some concerns about Jim's behaviour towards her, and while the woman had agreed it wasn't fair, she'd counselled Shadia to put up with it rather than risk a bad training evaluation. "If you want to take it further, you have two options," she told her. "You can file a formal report with HR or you can address your concerns directly with Jim. I'd suggest you do the latter, because if you go to HR, they're just going to ask you if you've raised your concerns with your boss. Either way, you should have a conversation with him."

"So you're saying that if I think I'm being harassed, I'm supposed to educate my harasser about why this behaviour isn't right?" Shadia asked. The training manager said she wouldn't have worded it that way, but the fact was that Jim had been with the company for more than a decade, and Shadia was a recent hire. Shadia understood what she was saying: she could be labelled a troublemaker.

And so she requested a meeting with Jim. It was scheduled for the following week.

I was appalled. The fact that Shadia was being counselled by her training manager to deal with the situation on her own, without support or much practical advice from the training manager or HR, was a concern. Asking the person being harassed to educate their harasser seemed an unfair burden—expecting the person with the least amount of power in the situation to take the lead on solving the problem. But Shadia didn't see a way out. The meeting with Jim had been booked, and now she needed to prep for it. "Will you help me?" she asked.

Of course I would, I told her. Over the next week, we spent the evenings practising what she'd say: how she'd outline her concerns, which examples she'd cite, preparing to prove her worth.

By the morning of her meeting, she'd spent hours planning what to say. Later that evening, she called to tell me what had happened. "You're not going to believe what he said to me," she said as she launched into the details.

She'd gone into Jim's office, notes in her hand, stomach in knots of apprehension. "I know my voice was a bit unsteady," she told me. "But I said what I needed to say: that I'd felt targeted with unfair feedback and expectations because of my responsibilities as a parent." She'd told him she felt he didn't respect her as a colleague and laid out her qualifications: she'd been a top student, had taken on leadership roles within university societies and clubs, and even as a junior employee, she was already involved in professional organizations. "Yes, I need a bit more flexibility than your average employee," she'd said. "But I know I've done excellent work."

His face had paled when she reminded him of a comment he'd made when she had said she needed some flexibility as a single mother: "Well, maybe this isn't the right job for you."

"Have you told anyone else about that comment, your concerns?" he asked her. She knew he meant HR. "No," she'd said.

"Okay, that's good. I do respect you. And it takes balls to come in and talk to me this way. But at the same time, I see your voice is unsteady and your hands are shaking. I've heard about your past history with your husband, that he was abusive. And I'm thinking you are feeling disrespected not because of what I've said, but because of your emotional baggage you carry from your past."

I couldn't help it: I had to interrupt Shadia as she repeated his words. "Are you kidding me?" I asked. "He said (a) you're imagining it and (b) it's your fault because of your past experiences?"

"I couldn't believe it, either," Shadia said. "As soon as he said that, I knew the conversation was pointless."

I had to agree with her: Jim was clearly an expert gaslighter. We talked through her options: she might have no other choice but to go to HR. While her conversation with her training manager had been informal, Shadia had made notes about it afterwards and hoped the woman would back her up. I told her I'd also confirm what she'd told me, including our prep work for her meeting.

The next morning, she texted me. "Just got called into J's office. He's recommending me for a job in another dept." She hadn't had a chance to contact HR, and while she still believed his behaviour was wrong, she also felt the cards were stacked against her should she opt to complain. At a time in her life when so much else was still unsettled, she didn't want to risk her job. I couldn't fault her decision.

Poster Woman

While I'd thrived working for Justin, when he was promoted two years later, I sensed it was time for me to move on. I'd been headhunted by another institution, and the opportunity seemed too good to pass up.

My new employer seemed dazzled by my visibility. My book came out just as I switched jobs, and they were happy to capitalize on it, touting me as their employee in congratulatory advertisements, internal and external speaking engagements and more. In fact, this public-facing advocacy and speaking was so demanding, it left time for little else, and they were fine with that. "You don't have any sales targets," I was told by senior management. "Just keep doing your speaking and community engagement—it makes us look good and helps build our business overall."

But a person's high-visibility success can also lead managers and others to miss the everyday challenges a marginalized employee continues to face, something that became clear to me in a conversation with my mentor John. John was a retired CEO I'd connected with while in university when he'd been part of a committee that had granted me a significant scholarship. He'd become both an advisor and a friend. One evening over dinner, I made a comment about the systemic barriers people of colour face in the workplace.

"But you're doing well," said John.

"Yes, but equality shouldn't require exceptionalism," I replied. The fact that I'd been able to climb the ladder wasn't a demonstration the workplace was equal: I'd seen mediocre white men ascend more quickly and with fewer challenges. "You've seen what I've faced," I said. "Yes, I'm doing well. But that doesn't mean systemic barriers don't exist."

It was a lesson that would play out again in my new job. On paper, things looked great. But here's how it worked in reality: I was assigned to a business unit. Each business unit has sales targets. Each manager is compensated, in part, on those sales targets. So for a manager, an employee with no sales targets reporting to you affects your bonus. My new boss welcomed me with these words: "Samra, I have only two rules for my team: Don't fuck with my family and don't fuck with my paycheque, because if you fuck with my paycheque, you're fucking with my family."

Before long, I was transferred to a marketing team. But the challenges continued. The department had never had an employee whose role was public speaking on diversity and women's issues, and no thought had been given to what I would do between speaking engagements. While the senior executives who'd recruited and hired me may have seen how the bank benefited from my speaking and advocacy work, the managers they'd assigned me to had no idea what to do with me. The night after I was named one of the Top 100 Most Powerful Women in Canada—an award the bank congratulated me for in newspaper ads celebrating diversity—a senior marketing executive suggested I was making co-workers uncomfortable with my visibility and that I needed to "tone down" my "sexy side-speaking stuff."

It wasn't the only microaggression I faced. After I left work at 4:00 p.m. one afternoon to pick up my daughter for an appointment, I was told I'd be dinged half a vacation day for leaving early. In meetings, I was asked to take notes when others at my level were not asked to do this. And so, when I wasn't giving speeches that made co-workers uncomfortable, I was a very expensive notetaker.

It was a lousy fit, and one that brought home the difference between diversity and inclusion in the workplace. Hiring diverse employees is easy. Creating an environment in which all can thrive takes commitment and effort. Later, I'd see an infographic about the trajectory many women of colour face that made me realize my experience wasn't unique: it showed women of colour hired as stars, but marginalized as "problems" when they pointed out issues within the organization and eventually "exited" or resigning out of frustration.

In the year preceding the pandemic, I'd done dozens of speaking engagements for my employer. Lockdown halted that work. And as with many people, the pandemic's pause button prompted me to step back and consider the path I was on. Was this the right employer for me? Was this really the work I was meant to do?

When Work—or Life—Makes You Feel Crummy

None of us feel great about work—or life—all the time. But when we feel bad for feeling bad, research shows we actually end up feeling worse, for longer. And when we try to put on a fake happy face, we undermine our own mental health and the strength of our work relationships. What's going on—and perhaps more importantly, what should we do?

Let's start with what happens when we berate ourselves for feeling crummy at work (or in other parts of our lives). One study, led by psychologist Dr. Emily Willroth at Washington University in St. Louis, looked at "emotion judgments"; that is, how people "think about and react to their initial emotions."[11] Dr. Willroth and her co-researchers found study participants who tended to judge their negative emotions negatively—to feel bad for being sad, fearful, angry, upset—were more likely to show symptoms of anxiety or depression and were more dissatisfied with their lives when compared to people who judged their negative emotions neutrally or even positively.

So, when we feel crummy, should we just grit our teeth and soldier on? Turns out that's not so great, either. An analysis of forty-eight mental health studies involving over 21,000 participants linked depression and anxiety to emotional suppression.[12] Studies in which people have been instructed to suppress feelings of pain or discomfort have found those who suppress are less able to tolerate pain in the long run than those who acknowledge their discomfort.[13] They're also more likely to have lingering negative emotions.[14]

And "toxic positivity"—papering on a fake smile or responding to negative emotions with reductive positive statements—isn't helpful either: saying "good vibes only" can lead us to ignore valuable emotional insights that bad or complicated vibes signal. One study that looked at workers in a variety of industries found people who pretended to be positive when they didn't truly feel that way may have made immediate interactions easier, but ultimately, they undermined their relationships at work. However, workers who genuinely looked for ways to find positive outcomes—what the researchers called "deep actors"—ultimately strengthened work relationships, were trusted more by co-workers and were more successful in meeting their work goals.[15]

So how should we respond when our work—or other aspects of our lives—provoke negative feelings? Emotions are data, and it can help to try to step back and view them in this way. Acknowledge the emotions you are feeling. Examine the situation that provoked them. What information are your emotions trying to convey to you? Then, taking into account this larger pool of information, you can choose what to do next. Accepting that you're having negative emotions doesn't mean you have to accept the situation that provoked them: look for the information inside those emotions to help you plan and move forward. Ultimately, you'll be happier—and your work relationships will be too.

Diversity, Yes; Token, No

I was visible. I was good at my job. I had a message about education, diversity and resilience that senior bank leadership felt aligned with the values they wanted to promote and that resonated with clients and the public. But I, and the managers I'd been placed with, had been set up to fail because of a lack of clarity on what my job really was and a lack of understanding of how that role fit—or didn't fit—within the bank's existing structures.

So how might things have been different? As I think about it, I keep coming back to another experience I had where I was explicitly recruited because of my diversity: the University of Toronto Governing Council. I'd never thought of applying to be on the council, but my mentor John encouraged me to put my name forward. "Isn't it all CEOs and executives?" I asked when he suggested it. I was a thirty-three-year-old recent graduate just starting my career—I didn't think I'd have a chance. Still, I applied and went through the interview process, where I talked about how my university education had literally changed my life, enabling me to build the courage and the resources to leave my marriage. In 2016, I was elected to the council. At the reception that welcomed new alumni governors, I stood out: there were seven older white men in black and grey suits, and me, in my red dress.

And then the chair of the college of electors, lawyer Scott Mac-Kendrick, approached me. "Samra, you might be wondering if you're here because of your gender, your skin colour or your age," he said after he introduced himself and shook my hand. "I want to say that we did want more diversity in the application pool, and that's why we invited you to apply, but after that, you went through the same rigorous screening interview and selection process everyone else did, and you're here because you stood head and shoulders above others we interviewed. You deserve to be here, and we want you, your thoughts and your ideas at the table."

I'm not sure if Scott remembers saying those words, but I remember every one of them, because those words were like keys unlocking a door for me. I wasn't the same as those older men who were also around the table—but I was as qualified to be there. Scott could have simply said nothing, taking for granted that since he felt he belonged, I must as well. But his words were important in letting me—and others—know my inclusion was deliberate and earned. His words were an act of allyship.

I later became the chair of the University of Toronto Mississauga campus council, a journey that took me from being a mature student on that campus to being its youngest council chair, and the first woman from a diverse background in that seat. In the council chambers, photos of former chairpeople line the wall: almost all men, almost all white. And then, there is my photo. As I took on the role, I vowed that while I might look different from the people in the photos preceding me, the people in the photos after me would look different too. Over my years on the council, I have nominated others from diverse backgrounds and mentored new council members as they came to the table, a responsibility I take seriously as I carve a path and create space for those who come after me. I may be one of a small group of "firsts" but I'm committed to making sure I'm not a "last."

Whispered Wisdom

I came to Canada at fourteen and quickly learned that to be successful, I had to be "Canadian," and was even told I had to give up my identity as a woman of South Asian heritage and an Ismaili Muslim. Fast forward twenty-five years to a pivotal realization: My multi-dimensional identity was an asset and my lived experiences could help create better experiences for employees and clients and for me. The power of authenticity!

ZABEEN HIRJI, RETIREMENT DISRUPTOR, FORMER CHIEF HR OFFICER, RBC

Moving from Diversity to Belonging

Diversity. Inclusion. Belonging. We sometimes mistakenly believe these words are more or less interchangeable. They're not. Diversity is simply inviting people to the table. Inclusion comes when we ask everyone at the table to share their ideas and views. But a better goal is to aim for belonging, when everyone at the table feels their ideas and views will be welcomed and heard. When people feel that they authentically belong, connection, resilience and engagement follow. For both leaders and team members, authentic relationships at work require being courageous in showing up as who we are. That requires vulnerability—and it can be risky, even scary. Our authentic self is often buried under layers of cultural and societal "shoulds," but with self-awareness and practise, we can unleash our authenticity—and let ourselves shine. How?

As a Leader

1. **GO BEYOND WORK:** Introduce fifteen-minute authenticity circles during regular meetings, where no work talk is allowed and staff are encouraged to engage in conversation about "rest of life" topics. People will find points of connection that are human, rather than driven by task, and ultimately feel better supported and connected at work.

2. **FORGIVE MISTAKES:** Successful teams allow room for learning, pivoting and growing together—which means allowing room for mistakes! Have compassion and kindness for yourself and others.

3. **TRUST YOUR GUT BUT QUESTION YOUR BIAS:** We're often told that great leaders "trust their gut"—and that's true, to a point. But sometimes our guts—our intuition—can reinforce the biases we've grown up with. Great leaders question their assumptions, check their biases and seek input, even when it makes them ask themselves some tough questions about what they've assumed is the right way forward.

4. **HAVE THE COURAGE TO SUPPORT DIFFICULT CONVERSATIONS WITH APPROPRIATE GUIDELINES AND FACILITATION:** Some workplaces have tried to create agreeable workplaces by banning disagreement—saying no to talk of politics or other difficult subjects. But pushing conversations underground isn't a solution, it's avoidance. Developing social

codes of conduct and circles of respect and can be healthier models for productive ways of tackling tough topics.

5. **BE DELIBERATE:** As I learned from Scott MacKendrick's welcome to the U of T council, it makes a real difference to be openly, deliberately welcomed. Don't assume people know they belong: tell them so. Then, ask how they would like to be supported. While the golden adage tells us to treat others as we would like to be treated, it's even more important to treat others as they tell us they would like to be treated. We don't all have the same experiences or come from the same realities. Being receptive to what others need starts with empathy, conversation and an open mind and heart, and is followed up with deliberate, thoughtful action.

6. **BE AWARE OF INCLUSION FATIGUE:** The people most invested in creating positive change in your organization can end up burned out and checked out if they're poorly supported or expected to carry the burden of doing this challenging work on their own. As well, managers and staff can become cynical about inclusion efforts that seem more like window dressing than real change. Persevere through inclusion fatigue at all levels with good support and a commitment to genuine transformation and results.

As a Person

1. **WATCH YOURSELF:** Observe yourself objectively as you move through your day, how you behave, think, respond, react. What feels authentic? Listen to your intuition, being mindful of discrepancies between your actions and your values. Practise listening to your inner voice, while challenging yourself to be aware of your biases.

2. **GIVE YOURSELF A GOOD TALKING-TO:** Talk to yourself as if you were your own best friend. Shun perfectionism. Give yourself positive affirmations. Visualize success, reward yourself for efforts and celebrate your achievements. It might sound like the kind of thing cool people make fun of. But a decade after I'd stood in front of the mirror pretending to give a university valedictory speech, I gave that speech at the University of Toronto. And I think that's pretty cool.

3. **SPEAK YOUR HEART, EVEN IF YOUR VOICE QUAVERS:** Having tough conversations can be daunting, but if it is safe to do so, seek the support you need (like the friend who asked for my help to practise her conversation with her manager Jim) and speak your truth. One note of caution: authenticity in the workplace carries distinct risks for marginalized people, which is why I say, "If it is safe to do so." Pause before sharing to assess the risk of additional harm, seek support from allies and be strategic in your timing: these are all wise steps.

4. **MAKE ROOM FOR MISTAKES:** "It's going to be a three-hour wait for a table." The waitress at the restaurant where I was meeting my friend Eric had just given me an up-and-down look that I knew meant she wouldn't budge—for me. But as soon as Eric—a tall, white man—arrived, suddenly a table opened up. "I can't believe that just happened," I fumed after we'd been seated. "I can't believe I just got denied service in the most diverse city in the world!" I wanted to talk to the manager, but Eric disagreed. "No, no, don't do that—I come here a lot," he said, protecting his privilege at the expense of my discrimination. I didn't say more in that moment, but over the next few days, my irritation grew. "Can we have a coffee?" I asked. As I explained how it felt

to be turned away while he'd been quickly seated, he got it. I could have silently fumed and cut Eric off, but that conversation was worth it because he's a friend and an ally. And, without prompting from me, he wrote a letter to the restaurant manager pointing out the difference in treatment we'd both received.

5. **DO YOUR OWN HOMEWORK:** Investing energy in a conversation with Eric was worth it. But if you're a person of colour or are otherwise marginalized, it's not your responsibility to provide on-the-spot anti-racism-or-any-other-ism education. If you're in a position of privilege, you're responsible for your own education about equity issues: you can google resources, read books and do the work without expecting people who live with the burden of racism or other marginalizing forces to teach you how to be better. And for those of us who are marginalized, we have the right to choose when to teach, when to fight and when to walk away.

6. **EMBRACE CRITICAL ALLYSHIP:** Go beyond "I want to help" and commit to using your expertise to reduce inequities. As Dr. Stephanie Nixon outlines in her work on critical allyship,[16] for those who are in a position of privilege, this includes learning about systems of inequality, speaking less and listening more while amplifying the voices of those from marginalized communities, working to build insight among others in positions of privilege, and not using allyship to enhance personal power.

7. **BUILD HEALTHY BOUNDARIES:** Foster connection with those who provide healthy support and establish clear, guilt-free boundaries with those who don't champion your authentic self. Say no to things you don't have the capacity for. Seek

feedback—but make sure it's from those who have your best interests at heart. And don't take criticism from people you'd never turn to for advice.

8. **PUT SELF-CARE FIRST:** It can be emotionally draining to engage authentically with those around us. Boundaries can be tough to define and tiring to maintain. And sometimes fatigue can pull us into a spiral of blame, directed at ourselves and others. For me, that self-blame unravels as a series of accusatory questions: Why did I let others make me believe I was "less than"? How did I let all those years go to waste, trapped in my marriage? Why has work often been so interpersonally challenging? Each question comes wrapped with anger, shame, guilt and pain. I once heard someone say we should treat mental health like dental health. For me, small acts of self-care—short meditations, walks outdoors, breathing exercises—are the equivalent of brushing and flossing twice a day. Time with a therapist is like my regular dental checkups and cleanings. Find what works for you and remember vulnerability is not weakness. Fear is not weakness. Asking for help is not weakness. And saying no to an unreasonable request—or simply one you can't take on right now—can be the best form of self-care of all.

9. **LEAN INTO AUTHENTICITY:** Authenticity is not a trait. It is a continuous practice, a way of life. Sometimes, we'll find ourselves in situations with people or in places that make us pull back, retreat. Sometimes, we're so overburdened with responsibility that we become disconnected from ourselves. That's okay. Authenticity is a process of knowing and re-knowing ourselves, discovering new facets of ourselves as we face new situations. Lean into your becoming.

Unconditioning Workbook

- As human beings, we have a fundamental psychological desire to be seen, accepted and respected for who we are. But that desire is balanced against another set of sometimes conflicting needs: the need to fit into the community around us. As a result, we are constantly calibrating our inner and outer selves in order to establish and maintain connections in the community in which we find ourselves, as we seek to find friends and companions, to get work and to be successful.

- Those of us who are not white face additional pressures to conform: to the larger society's norms (often not "colour coded" but reflecting the dominant white culture) as well as to our respective religious, cultural and community-specific norms. We are often expected to represent our communities "well" out there in the world. It's hard to be yourself when you are carrying so many "shoulds" on your shoulders.

- The message we often get from society is that "you, as you are, are not enough." But when we connect with our authentic selves, we can begin to see our authenticity not as a barrier preventing us from being "enough," but as a source of strength to become "more."

- Authenticity—in the workplace and elsewhere—builds resilience because we can take more risks and bounce back from setbacks when we are supported in being true to our values and our strengths.

- People from marginalized groups face real barriers in the workplace, including, but not limited to, microaggressions that add to our psychological load and drain our mental and emotional energy.

- Good managers don't manage from fear—they manage through support. This is the difference between being a leader and being a boss.

- Hiring diverse employees is easy. Creating an environment in which all can thrive takes commitment and effort.

- If you are a person of colour or otherwise marginalized, it's not your responsibility to provide on-the-spot anti-racism education. You have the right to choose when to teach, when to fight and when to walk away.

- If you are a member of the dominant culture, you are responsible for educating yourself about equity issues. Google resources, read books and do the work without expecting people who live with the burden of racism or other marginalizing forces to teach you how to do better.

- In the workplace and elsewhere, don't take criticism from people you'd never turn to for advice.

- Make time for self-care. (See more on this in Chapter Ten: Care Package.)

- Authenticity—at work and in the rest of your life—is not a trait. It is a continuous practice, a way of life. Authenticity is a process of knowing and re-knowing yourself, discovering new facets of yourself as you face new situations. Lean into your becoming.

Reflection: Belonging

We've all absorbed messages from our families, workplaces, cultures and experiences about whether we belong, whether we're accepted. Often these messages aren't spoken explicitly and are instead embedded in actions, encoded as subtle signals that remain unstated, but shape our behaviour nevertheless. The first step is to articulate them. Here are some that shaped me:

- I need to dream small because I'm a woman.
- I need to make my mothering invisible in the workplace or I won't succeed.
- My brown skin and Pakistani heritage make me a stranger in some workplaces, someone who might be *let* in but not *welcomed* in.

For me, the damage caused by these messages is best healed with the insights I've found as I've pulled them apart:

- When someone tells me to make my dreams smaller, they're showing me their limits, not mine.
- My children are a source of strength, insight, humour and humanity. A workplace that doesn't welcome me as a mother is a workplace that doesn't deserve the benefits of my success.
- Whether or not you welcome me, I belong here and I will do all that I can to hold the door open for others. And even if someone doesn't pull up a chair for me at the table, I will pull one up for myself.

What have you been told about where you belong, whether explicitly or through the actions and behaviours of others? How can you recast these messages into your inclusion mantra?

1. A negative message I've gotten at work or in other situations about whether I belong is _____
_____
_____
_____.

2. I choose to reframe this message as an inclusion mantra by tapping into the strength within that makes me distinct: _____
_____
_____
_____
_____.

Whispered Wisdom

I'm very proud of the career I have built in a male-dominated area of law. Over the years, I've always been surprised when people assume I didn't face obstacles in many different forms. There have been times in my career where I have felt like broken glass that is Scotch-taped together. But—and this is the key—I've always pushed through and been stronger for it.

LEILA RAFI, PARTNER, McMILLAN LLP

CHAPTER EIGHT:

Creating Your Team

In the photo, I am lobster-bibbed and ready to dig in. "Ready for yet another lobster feast—I'm in seafood heaven!" I texted my friend and mentor John. I was nearing the end of my Quebec road trip. When I'd told John my plan for my solo mind-clearing journey, he'd made me promise to send him a daily snapshot. He knew I'd be in touch with my daughters each day, and we both knew I could look after myself, but it was still nice to know he'd follow up if I didn't check in. Smart adventures include safety nets.

Will You Be My Mentor?

I'd met John almost a decade earlier. "Can we meet for coffee?" It was a question I'd posed to each of the members of the University of Toronto committee that had awarded me the John H. Moss Scholarship, the university's highest honour for undergraduate students. In the year after I'd left my marriage, the scholarship made it possible for me to pursue a master's degree in economics, something that would otherwise have been difficult for me as a single mother of two young daughters. I'd asked the university for the contact

218

information for the committee members, as I wanted to thank each in person.

"I'll do you one better," responded John Rothschild, then CEO of Prime Restaurants and chair of the committee. "Let's do breakfast."

I didn't intend to do more than say thank you. But as we chatted over our morning meal, we hit it off. Still, I wasn't going to overstep. Then John opened the door. "What more can I do for you?" he said as our time together wound down.

"Will you be my mentor?" I blurted. I wasn't even sure what I meant; I just knew the man across from me was astute, intelligent—and kind.

"Absolutely," he replied.

In the months that followed, we met regularly for coffee, talked about my studies, my dreams for the future. I told him about my girls, shared details of my past. When discussing a situation, John never told me what to do. "I'll tell you my thoughts," he'd say before offering them, "but I'll support you in any decision you make, even if it's a decision I wouldn't have made." To help me clarify my thinking, his preferred tactic was to challenge me to convince him of why I wanted to do something. Crafting my argument inevitably led me to reaffirm my decision—or talk myself out of it. John wasn't someone who beat around the bush: his questions were direct, but he also listened and was open to the perspective that perhaps a young, brown woman experienced the world differently than an "established white guy." Over time, John has become my biggest mentor, often the first person I call when I need advice, comfort, encouragement or a sounding board—and the closest thing I have had to a healthy parent.

John wasn't my first mentor, but this was the first time I deliberately asked for such help. I'd found my first mentor, Professor James

Appleyard, by accident at the start of my university journey. Then, I was one of seven hundred students in an undergraduate management course, a twenty-eight-year-old woman in a hijab in a sea of eighteen-year-olds. I was doing well in the course—really well, scoring 98 percent on a test. The thing was, I knew it should have been 100. The percentage would make no difference to my overall grade, but it was the principle: I'd answered the question correctly. And so I booked an appointment with my professor.

The exams had been marked by his teaching assistants, and the rules of the course were that if you challenged a mark, the professor would review and re-mark your whole exam—so your mark might go up, but it might also go down.

I handed Professor Appleyard my exam. "I'd like you to re-mark it," I said.

His eyebrows shot up when he saw my mark. "Okay," he said, smiling. "This is the first time a student has asked me to re-mark a test with a 98 percent. Why don't you take a seat?" He reread it as I waited, then looked up. "I don't think my TA could have written a better answer," he said, adjusting my mark to 100 percent. "So tell me your story."

I explained I was a mom with two daughters, going to school part-time while running a daycare from home to pay for my tuition.

"Why don't you apply for some scholarships and bursaries?" he asked.

"University scholarships are linked to student loan status, and I don't qualify because of my husband's income," I replied. The same went for bursaries. He didn't ask why my husband wasn't helping with my school expenses.

"What about external scholarships?" he said. I hadn't heard of them. He advised me on how to apply and offered to write me the reference letter I'd need. Not long after, he gave me a copy of the recommendation he'd composed. I think now that he wanted me to see what he'd written. It was glowing.

I read and reread that letter. It was the first time I'd caught a glimpse of how someone outside my family, outside my community, saw me: skilled, talented, exceptional.

Not every teacher had been so supportive. As a youngster, I'd been in situations where my intelligence had been dismissed or viewed with suspicion. In elementary school, our music and social studies teacher, Mrs. Baqri, was known for her high standards and tough tests emphasizing memorization of long answers. I was eager to impress her, and so for our first test, I diligently memorized the sections she said might appear on the exam. The day of the exam, proctors watched over us to make cheating impossible. I turned over my paper and started scribbling furiously. We were to choose three of the six questions to answer, but I answered them all. After she marked the exams, she accused me of cheating and quizzed the students who sat around me about whether they'd seen me copying my answers. My parents were called in and I was given a zero. The lesson was clear: don't exceed expectations, or you'll be punished.

As someone who has survived repeated trauma from people who were supposed to teach, protect and even love me, learning to trust didn't come easily to me. I thought people would reject me if I wasn't a version of myself tailored to their needs, meaning I learned to hide and repress my authentic self. I'd learned that, for girls and women especially, being exceptional made you a target. And I believed connecting with others meant giving them what they needed while pretending to have no needs of my own, leaving me isolated in exhausting, one-sided connections.

I hadn't asked my university professor for help. But he'd sensed I needed it and gave it, without expecting anything in return. One voluntary mentor opened my eyes to the value of truly connecting with people in my life. Since then, I've successfully created a network of friends and mentors whose insights and support have added immeasurably to my life, personally and professionally.

Making those connections can feel risky. For some of us, admitting we want help places us in an uncomfortable one-down position; it means being vulnerable enough to admit we don't know it all. There's the ego risk of being turned down, the potential embarrassment of being turned away. But as I learned with the professor who offered mentorship and the businessman who said yes when I asked for his, smart, accomplished people know they are strengthened by their connections and enriched by others as they reach out. Their understanding of the world expands as they help others expand their own knowledge. When I've reached out, I've always had more yeses than noes. I've worked hard to pass it along with yeses of my own, while being generous in understanding when someone does say no—and I hope others understand when I sometimes say no as well. (Connections matter—but so does self-care. You can't mentor anyone when you overextend yourself.)

But here's something I didn't expect when I took that first risky step of asking for John's help: reaching out has become one of my superpowers. To tap into it, I've had to unlearn the lessons of isolation and suspicion that trauma so often fosters, to quiet the voices that told me no one would help me—or if they did, I'd pay for it later. In a world that places a high value on independence, the question "Who can I ask for help?" can sound like weakness, but in fact, it's a step to connection, strength—and sometimes, friendship.

Still, it took me some time to recognize something that might have been obvious to someone viewing my network from the outside: particularly when it came to mentors, it turned out I had a woman problem.

Whispered Wisdom

Practice patience and empathy
with yourself and others. (However, do
reserve a little hostility for assholes.)

ALEXANDRA GILLESPIE, VICE-PRESIDENT,

UNIVERSITY OF TORONTO & PRINCIPAL,

UNIVERSITY OF TORONTO

MISSISSAUGA

Who Ends Up in Our Circle

"Well, what happens, happens," said the colleague I was chatting with. We'd been talking about who ends up in our network of professional and personal connections. "You meet people: some stick and some don't."

That's how many of us approach it, forging friendships and creating networks haphazardly based on who happens to cross our path or ends up seated in the cubicle next to us at work. And serendipity can work magic: I could have ended up in a different section of that introductory economics course with another professor and not made a connection that helped change my life the day I asked for my exam to be re-marked.

As discussed in the parenting chapter, humans are born needing to connect with each other, first with our key caregivers, then with those in what is usually our family group and community and, as we move on through life, with friends, partners and colleagues.

We're wired to attach. These relationships are essential to our feelings of belonging and contribute to our self-esteem; those who lack a sense of belonging are particularly at risk for depression, for instance.[1]

Many factors affect those connections, but one theory suggests that the feeling we have when we "click" with another person or group stems in part from a "shared reality," a tendency to form closer relationships with people who view the world the way we do.[2] Interestingly, though, simply having a single large circle of friends and connections in the same community or group isn't a predictor of self-esteem, but belonging to multiple circles is.[3] It turns out it's better to be at the heart of a Venn diagram of many groups than to be a dot floating in a single, bigger pool. These multiple group connections might help in more than one way. If we have links to many groups, our entire identity isn't tied to adhering to one group's beliefs and standards, and so if our connections are weakened or strained in one area—or if we're questioning that group's values, behaviours or "reality"—we have other supports to fall back on. Each circle or community will have its own goals, values and beliefs—a set of lenses through which it views the world. When we belong to multiple groups, we are exposed to multiple points of view, which I would argue pushes us to develop our personal beliefs in a richer, more nuanced way, potentially boosting our inner support mechanisms as well.

Still, our life experiences have an enormous impact on *how* we attach. Those of us who have experienced trauma as adults or in childhood—physical, verbal or emotional abuse or neglect—may develop attachment styles that complicate our ability to form healthy friendships and intimate relationships, especially the way we manage the boundaries within relationships. Counsellor Nedra Glover Tawwab puts it this way in her book *Set Boundaries, Find Peace*:

- People with "anxious attachment" tend to have porous boundaries, constantly seeking validation, wanting to be close but pushing people away, engaging in attention-seeking behaviours, and experiencing paralyzing fear that the relationship will end.
- People with "avoidant attachment" hyperfocus on the negative aspects of a relationship, look for reasons to justify the feeling that the relationship isn't working, worry about loss of autonomy and struggle with self-disclosure, often opting for "my way or the highway" rigid boundaries.
- People with "secure attachment" have a healthy sense of self, are comfortable sharing feelings, regulate their emotions during disputes, allow others to express their feelings without overreacting—all markers of healthy boundaries.[4]

One of trauma's most toxic effects is its disruption of our understanding of boundaries. When we grow up in healthy circumstances, we learn to see and set healthy boundaries, to recognize what we need to feel safe and to communicate those boundaries clearly and confidently. We learn that it's okay to say no to physical contact, emotional manipulation and direct requests we're not comfortable with, to hear others when they say no—and to speak our yes with clarity and enthusiasm. But families, communities, schools and workplaces that aren't healthy teach us we don't have the agency to say yes or no: we're pressured to please others even when it harms us or puts us at risk.

So what happens when we move out into the world? Some of us become people pleasers, ignoring our own needs as we strive to ensure we give everyone around us what they want. Others become black-and-white rule setters, enforcing a "my way or the highway" approach to interactions, unable to accommodate the boundaries of others because we fear that bending will break us. When our boundaries are too loose or too rigid, our relationships suffer. Acknowledged or not, resentment bubbles away under the surface for the pleasers, while the rule setters drive away those who won't acquiesce to their will.

Specific experiences may also colour who we connect with. While it's true that patriarchal cultures are pervasive, the community in which I grew up was among those still adhering most strictly to conventional male and female roles: men had the power, and women had the power men let them have. You'd think this would create strong bonds among those typically excluded from power—women. But what it often does instead is create competition for whatever power is up for grabs, alongside a keen awareness that it is better to be the enforcer of a husband's or father's power within a household than to be powerless outside it. It's a terrible double bind: remaining connected—a basic human need—means playing by the community's standards of male power and authority, and what little agency individual women have is often attached to enforcing those patriarchal standards. Ironically, I wasn't surprised when men wielded their power in ways that harmed me—but I was always surprised when women did. Within my family, my father claimed me and one of my sisters as "his" allies in his battles with my mother, and my mother blamed . . . my sister and me. As a teen bride, I hoped for a good relationship with my mother-in-law—but instead endured abuse at her hands because she finally had another woman in the family with less status than she had. After I escaped my forced marriage, completed university and entered the work world, I often found myself in positions where I seemed to be competing with other women for one of the limited positions or honours designated for women or people of colour—and so we seemed to be pitted against each other rather than being evaluated as part of the overall pool of candidates eligible for all the spots. In the banking world, for instance, I often had positive interactions with senior women in leadership positions many levels above me, but then my direct female managers acted as if they viewed me as a threat. Yes, there were opportunities for women—but in what was still very much a patriarchal system, the message to women in middle management was that only a select few would get to rise through the glass ceiling. "If she gets ahead, I won't" was a common mindset.

My friendships with women were also complicated by my early isolation in Canada: I'd had virtually no friends during my marriage. After it ended, I socialized most with students—men and women— within the Muslim Pakistani community, where relationships were complicated by tension between the familiarity of shared social backgrounds and the push and pull of adhering to the community's standards for how women should behave. The actions I'd taken in leaving my marriage made my position in the community precarious, often placing me outside the boundaries of what was considered acceptable. Some viewed me as a bad influence, while other women who had experienced similar abuse saw me as a potential ally, like my friend Nasrin.

Not long after my marriage ended, I became friendly with a Muslim family I met through a local mosque. At the time, I felt supported by them, but looking back, I see now I was perhaps a kind of "project" for them: the divorced woman they were going to help get back on a proper Muslim path. It was this family's matriarch who tried to push me into marriage with a sixty-year-old man in Pakistan, since, as she put it, I couldn't expect much else as a divorcée. In her eyes, any marriage was better than no marriage.

Around that time, I met Nasrin. We were close in age, and she too had left an abusive marriage, though she'd been unable to keep her children with her and so they remained with their father. We bonded over shared challenges: we were both in school trying to better ourselves, in precarious positions within the community and struggling with ex-husbands whose behaviour made life difficult. Over time, I gradually pulled away from the community that judged me as a failure and possibly dangerous for leaving my marriage, while Nasrin stayed deeply connected to it. Still, we remained friends.

It wasn't an easy friendship, though. Friends should be the people you celebrate successes with and seek support from during hard times, but both were difficult with Nasrin. When I was accepted for my first TEDx Talk, she turned down my invitation to attend the conference. "Why?" I asked. "Because I'm jealous," she said matter-of-factly. I was so startled, I laughed, thinking she was joking—but she wasn't. When she showed up at the last minute, she seemed to expect effusive praise for being there at all, the kind of toxic emotional withholding game I'd later recognize in unhealthy romantic relationships. When I turned to her for support during a difficult time with one of my daughters, her response was cruel: "It's no wonder she ran away, with a mother like you." Nasrin's judgment of me stung, and it wasn't confined to my parenting. She criticized me for dating, too.

Still, we remained friends. "Why?" One of my daughters asked the question I likely should have asked myself. "She gets me," I told her. "We're from the same background, we've been through similar things. I don't have to explain things to her." Nasrin and I bounced back and forth between connecting and disconnecting, with the door to our friendship swinging open and shut. It was a relationship filled with drama, the kind some might file under the heading "frenemy" and psychologists call "ambivalent." Researchers Bert Uchino and Julianne Holt-Lunstad have shown that these ambivalent relationships can be even more harmful than straight-up negative ones.[5] At least with an enemy, you know where you stand. But frenemies send us into a spiral of second-guessing, rumination and uncertainty that can spike our blood pressure[6] and ruin our sleep.

Nasrin wasn't my only female friend. There were others with whom I also shared similar cultural backgrounds and experiences. But as with Nasrin, some of those relationships suffered as I moved beyond the boundaries my community sought to impose and my world grew larger than the trauma I'd survived.

There's a quote from Ernest Hemingway's novel *A Farewell to Arms* that shows up frequently in social media posts and elsewhere. You might recognize it: "The world breaks everyone and afterward many are strong at the broken places." It's a line that resonates with many of us who have survived trauma, offering hope and strength in the aftermath of difficulty. What it doesn't say is that sometimes our broken places become the sites of connection with others whose experiences are similar. As anyone who has bonded with co-workers dealing with a crummy boss or played on a team during a losing season can attest, connections can feel stronger when you've weathered a storm together or shared a common experience or history. Bonding over righteous outrage, coming together against a common foe, encouraging each other in the face of adverse conditions: all can make a friendship feel tight and strong. And some of those relationships may outlast the tough times—though it's also true that once we've moved on from a situation or threat, we sometimes find we don't have much in common except for the shared memories of what we went through.

As I moved on from my marriage, completing university and embarking on a career, the trauma that had once seemed to dominate my life became a proportionally smaller part of it. My life was about more than surviving bad things—it was about embracing the good and thriving as well. And I discovered that while we may be strong at our broken places, the relationships that grow from those broken places might not be. Kindredness built on shared brokenness can keep us tied to that brokenness, especially when our healing journeys diverge.

Not every friendship born out of shared trauma is fated to end—and not every supportive connection forged in trauma is fated to become a friendship. Support groups, for instance, can be powerful sources of encouragement and understanding for those who have experienced similar difficulties, and we can value the contributions

Whispered Wisdom

I'll be honest: I was a hard-ass most of my career, hard-driving and, of course, under so much pressure as a partner in a law firm with children, and a lot more to deal with. Then a bomb within my family made me drastically cut back my hours and career. It felt like I had to crank it down from being a nuclear reactor to a candle, packing my aspirations up into a little box.

Who knew being blown to smithereens would be a good thing? With my sights shifted, I saw far more important challenges to be tackled, from within my city to across the globe. As my life is now solely spent supporting and amplifying others, my impact has spread into a multitude of domains, helping to create a new generation of little nuclear reactors, powering up for good.

Do I miss spending my time trying to triple my billings? Ask me something harder.

WENDY REED,

LAWYER, PHILANTHROPIST, MENTOR. REWIRED & REBOOTED.

of others around the table without taking the next step to friendship. But leaving behind relationships—friendships and romantic bonds—built on brokenness is hard. It feels cruel to say, "We don't have much in common anymore." We excuse unkind or even toxic behaviour because we know what the person has been through and don't want to be the shitty friend who walks away from someone who is struggling. But don't we deserve more than to be treated poorly by the shitty friend we hesitate to walk away from?

Nasrin and I weathered more than one friendship breakup. Until we didn't.

And while I knew the friendship wasn't a healthy one, still a part of me wondered, was I the shitty friend in this story?

From Dramatic to Deliberate

What do you think of when you hear the word *networking*? It's got some ick to it, doesn't it?

We live in a culture that often views deliberately seeking out and connecting with people as a kind of gold-digging. In my experience, we accept networking may be necessary in business or to move ahead professionally, but still, many of us think . . . *yuck*. And the suggestion that we might want to be even a little bit deliberate in seeking out friendships has the whiff of desperation, neediness or even horror movie manipulation to it. It's as if we believe friendships must be accidental to be real.

It's a bit like how we view romantic relationships: we're surrounded by movies, books, songs and other messages suggesting it's not real love unless it catches us by surprise. But the reality is, many of us are pretty deliberate about seeking romance these days. We sign up on dating apps, review people's profiles, swipe left or right. It's true: we might still meet our match in the coffee shop lineup or when we move back to our hometown to rescue the family business from ruin (oops, sorry, I think that's a Hallmark movie plot sliding in). But it's also okay—and more likely than ever—to meet our mate online, with recent surveys suggesting one in eight Americans have married someone they met online[7] and one in four currently engaged couples met online.[8]

Here's the thing: I believe that especially for those of us who have grown up with and around unhealthy relationships, our accidental or "natural" friendship patterns can lead us to keep repeating the unhealthy relationships of our pasts. We need to unlearn how we make friends, forge professional connections and, yes, find romantic partners as well, leaving behind the drama of our pasts and taking deliberate steps to choose more wisely. Sure, some of those connections may happen serendipitously—but whether we decide to pursue them or not is still up to us, a deliberate choice we get to make.

So why do we cringe a bit about this? I think it's rooted in confusing being deliberate with being transactional. When we view potential connections through a transactional lens, we're asking ourselves "What can this person give me?" We might, if we're viewing it as two-way, add "And what can I give them?" But there is very clearly an element of tallying concrete benefits, of measuring how a connection enhances our status or wealth. Being deliberate isn't quite the same: the questions we ask are more along these lines: "Is this person good for me and I for them? Are we good together?" The lens becomes much wider, one of evaluating the potential positive (or negative) impact people have on each other emotionally, intellectually and even spiritually. And, of course, the connection you offer someone else has value to them as well: all of us want to be connected, seen and valued for who we are. It's the difference between asking "Am I better with this person?" versus "Am I richer with this person?"

And "Am I better?" isn't such a bad question to ask.

Whispered Wisdom

You have more creative power than you can fathom. Everything is available to you. *Everything.* Think about the life you want. Think about how you want to feel each day, the experiences you want to have, the kinds of people you want to be around. Let that be your compass for your priorities and daily practices. There is nothing too big or too grand for you to want to be, have or pursue. After all, why NOT you?

KELSEY KOMOROWSKI

Tackling My Woman Problem

"Be a woman other women can trust. Have the courage to tell another woman directly when she has offended, hurt or disappointed you. Successful women have a loyal tribe of loyal and honest women behind them. Not haters. Not backstabbers or women who whisper behind their back. Be a woman who lifts other women." When this popular online quote from African American lawyer and journalist Sophia A. Nelson showed up in my Instagram feed, I found myself nodding in agreement . . . and then pausing. Was I a woman other women trusted? Was I surrounded by a tribe of other women? Did I lift other women up?

I knew I *wanted* to be. In fact, I'd begun to build a not-for-profit program aimed at lifting other women up, matching women leaving abusive situations with mentors. But as I looked around me, I also knew I wasn't there yet. Of course, I had women in my social and professional circle. But my mentors were mostly men, and I often found myself holding back in female relationships because my experiences with my mother and mother-in-law and the judgment I'd felt from women within my community and at work made me wary. *I need to work on this*, I thought.

And then a woman I'd met professionally called. We'd crossed paths at various events and I'd enjoyed speaking with her, but our connection hadn't progressed beyond that. Now, she was inviting me to a women's luncheon at a downtown restaurant, a networking gathering where she brought together professional women from a variety of fields. I wasn't sure I measured up. I'd just written my book, but the others at the table still seemed more accomplished than me, further along in their careers, more advanced in their fields. When I expressed my doubts to her, she pushed them aside. "Come," she said. "They're all great women!"

I wasn't sure what to expect, but as we took our places at the table, our host's genuine warmth and interest set the tone. "Why don't we go around and tell each other who we are—not what we do, but who we are?" she said. It was exactly the right question, as each woman shared what mattered to her. One talked about growing up in a homophobic environment and now being a mom to a child born male who was exploring wearing feminine clothing, and how glad she was to be able to simply say "You be you, kid" to the child she loved, breaking the cycle of biases she'd been raised with. Another talked about her challenges of feeling like an imposter at work.

There was a small element of transaction to the conversations: she also asked us to share one thing we'd like some help with. But that transactional element felt grounded in connection and generosity rather than focused on tallying a balance sheet. Though the economist in me realized it was mathematically impossible, I think somehow we all left feeling we'd received more than we'd offered.

My ask that day? I was in the early stages of setting up my charity,

Brave Beginnings, but was struggling to sort out next steps. "I can help," piped up one woman, a retired lawyer.

Later that evening, I sent our host a note. "You know, I've always been hesitant to connect with women," I confessed to her. "I grew up seeing women subvert rather than support each other. But today I truly felt the power of how women can lift each other up. Thank you for that."

In the months that followed, new friendships with some of the women I'd met that day deepened. There were moments when the voices of my past whispered in my ear. *They're more successful than you. You're not their equal,* the voices grumbled, echoing the suggestions of my childhood that another woman's success was my defeat in the fight for power's crumbs. But now I could recognize past patterns, be deliberate in rejecting them. I was discovering we don't have to fight for crumbs when together, we can make bigger pies.

Now, a few years later, my network of friends, colleagues and mentors is richer and more diverse than it has ever been. I love hanging out with Elizabeth, who is pursuing her Ph.D. and conducting research on social justice, our conversations swinging from super-serious to super-silly. Wendy is like the big sister I never had, always ready with a pep talk and sound advice. I've learned so much from two Jennifers in my circle, one a woman of colour at the forefront of her field whose example challenges me to break barriers and the other my foodie and travel partner whose authenticity inspires me. My friend Kelsey inspires me with her leadership skills and in our downtime is my favourite slumber party, girl-talk pal. I'm dazzled by the enthusiasm and strategic thinking of my agent, Samantha, as she encourages me on my path. Emma has been not just a friend to me, but has also formed a deep friendship with Kinza. Ann is my vision-boarding buddy. And Elisabeth's leadership and courage inspire me endlessly. I value the advice I get from the medical professionals I've sought guidance from in navigating my new field—and look forward to friendships blooming from some of these new connections. They make me better—a better person, a better friend and, I hope in the future, a better doctor. And I trust I make them better too.

The Secret to Better Relationships? Better Boundaries.

Healing from trauma requires a strong support system, and healthy boundaries are key. Nedra Glover Tawwab's book *Set Boundaries, Find Peace: A Guide to Reclaiming Yourself* is an excellent resource if boundary issues are making it difficult for you to find and nurture authentic friendships and other relationships. These are some of the boundary lessons I've learned along the way.

- When people treat us badly, they aren't telling us who we are, they're showing us who they are.
- It's okay to let go of places and people you've outgrown. Think of yourself and the people in your life as a tree: you are the trunk at the core, with each branch representing a specific relationship. Some of the branches are healthy and vibrant, our most enduring and nourishing connections. Some grow for a while but then stop thriving and eventually break off—they're the relationships that might have been right at a particular time in our life but simply weren't enduring. And then there are the branches that are sick or toxic. These are the relationships we need to actively prune, cutting them out before their wounds threaten the health of our whole tree. This pruning isn't easy: women especially can face heavy social pressure to "heal" the damage in a relationship or another person, putting themselves at risk

when pruning that relationship could be the healthier choice.

- Resilience is a team sport, fostered and maintained in community, through our connection to others. Surround yourself with people who lift you up—and whom you lift up in turn. Build a mutually supporting cheerleader squad.

- Asking for help isn't a sign of weakness, it's a signal of the strength we can build together.

- Not every relationship will last forever, but that doesn't mean it wasn't successful. And there will be times we'll face rejection. But rejection is not an end point—it is an opportunity for redirection, a chance to learn and seek a better outcome in our next friendships.

- Good relationships are reciprocal. Carrying those we care for in our heads and our hearts, looking for and creating opportunities to make their lives better, is essential—just as we hope those in our circle will do for us.

- Jealousy can be transformed into inspiration. When you look at someone else's success, if you feel a pang of jealousy, acknowledge it without being hard on yourself (we have all been fed that faulty script) and then reframe your thinking. Think of it as a collective success, as inspiration to carve your own success path.

- Healthy boundaries don't shut hurt out—but they do help us to avoid internalizing the shame. In the years before I worked on developing healthier boundaries, I would often carry someone's hurtful words inside me for months or even years after they'd spoken them, internalizing their judgment even when their words were unfair or untrue: one boss's accusation that I wasn't serious about work as I juggled parenting responsibilities made me wonder if I was a good employee, and my mother-in-law's constant judgmentalism about my housekeeping standards had the power to trigger self-doubts about whether I was setting a good example for my own daughters. When I started to work on my boundaries, I thought the goal was to develop an emotional Teflon shield, so that others' words would simply bounce off me. I've realized over time that shutting out emotions isn't the goal. Now, rather than Teflon, I aim for a protective bubble, one that lets me see what the other is saying, and evaluate, in a healthy, objective way, whether there's anything within those hurtful words or actions that I should consider. Yes, I may be hurt by someone's thoughtless or even deliberately cruel words or actions, especially if they come from someone I care about, and it's okay to feel that pain. I'm strong enough emotionally to withstand and recover from it. But I've also discovered that hurtful words often reflect the accuser's mindset more than they reflect reality. Feeling hurt is human. Internalizing the shame of someone else's hurtful words is a choice, one worth the effort of unlearning.

Whispered Wisdom

Too often we dwarf our potential by self-censoring our dreams. There is an authentic self in us that is in the making, and awaits full awakening. Let us be wake-up calls for one another!

HALINA VON DEM HAGEN

Unconditioning Workbook

- Reflect on the Ernest Hemingway quote "The world breaks everyone and afterward many are strong at the broken places." Sometimes our broken places become a point of connection with others whose experiences are similar. This kind of bond can be powerful, and some of those relationships may outlast the tough times. But we may also find that after we've moved on from a bad situation, we may not have much in common except for the shared memories of a painful experience. Life is about more than surviving bad things—it is about embracing the good and thriving as well. It is okay to grow apart, especially if a relationship is keeping us tied to brokenness.

- We live in a culture that often views deliberately seeking out and connecting with people as a kind of friendship gold-digging. But especially for those of us who have grown up with and around unhealthy relationships, our accidental or "natural" friendship patterns may lead us to repeat the unhealthy relationships of our past. Being deliberate in who we seek to connect with can help us leave behind the drama of our pasts and choose future relationships more wisely.

- *Deliberate* doesn't mean being *transactional*. The question to ask isn't "What can this person give me?" but "Is this person good for me and I for them?"

- The messages from our families or communities of origin may have taught us to think that another's success is our defeat—especially for marginalized people, who may be told there are a limited number of seats for "people like them" at the table. It's important to seek ways to stop fighting for power's crumbs and instead work together to make bigger pies.
- Smart, accomplished people know they are strengthened by their connections and are enriched as they reach out, their understanding of the world expanded as they help others expand their knowledge.
- Connections matter—but so does self-care. You can't connect with or mentor everyone.
- In a world that places a high value on independence, asking for help can seem like weakness, but in fact, it's a step to connection, strength and sometimes friendship.

Reflection: Mind the Gaps

We aren't all born into happy families or healthy communities. But we can create a chosen family, an intentional community. We can foster friendships deliberately, actively selecting who we welcome into our lives and reconnecting with the inner instincts we all possess that tell us who has our best interests at heart.

Imagine your desired life—improved yet attainable: What kinds of people would be in it? Would there be more laughter? More social activism? More art or music? More business acumen? More children? More old people? A wider variety of backgrounds? Someone who knows how to spin a great yarn, loves to garden or can do a magic trick? Create a list that is as serious and silly as the answers that pop into your head. Or, if you're better with visuals, create a friendship mood board with images that represent the kinds of people you'd like to have in your life.

Look at the circle you have: Who in your circle already aligns with what you wish for? What are you doing to nurture those relationships? How are you making their lives better?

And where are the gaps? Identify one or two types of people you'd like to add to your world. Brainstorm: Where might you connect with someone like this? Who in your circle might already be connected to others like this? Can you sign up for an activity, take a course or join a group where someone like this might be found? Do you already know someone like this—and if so, can you ask them out for coffee or to join you and others for a social event?

Make a list. Reach out. Repeat. Review in three months. And keep going!

1. In my desired life, I imagine having friends who ＿＿＿＿＿＿
＿＿＿＿＿＿＿＿＿＿＿＿＿＿＿＿＿＿
＿＿＿＿＿＿＿＿＿＿＿ ＿＿＿＿＿＿＿＿＿
＿＿＿＿＿＿＿＿＿＿＿＿＿＿＿＿.

2. In the life I have now, my circle includes friends who possess skills and attributes I admire, such as ＿＿＿＿＿＿＿＿＿
＿＿＿＿＿＿＿＿＿＿＿＿＿＿＿＿＿＿
＿＿＿＿＿＿＿＿＿＿＿＿＿＿＿＿＿＿
＿＿＿＿＿＿＿＿＿＿＿＿＿＿＿＿.

3. I nurture my existing connections by＿＿＿＿＿＿＿＿＿
＿＿＿＿＿＿＿＿＿＿＿＿＿＿＿＿＿＿

_____
_____
_____.

4. In my circle, I would like to add people who _____
_____
_____
_____
_____.

5. Some places and ways I might connect with people like this include
_____
_____
_____
_____.

6. As a first step, I am going to_____
_____
_____
_____
_____.

Whispered Wisdom

Life can be blissful when you surround yourself with people
who don't judge you and people who believe in you.

TINA SARELLAS, RBC REGIONAL HEAD CORPORATE CLIENT GROUP

CHAPTER NINE:

Questions of Faith

I felt as if I were in the presence of God. And I'd been directed there by a stranger on a beach.

I'd stopped to stretch my legs with a stroll along a stretch of what looked like deserted shore, and so I was surprised to see a woman perched in the shelter of the rocks along the shoreline, her head buried in a book. She looked up and smiled; I said hello and with some help from Google Translate, we bridged the gap between my broken French and her limited English. "Are there sights in the area I shouldn't miss?" I asked her. "Yes, yes," she said, naming the Mingan Archipelago National Park Reserve a few kilometres away. We chatted some more before I set off back to my car.

That evening, I punched the park name into my phone. Made up of more than a thousand islands and islets in the Gulf of St. Lawrence, the archipelago is home to dozens of monoliths, large limestone rock formations carved by winds and water over millennia. The next day, I punched "Mingan" into my GPS and arrived at Havre-Saint-Pierre early in the morning to join the six-hour boat tour to Île du Fantôme, Niapiskau Island and Quarry Island.

After brief excursions to the first two islands, we had two hours to ourselves to explore Quarry Island. Tide pools of barnacles, urchins and sea stars dotted the shoreline. In the distance, seals bobbed in the waves. As I sat on the rocks, I watched the salty spray of the gulf's waves rise above the shoreline's rocks. Gulls and other seabirds soared and swooped in the sky above me. The summer air was bracing, the breeze fresh and pure. With each breath, a powerful feeling filled me. I felt as clean and pure as the air I took into my lungs.

This is like what God's love must feel like, I thought as I inhaled. *This feels like the universe's love.*

I wasn't picturing some deity sitting on a throne, judging people and directing them to heaven or hell. What I felt that day was a deep love, a connection to humanity and nature, to the source of that light, that love. Some might call it God. I prefer "universe."

Why Talk about Religion?

It's hard to talk about faith and religion, isn't it? It's a topic we often avoid, out of politeness or fear. We don't want to offend or alienate. We don't want to *be* offended. Some of us feel compelled—indeed are told by religious leaders that we have a duty—to proselytize, to convert others to our one, true faith, thereby saving them from damnation. Others among us roll our eyes at these religious campaigners, ignoring their knocks at the door, discarding the literature they leave behind. Some leaders warn us away from people of other faiths or those who subscribe to no faith at all, convinced these others are a threat to our souls, a potential contaminant. And for those of us who have experienced religion's sting—seen it wielded in harmful ways—it can be tough to talk about our experiences. Those who shape our religious upbringing may see us as sinners or betrayers, while those outside that community may use our words to confirm their worst biases about others of our faith—and those who don't subscribe to any particular faith may find it all boring, baffling.

So why talk about it at all? The challenge is that religion and faith—which I view as two separate things, though they may certainly intertwine—can deeply influence the way we view the world. For those of us who grew up in religious households or communities, religion often provides a model for parenting, the relationship with God modelling for the parent-child relationship. Religious leaders often articulate specific guidelines around the relationships between men and women. There may be judgments about sexuality and sexual relationships, and LGBTQ2S+ people especially may be subjected to trauma and marginalization in religion's name. Embedded within the religion may be attitudes about our agency and ability to control our life path, about accountability and reward for "good" behaviour, about punishment of those who falter, about the role of questioning and critical thinking and about charity and attitudes towards those viewed as sinners.

While people outside our communities may view our religion as a monolith, within it, there may be a wide range of beliefs, interpretations and approaches. Not every Muslim believes the same things, just as there are variations in belief within Christian, Jewish, Buddhist, Hindu and other faith communities. And there are commonalities among fundamentalist groups—also referred to as "high-demand, high-control" faith communities—that cut across belief systems. As psychotherapist Krystal Shipps writes, a high-control faith community—whether Christian, Muslim, Jewish or otherwise—is one "that requires obedience; discourages its members from questioning its rules, principles, and practices; expects subservience and loyalty; discourages trusting relationships outside the group; perpetuates the notion that those within the group are right and superior to those outside of it; promotes extreme or polarizing beliefs; and expects its members to suppress their authentic selves in exchange for the sense of belonging and security the group offers."[1] For faith communities like this, a common refrain is that whatever is happening to us now, no matter how difficult or apparently unjust, will make sense in the afterlife or, according to some faiths, has even been caused or influenced by things that happened in a previous life. The combined effect can be to avoid dealing with issues in *this life*. There's little incentive to develop the emotional skills to confront and seek to change emotionally unhealthy—even dangerous—situations if they are part of a greater plan we're not able to see.

So why talk about religion? Because we learn a lot about how to view the world from the religious traditions within which we were raised. These may be lessons that help ground us, comfort us and assist us in navigating our lives. They may also be lessons that limit us, make us vulnerable to abuse and close us off from the possibility of emotional health.

About 85 percent of the world's population identify with a specific religion. While we tend to think of religious affiliation as somewhat fixed—we say "I am Muslim" or "I am Catholic," identifying ourselves with our religion—the reality is that for many, their religious identity will change in their lifetime. Nearly one-third of religious people in the United States switch to another religion during their lifetimes,[2] while many others will leave religion behind altogether: from 2007 to 2021, the percentage of Americans describing themselves as having no religious affiliation grew from 16 percent[3] to 29 percent.[4] Shifting our religious views can be a significant life event for people, with major negative *and* positive impacts.[5]

How can we *not* talk about religion?

Lessons in Faith

I can't talk about religion without talking about my mother.

When I first wrote this section, the opening lines read: "My earliest memories of Allah are of hell, a fiery place of punishment for those who have failed to live up to Allah's demanding expectations." But of course, these aren't my first memories of Allah—they are my first memories of my mother talking about Allah.

What were the reasons my mother gave for why someone might end up in hell? I could be sent there for eating with my left hand. I might be banished for missing a single prayer during the day. Or failing to put my toys away. Or speaking back to her.

The messages were confusing, though. "Allah loves his human children seventy times more than a mother loves her children," my mother would tell us. But if Allah loved us, why did he test us, threaten to punish us? "The easier you have it, the less Allah cares for you," my mother would say. "Allah tests those he loves the most. Our hardships will be rewarded in the afterlife." And if we failed his tests? We would be cast out, banished, isolated from all we loved.

Still, there were ways we could demonstrate our faith. "Samra, you must recite now for our guests!" My mother beamed in pride as she pushed me to stand in front of her dinner guests, my aunties and uncles, family friends and neighbours gathered in our living room. I was just six or seven, happy to please my mother with the verses I'd memorized from the Quran. I drew a breath and began, and the words tumbled out of me.

"You are such a good girl!" our guests exclaimed as they praised my diligence in learning the verses. The irony? I didn't understand the Arabic words I spoke or their deeper religious meaning: it was simply rote memorization. Still, I knew they were holy words. I knew reciting them made my mother, and the people around us, proud of me. I hoped they made Allah proud of me too.

In my mother's view, life was mysterious and whatever happened was Allah's will. Our duty? To demonstrate our devotion to Allah through our prayers, thoughts and actions, to never question, criticize or argue about Allah's commands and to ignore Shaitan, the devil who tempted us to sin with his whispers and who cackled with laughter and delight when we were bad. My memorized verses were one way of showing both my devotion and hers: only a devout mother could have raised so devout a child!

The lesson I absorbed, first through my mother's words and then through the imams, at the mosque and elsewhere: Allah's love was conditional, based on obedience to him—and if I failed to be obedient, I would be cast out, cut off from my family, my community and all that I knew.

The lesson underneath: my mother's love was conditional as well, based on obedience to her and her beliefs, and if I failed, she would cast me out.

But devotion wasn't a guarantee that all would be well. In our home, it frequently wasn't. And while my parents fought, I prayed. Sometimes I recited the prayers we'd been taught. But more often, my prayers were in my own words. *Please make my father a better man. Please stop my parents from fighting. Please make my mother love me.* Sometimes my prayers were questions about matters big and small. *Why do you let my mother be beaten? Why can't girls play sports? Why do you make some children street beggars when others live in comfort?*

As I grew up, the list of possible transgressions grew, many of them connected to beliefs about women, purity and temptation: I wasn't to touch the Quran while on my period. Showing too much skin was sinful, as was anything else that drew male attention, intentional or not. At twelve, when I told my mother a male relative had groped my breasts, I was the one banished from the next family gathering, my changing body blamed for being too tempting rather than the adult male blamed for assaulting me. My forced marriage was a way to protect me from him and men like him—or was it a way to protect them from the temptation of my body? Either way, it was my body that was the centrepoint of sinfulness, both a jail and a trap.

And once married? Disobeying my husband was a sin. Refusing sex with him was a sin: there was no such thing as marital rape because a wife had no right to say no to a husband's desires. But also, as a woman, enjoying sex was a sin. Using contraception was a sin as well. My body was a vessel, not my own.

Even so—and despite the example of my parents' own marriage—it didn't seem possible to me that Allah would want me to be beaten and terrorized in my own home. But when I turned to the imam at my mosque for advice on the abuse I suffered at my husband's hands, his initial support evaporated after he spoke to my husband. "You know, sister, your husband is so remorseful. You must give him another chance." A second imam told me my only choices were to stay with my husband or marry someone else. "You cannot go against nature," he told me. "Allah's law says you must not live on your own as a woman." This world is temporary, but the afterlife is forever, I was told. By suffering now, I was ensuring my place in heaven.

Over the years, I have heard from countless women from other faiths that they too had been counselled to stay with abusers. Patriarchy cuts across religious lines.

What did my mother say, who had stayed with a husband who beat her? I was to pray—and to stay. Divorce was a sin that would bring shame on us all.

And after I was divorced and began to rebuild my life? My mother, by then a widow herself, shifted her interpretation: Perhaps Allah's plan was for me to be abused and divorced so I would end up on my own and could look after her. Allah was giving me success as a test, lifting me up only so that my fall, when it came, would be even more painful. If I failed to stay on the path Allah had chosen for me, I would have an accident that would destroy my brain, tear my limbs from my body, burn my skin for all eternity. Sometimes she sounded almost as if she were wishing these things upon me to prove her own delusions right rather than warning me against them.

When she came to visit, I tried to avoid conversations about religion. And then I heard the stories I'd grown up with tumbling from my then-eight-year-old daughter's lips. Saarah and I were cuddling at bedtime when she started to cry. "What's wrong?" I asked.

"I was standing on the balcony after school, singing my songs," she told me through her tears, "and Nani said singing is haram, and on the day of judgment, Allah will put a hot coal in my throat and then my throat will burn forever." Her sister's drawings were haram as well, she'd been told, and so on judgment day, Kinza too would be tested, challenged to bring her drawings to life, and when she failed, she too would burn forever.

I wasn't going to have the images that haunted me—of hellfire and agony and isolation from those I loved—haunt my daughters. I told my mother there would be no more talk of Allah's punishment in my home.

I was stepping away from my mother's version of religion. I didn't see until later that I was stepping away from my mother as well.

Connecting through God

Often when we talk about religion, we talk about it as if it is a matter of belief in and relationship with a particular deity or conception of that deity. And many faithful people do speak of their personal relationship with their God, conversing with them through prayer, expressing love for them. But that relationship isn't the only one connected to the religion to which we adhere: our relationship with God is intertwined with our family relationships and connections to a wider community of faith. For those of us who are immigrants or children of immigrants, our faith community can be a powerful connection to a global community or country of origin, a lifeline to familiar beliefs and values in a new place where we might otherwise feel isolated, under threat or singled out. Religion isn't just about what we believe in: it's about who we're connected to.

And those beliefs and connections have an impact on our physical and mental health. Many studies show that people who identify themselves as religious are physically healthier, live longer and report being happier than less religious or non-religious people.[6] Other studies have found that attending religious services can even provide some protection against coronary heart disease and lower your likelihood of having diabetes and hypertension.[7]

Why? The answer is layered. Religious beliefs can help us cope with life's difficulties and improve our mental health by setting our difficulties within a larger, more meaningful context, which allows us to remain more optimistic in the face of adversity. The impact of social support is also important: studies show that the connections to others forged through participation in ritual and religious community can give us access to mutual support, so we have help and other resources when we need them, which helps us avoid ill health and cope with it more effectively when we face it.[8]

But religion isn't a uniformly positive force. The structures and strictures that give comfort to some may be used to harm others. The explanations of the world and why some people suffer while others succeed may make sense to some but raise questions for others. And the relationships that provide social support may also be used to exert social control over those viewed as disobedient, disbelieving or dissenting. For those raised in communities of belief, recognizing religion's less positive attributes can lead to questions and doubts, which some resolve by "reconfiguring" their beliefs—perhaps choosing to move to a new mosque, church or temple—while others "deconvert" or "disaffiliate" and leave their religious communities altogether.[9] It's often a difficult process; those who experience it describe it as a significant life event that involves emotional stress, guilt and loneliness—but can also result in "joy, freedom, relief, gratitude and empowerment."[10]

Finding Our Way

When I stepped back from my mother's version of religion, I felt unanchored. I still believed in a higher power. I believed in the positive values I'd seen expressed in my community: the importance of education, the obligation to give back and support others who are less fortunate. In my soul, even in my most difficult moments, I'd always harboured a deep optimism that things would work out and felt grateful to God for equipping me with the skills I needed to navigate life's storms. As I look back, I know there were likely moments when my optimism made me stay longer than perhaps I should have, when I believed my hope for my marriage—that it would be transformed into a loving relationship—might come to pass. But that same optimism kept me moving forward too, one step at a time, to complete my high school courses, to set up my home daycare, to save the money I needed to pay for university. I didn't always know where the next step would lead me. But despite the tales of a wrathful God that I'd grown up with, part of me believed more strongly in God's love than their anger—a love seventy times stronger than a mother's, so much larger than we can imagine.

And on that rocky Gaspé shore, I felt that love.

It is a love that doesn't want girls to be held back from education. A love that doesn't want any woman abused in the name of religion and duty. It is a love that treats LGBTQ2S+ people with respect and dignity. It is a love that holds us accountable when we cause harm to others—and wants us to love ourselves enough to hold ourselves accountable as well. It is a love that urges us to live every single day as if it is a miracle. It is a love rooted in connection and caring, in humour and humanity, in lifting up and not putting down. It is a love that welcomes our critical thinking, a love that does not fear our questions and our doubts.

It is not a vision of God's love that my mother shares. As I gained clarity on my beliefs, our contact dwindled. Despite my efforts to steer our conversations to non-religious topics, it was hard to avoid speaking about religion with someone whose entire world view is infused with religious explanations. At my next birthday, my mother left me a long voice message, her words and tone thick with judgment as she ended by saying "I hope Allah brings you wisdom."

I believed God had. I don't think she would agree.

Navigating Your Spiritual Journey

For those connected to religious communities, navigating a path to your own spiritual beliefs—or leaving spirituality behind altogether—can be complicated and difficult. This is particularly true for those whose beliefs diverge from the community in which they were raised, where religious belief is entwined with connection to family and community, and rejecting aspects of those beliefs may threaten critical supportive relationships. If you've also been shamed, blamed, abused or otherwise harmed in the name of your religion, you may also be navigating complicated feelings of anger, self-blame, sadness and more.

The questions I asked about my faith had bubbled within me from childhood—questions about why some people were poor and others not, why my mother was abused, why girls were given brains to think if we were not supposed to use them. Later, I struggled with the grown-up versions of those questions in my marriage: Why I should be abused. Why I would be given a brain if not to use it. But it wasn't until I was safely out of my marriage and had forged connections beyond the confines of the community in which I lived that I was able to start to safely make choices based on my questioning. I couldn't take those steps without first building some bridges.

It's not surprising, is it? We're wired to seek support and provide it to others, and religious communities are powerful sources of connection, as well as support and control. Studies of those who have left religious communities show those who cope best tend to share characteristics with those who do well after any traumatic life event: They tend to think for themselves, measuring at high levels for self-esteem and tending towards reflection. They have or expect to have good social supports and, specifically for those questioning their faiths, social supports that extend beyond their religious community. And economic independence helps too.[11] (One note: many of the studies focus on those who have left Christian communities, and few focus specifically on the experiences of immigrants or those who are otherwise marginalized within the larger culture. There's lots of work to be done here!)

Each person's path is unique. You may find answers to your spiritual questions within your current faith. You may discover a deeper connection to another community of faith. You may, like many, shift to describing yourself as spiritual though not religiously affiliated. Or you may decide that atheism is your truth. What will help on your journey? Seeking clarity on what matters to you—your values—as well as taking steps to ensure your overall mental and physical health will all work in your favour. You may find support in a new community of faith, but strengthening your overall web of connections could be just as valuable, or more. For me, having social and professional circles that include people from many backgrounds both challenges and informs me, pushing me to explore new ways of seeing and being.

An Answered Prayer

They were words I never thought I'd hear my mother say: "I'm proud of you, proud to tell people that you're my daughter."

I'd called my mother in Pakistan to check in on her. Since I'd told her I wouldn't tolerate the more judgmental aspects of her religious views, we'd fallen into a cycle of lengthy silences and occasional phone calls. She knew I was in medical school, though following the pattern of a lifetime, rarely asked questions about what I was doing. This time I was surprised when she asked about my studies. I'd just completed my child psychiatry rotation and was brimming with enthusiasm for the work I was doing, something I'm sure came through in my voice as I told her about it.

And that's when she said it: "I'm proud of you, proud to tell people that you're my daughter." After a lifetime of waiting, finally hearing the words four-year-old me once lingered at my mother's bedside hoping for, I felt . . . not much.

In the days that followed, I returned to our conversation. The joy I'd expected to feel hadn't materialized, but in its place, I felt instead a deep sense of liberation. That inner four-year-old didn't need my mother's affirmation, because she already had mine. She knew she was worthy. Knew she was loved. Knew she would be protected. Not by my mother, but by me, and by the web of healthier connections I had forged over time with those around me. My happiness didn't rest in my mother's hands. I held it in my own.

Whispered Wisdom

When faced with challenges or experiencing failure, I try to look at the bigger picture to keep things in perspective, and to push through the noise and voices intended to dim our light and rein in boldness and confidence. At my core I believe that part of my purpose is to be of service to others, helping others recognize and strive to achieve their potential. Fundamentally, it is faith, values and positive actions that create the guideposts to nurture purpose and build character and resilience.

These five core choices have always been my North Star:
I choose:

1. faith, values and practices that ground me, build resilience and give me peace and purpose
2. helping other women unlock their full potential
3. to get up when I fail or fall down, which sometimes means leaning on others and having the courage to ask for help
4. not to be limited by other people's biases or the limitations they try to place on me
5. a mindset and posture of continuous learning and growing

HARRIET THORNHILL, RETIRED RBC EXECUTIVE

Putting on Your Twenty-Seconds Gloves

To me, faith is not a destination, it is a journey. Our routes may vary, and I strongly believe it is important for each of us to be in our own driver's seat, freely choosing the road we travel. Questioning our faith can be difficult, and in some situations, dangerous. If you are re-evaluating your beliefs or adherence to a particular religious community, you may opt to discuss your concerns within your community. It may also provide good balance and support to seek wider input: from friends outside your faith or from a professional counsellor who can help you work through the challenges you face. Or you may opt simply to build social connections that are not linked to faith or religion at all, focusing instead on connecting with people and communities aligned with your values. See the reflection at the end of this chapter (What do you believe in?) if you're having trouble articulating what those values are.

There may be people in your life you want to stay connected to— because they are family, because you feel loyalty or concern for them— whose judgment of you with regards to your spiritual or other life choices feels toxic. Handling these interactions isn't easy. What has helped me? My twenty-seconds kitchen gloves.

I first saw these gloves advertised on television as being strong enough to withstand carrying burning hot coals for twenty seconds. And I realized that in life, sometimes we just need twenty-seconds gloves we can use to pick up the coals and get the job done. When I'm faced with dealing with someone I know will be difficult, I do the mental and emotional equivalent of putting on my twenty-seconds gloves. I go into the interaction knowing what my goal is. I do my best to ensure the path is clear and that I can move as efficiently as possible. I put on my gloves— my emotional protection—get in, move the coals and get out.

Unconditioning Workbook

- Our view of the world can be deeply influenced by the religious tradition within which we were raised. These lessons may help ground us, comfort us and assist us in navigating our lives. They may also include lessons that limit us, make us vulnerable to abuse and close us off from the possibility of emotional health.

- For those of us who are immigrants or children of immigrants, our faith community can be a powerful connection to a global community or country of origin, a lifeline to familiar beliefs and values in a new place where we might otherwise feel isolated, under threat or singled out. But for those of us who are marginalized within our faith communities, it may also present real barriers to our individual growth and our full participation in the world around us.

- Seek clarity on your own values. What matters to you? If you choose to leave your current community of faith, seek social supports that extend beyond your religious community.

- Values are dynamic: shaped, challenged and reshaped by our lived experiences and the wisdom we gain over time.

Reflection: What Do You Believe In?

"If you don't stand for something, you'll fall for anything." Variations on this quote show up on Pinterest boards and Instagram feeds, attributed to Malcolm X, Alexander Hamilton, Scottish clergyman Peter Marshall and others. While we may not know for certain who coined the phrase, the words ring true: knowing what we value provides clarity when it comes time to make choices about how to live our lives.

Values are dynamic: shaped, challenged and reshaped by our lived experiences and the wisdom we gain over time. You might have been raised within a community where bias against another group is accepted as the norm, a value that may be tested when you come to know someone from that group. You may push and pull against values and judgments applied to yourself as well. One example from my own experience: A colleague once described me as "selfless" when he praised work I'd done to mentor others within our team, and I took the label on with pride. But as I struggled in my life to set good boundaries with others, grappling with the idea that I was being selfish for looking after my own needs, I realized that being "selfless" was a value I no longer ascribed to. I needed to find ways to understand my responsibilities to others—and myself—in more nuanced terms. My values had evolved.

And sometimes living up to your values comes with a cost. Early on in my speaking career, I was hired to give a presentation at a Pakistani event. The week before, the planning committee—all men—asked me to do a run-through of my speech. In it, I talked of how my marriage had involved physical, emotional, verbal, financial and sexual abuse. I could see heads shaking as one of the men challenged me about sexual abuse: "How is that possible," he asked, "if you were married?" I gave an example: my husband pressuring me into having sex in the days after my father died, despite my grief and my clear wish not to. They weren't convinced. "It's obvious you have become too modern, but you can't talk like that in front of our culture," they said. "They can't digest it." Then on the day of the speech, I delivered the line onstage as I had first written it, including the reference to sexual abuse, because I knew there were many women in the audience who needed to hear it, who were themselves being subjected to abuse (including sexual) by their husbands. I wish I had heard someone say it when I was going through it. I knew I wouldn't be asked back, but staying true to my values and speaking clearly about the reality of non-consensual, coercive, manipulative sex within marriage trumped any obligation to be a good girl and do as the organizers wanted.

What are your values? And are you living your life in a way that aligns with those values? How do you know? Use this exercise to articulate what you stand for:

- **PICK YOUR TOP TEN:** Search online using the keywords "core values list." You'll find links to lists from many sources to inspire you. One of my favourites? Brené Brown's downloadable "Dare to Lead List of Values."[12] Review the lists you see, and come up with your personal top ten: Which values are most important to you? Not sure which to pick? Think about who you most admire: What values do they embody?
- **DEFINE YOUR VALUES:** Once you have your top ten, spend some time defining each of those values. What does each word mean to you?
- **ALIGN YOUR LIFE:** Are you living according to the values you've listed? Which values are most present in your work life? Your family life? Your friendships? Your life in your community? Within your faith group? Are your values in conflict in any of these areas? What steps can you take to align your life with the values you wish to live by? Go back to the "best possible life" exercise at the end of Chapter Six: Do the values you've chosen align with your best possible life?

Doing a values inventory like this can be especially helpful as you approach—or cope with—significant life changes, to help clarify what matters and deserves your attention.

1. My top ten values are:

Value   I define this as . . .

_____   _____

_____   _____

_____   _____

_____   _____

_____   _____

_____   _____

_____   _____.

_____   _____

_____   _____

_____   _____

2. The values most present in my work life are_____

_____

_____.

3. The values most present in my family life are_____

_____

_____.

4. The values most present in my friendships are_____

_____

_____.

5. The values most present in my community life are_____

_____

_____

_____.

6. The values most present in my faith are_____

_____

_____

_____.

7. As I review these lists, I see the following gaps:_____

_____

_____

_____

_____.

8. Steps I can take to address these gaps include: _____

_____

_____

_____.

CHAPTER TEN:

Care Package

My time on the road was coming to the end. After I packed the car for the final drive home to my girls, I paused for a coffee and a short Instagram post. "Some of the greatest insights come up when you give yourself the time and opportunity to connect with your own thoughts and feelings," I wrote. "I feel like I'm on two journeys right now. One is sightseeing through Quebec. The other is an internal journey of greater self-discovery and love. We hold so much wisdom and insight within us. When we tap into it and trust our intuition, we find the answers we're looking for—the ones that were there all along."

I'd set out on this journey as an exercise in self-care. It wasn't something that came naturally to me, this pausing and listening. But months earlier, just before the pandemic, my body had delivered a message I couldn't ignore.

It was the month leading up to International Women's Day, and I was on a speaking tour that had me scheduled to give more than twenty speeches in a few weeks, criss-crossing the globe. I'd been to Africa in 40 degree Celsius heat. I'd flown to Saskatchewan where it was minus

30. Then it was on to Atlanta. Then back to Toronto and a connecting flight to Vancouver. I'd packed the trips tightly to minimize my time away from home, but while the schedule was gruelling, I felt happy. It's true, I wasn't taking great care of myself: my gym visits had gotten squeezed out by travel, my sleep was patchy because of time zone changes and I hadn't had any real downtime in weeks, but everywhere I went, people were telling me how much my message meant to them and what they'd learned from my story. Their engagement was like oxygen to me. I love inspiring audiences and helping people find their "aha" moments. I didn't realize I was about to have one of my own.

As I boarded the plane for my eleventh flight of the week, I felt good, riding the natural high of connecting with people and doing work I love. But as I sat down in my seat, a wave of unease washed over me. It felt as if a weight were literally crushing down on my shoulders as another pushed like a knee against my chest. My vision started to swim as dizziness overtook me and hot-cold clamminess enveloped me like a damp blanket. I could feel myself struggling to breathe as I grabbed for the vomit bag in the seat pocket in front of me.

I don't know if I pressed the call button or my seatmate did, but in moments, a flight attendant was standing over me, swiftly joined by two doctors who were passengers on the flight. Their opinion: not a heart attack, but an anxiety attack. I wasn't in any real danger—though my body seemed to think I was. As my breathing returned to normal and my other symptoms abated, I struggled to understand it. I wasn't in crisis. I'd been flying since I was a child and was on my way to do something I loved to do. What was going on?

Balancing Act

In many ways I was lucky: my life was out of whack because I was doing too much of something I loved to do. That isn't always the case.

Imbalance can just as often—probably more often—come when we're overloaded with things that don't bring us joy, obligations that drain us as our to-do list overflows with got-tos, don't-wannas and holy-shit-not-this-agains. And while, yes, anyone can be overloaded, women in particular juggle complex and competing responsibilities that leave us particularly vulnerable to being overburdened. A 2022 survey of Canadian mothers by the Canadian Women's Foundation found that almost half of mothers said they had "reached their breaking point" compared to about one-third of dads. Two-thirds of moms were concerned about their physical and emotional health. Half of all moms surveyed said they found it exhausting to balance work and child care responsibilities, and almost as many said they struggled to keep up with work demands—not surprising since the majority of moms reported doing more than their spouses to manage family schedules and activities, support children's education and make arrangements for caregiving when schools were closed or kids were sick. (Only about 20 percent of dads said they carried a heavier load than their spouse in these areas.)[1]

Those themes are echoed in other global surveys of women (moms and not). A Deloitte survey of five thousand women in ten countries found almost half felt burned out, rating their mental health as poor or very poor, with women in ethnic-minority groups being more likely to feel burned out and less comfortable talking about mental health or seeking workplace support to cope with it.[2] A 2021 McKinsey study of women in corporate leadership positions found women leaders were stretched thinner than men in leadership, with more than 40 percent of women leaders saying they were burned out, compared to just over 30 percent of male leaders.[3]

While the pandemic added layers of complication to all our lives, the flexibility some had as their jobs allowed them to shift to working from home helped. Some with flexible arrangements found it easier to balance work and home,[4] and the vast majority of those who had worked from home wished to continue to do so at least part of the time.[5] (Though there were downsides as well: women climbing the corporate ladder said working remotely meant they were excluded from important meetings and opportunities.[6])

That picture is even more complicated for low-income earners. While money doesn't necessarily buy happiness, being financially stretched sure doesn't help. Women still typically earn less than their male counterparts, racialized women especially so.[7] That means we're less able to "buy" balance by paying for services, supports and relaxation, and more likely to face the added burden of worrying about having the money to pay for the necessities for ourselves and our families.

Sounds crap-tastic, right?

Set this against the backdrop of political upheaval, climate change and other twenty-first-century challenges and it's kind of surprising we aren't all collapsing in heaps as waves of anxiety wash over us. While there are significant, valid arguments for making systemic and cultural changes to address these challenges and barriers, on a day-to-day basis, each of us is faced with figuring out how we're going to cope. And there are times when it can feel like we've got no more power than a leaf in the wind.

How Do You Do?

As Dr. Shauna Shapiro points out in *Good Morning, I Love You: Mindfulness and Self-Compassion Practices to Rewire Your Brain for Calm, Clarity and Joy*,[8] we often respond to difficult situations by blaming ourselves (being paralyzed by shame or, at best, berating ourselves as we seek to whip ourselves into shape) or by trying to make ourselves feel better with positive self-talk. Blame and shame don't help because they shut down the learning centres in our brain. Trying to give ourselves a self-talk confidence boost might work in the moment, but our good feelings about ourselves can dip again if we're feeling low or face another challenge. Dr. Shapiro advocates a third option: self-compassion, which means that no matter how we perform, we are worthy of love and care. Our worth is inherent, not dependent on what we achieve. Mistakes are part of success. Setbacks are part of the journey and don't make us weak—they make us human. This self-compassion allows our brain to remain open to learning, assists us in creating the emotional distance to think rationally about what we're experiencing and allows us to respond appropriately to the situation.

But self-compassion isn't where many of us land: instead, we get caught in a loop of worry and control. Dr. J.M.G. Williams, one of the founders of Mindfulness-Based Cognitive Therapy (MBCT), describes this as being caught in "doing mode." Doing mode isn't necessarily bad: it's the process by which we choose a goal, evaluate the gap between our current situation and that goal and figure out how to achieve the goal, based on what's worked for us in the past and what we anticipate will work for us in the future. Dr. Williams calls this a "discrepancy-based" mode, because we're basing our plan of action on what we see as the discrepancy between where we are now and where we want to be.[9] Doing mode can be useful in all sorts of practical situations: navigating the route from home to the grocery store, cooking a meal, setting up a process for completing a task at work—literally "doing" all kinds of things.

But doing mode isn't as effective in managing our personal, internal world of thoughts and feelings. Doing mode toggles us between the past and the future: we're looking ahead to where we want to be, and we're basing our plan on how we got somewhere in our past experiences. But when dealing with emotions, that "doing" plan is a swaying bridge loosely anchored between an imagined future and a remembered past. When in a worry loop, it's easy to get caught imagining multiple versions of future catastrophes and trying to devise plans to turn down the volume on the anxieties bubbling up as a result.

Doing mode can look like you're applying a logical process to a problem, but often we get caught in an emotional vortex, trying to manage the feelings bubbling to the surface by developing one distracting "solution" after another.

Dr. Williams's advice? Shift to "being mode." In being mode, we're not preoccupied with toggling between the past and the future: we're simply being, noticing what is actually happening in the present with more psychological distance, which then allows us to make more intentional choices.[10] The difference can seem subtle when we talk about it in abstract terms. Here's a recent soundtrack of my own, when I was caught in a worry loop about rising mortgage rates:

DOING MODE: "This is scary. I need to check the mortgage rates again. Are they up today? God, if they keep climbing like this, the whole market is going to cool and the value of the house is going to drop. Then I'm never going to make back that money I've put into the kitchen. God, what if I flunk out of med school? By the time I go to renew my mortgage, they'll never refinance me. I'll lose the house. I'll be broke. I need to check my account again. I never should have agreed to this reno. What was I thinking?"

What might that sound like if I slipped into being mode instead?

BEING MODE: "I'm feeling scared. I can feel anxiety bubbling up, fluttering in my chest. I'm worrying about money and the financial choices I've made. I feel like I'm twenty-five, trapped in the house. I don't feel safe."

The differences? In doing mode, I'm responding to emotions by trying to "solve" them without pausing to observe where the emotions originate and what they might be telling me. Sometimes there is a "problem" to solve—but sometimes old emotional patterns are being triggered by new circumstances and the problem we're leaping to solve doesn't exist or isn't what we think it is. It's as if we're trying to speak to an echo and are then surprised when the conversation derails. In being mode, I'm acknowledging the emotions and stepping back to observe them.

Later, I can sit with what I've observed and try to understand why those feelings bubbled up. Decoding them doesn't always come quickly: sometimes understanding their origin can take days or more. But as I've learned to exercise my "being" skills, those insights do come more quickly, helped by the fact that I'm not throwing random "solutions" at my emotions that simply complicate the situation. In this case, as I sat with what I observed, I realized that the money worries I was feeling were rooted in what it felt like when I was married and had no control over my own money. But that wasn't my current situation. I was no longer that scared twenty-five-year-old. I was a forty-year-old with lots more life experience and an economics degree, and on my way to being a doctor, with money in the bank and the skills to support myself. I can't control interest rates or house prices. But I have the skills to figure out what to do if things do go wrong.

All of this may make sense when we're talking about negative emotions bubbling up, but how does any of this apply to situations when things seem to be going well but then get knocked sideways? Situations like, oh, I don't know, maybe having an anxiety attack on a plane when you think you're fine?

What was happening on that plane? I was feeling great, getting all kinds of positive feedback. But how was I, really? Let's slip back into the doing and being soundtracks.

DOING MODE: "Wow, I'm doing great. That last speech went really well. The woman who came up to me afterwards said she'd learned so much—that made me feel good! I can't wait to get to Vancouver. The next group I speak to will be interesting: lots of human resources people in this one. I hope they'll get something out of what I have to say. I love the energy I get from being onstage—it's such a boost!"

BEING MODE: "I'm feeling good. The reactions to my last speech gave me an energy boost—they filled up my bucket. But I am a bit tired. My sleep is a bit off. I can feel some nervous energy buzzing through me. I miss Kinza and Saarah. Now I'm on this plane for three hours with nothing to do, and I can feel my energy level dipping down again. It'll be quite a while before I'll get the boost I feel when I'm in front of an audience. And I think I'm too wired to sleep."

From the outside, it might look like I'd be better off sticking with doing mode in this case—at least I'm telling myself I feel good! But underneath the soundtrack in my head, my body's energy level was dipping and buzzing, and as my brain tried to ignore the fatigue and mixed feelings about my travel, those emotions still hummed through my body, seeking a way to be heard. The more I pushed them down by focusing on the boost I'd get from speaking, the more they looked for a way out. And they found one: an anxiety attack.

Other common examples: the way students get flattened by cold bugs immediately after exams, or when we get sick just as our vacation starts. In both cases, we're running on adrenaline, powering through to a deadline. And the moment the pressure is off: *crash!* Our body's energy overdraft comes due, and we're forced to rest, reboot and recharge.

There is a popular belief that we only experience burnout when we're doing things we don't like. But when we do things we love and care about, we may in fact be more susceptible to crashing as we over-extend our emotional energy. That's what happens when we experience compassion fatigue, common especially among those in helping professions, such as medicine.

I thought my "happy" bucket was full. After all, I'd filled it with the buzz from speaking, the warmth of the response from audiences and the enjoyment from travelling to new places. But life is more complex than a single bucket waiting to be filled. Overloading in one area doesn't satisfy us, it leaves us unbalanced—something our brain might ignore but our bodies will eventually find a way to tell us.

Whispered Wisdom

Love comes with hurt. Liking comes with hurt. Connection comes with hurt. In our attempts to shield ourselves from the hurt, we limit our growth, our newness, and our freedom to be, to live, and to thrive.

FOLUKE AKINBOYO, MA, RP

Riding the Wind

If you were walking through parts of tropical Asia—in India or Pakistan, say—you might happen upon what looks like a leaf striated in shades of biscuit, brown and yellow, its sections marked with darkened veins. It's the kind of thing you expect to be picked up by the breeze and blown along. But if you're lucky, you'll get to see the *Kallima inachus*—the orange oakleaf butterfly—open its wings to reveal its three-to-four-inch wingspan in all its blue, orange and black beauty. That leaf is actually an insect that thrives in areas with heavy rainfall. It's adept at avoiding danger, a powerful flier, skilled at navigating erratically when pursued by birds and able to disappear into foliage, where it uses its leaflike camouflage to hide in plain sight. Like the orange oakleaf butterfly, we too have the capacity to weather rainy days, use the wind to our advantage and outwit our foes—but we need to care for ourselves if we're going to do it well.

What does self-care look like? The definitions and categories of self-care are broad. The World Health Organization talks about self-care as involving tools that support "individuals, families and communities to promote health, prevent disease, maintain health, and cope with illness and disability with or without the support of a health worker,"[11] and many definitions include emotional, mental and spiritual well-being; physical health; interpersonal relationships; connections at work and in the community; and even our relationship with the natural world or the planet. I think of it this way: self-care involves our inner selves, our physical selves and our connected selves and includes the steps we take to be well, stay well and cope well.

Many of us feel self-care is only possible for those with "enough" time and money while others feel guilty spending time (and money) looking after themselves.[12] One multi-country study of self-care during the Covid-19 lockdown found that while self-care activities improved people's well-being, the higher the level of their perceived stress, the more difficult they found it to engage in self-care—so self-care became tougher to maintain just when it might have been most helpful.[13] And there isn't a one-size-fits-all solution: our individually unique and shifting circumstances mean my self-care needs may differ from yours, and my needs today may look different from my needs tomorrow or next year. Still, self-care does make a difference to overall mental and physical health: eating well, sleeping well, getting regular exercise, forging and maintaining healthy interpersonal connections, engaging in satisfying work and hobbies and articulating and pursuing a purpose in life all contribute to creating and maintaining well-being. Studies show us that engaging in self-care helps us deal with stress and improves our perceived quality of life.[14] And we don't have to be perfect to be better. Even changes made later in life can be beneficial: a study of more than three hundred thousand adults, for instance, found even those who shifted from being less active to being more active later in life decreased their risk of heart disease, cancer and early death.[15]

Pull Up the Weeds, but Plant Some Flowers Too

When we reflect on self-care, it's easy to slip into thinking about it as if we are weeding a messy garden, pulling up bad habits. And sure, it's worth considering how we can limit or change behaviours that aren't healthy. But when it comes to what we want to add to our garden, it can be just as easy to carry over the attitude of "only if it's good for us" and opt for, well, replacing the weeds with nothing but kale. Don't get me wrong: kale is great—crunchy, packed with nutrients, and its leaves can even be pretty. But seriously, no one really wants a garden filled only with kale. Or even only with vegetables. Yes, look for self-care steps that boost your physical and emotional health, but leave room for pleasure and beauty as well: the equivalent of flowers with amazing colours and beautiful scents whose sole purpose is to add joy to your garden-life picture.

A nutritionist I know talks about how important "satisfaction" is to building a healthy diet and choosing what's on your plate: if what you're eating doesn't leave you satisfied, no matter how high its good-for-you score is, you're going to go in search of something else to munch on. The same principle applies to life: feeling accomplished, productive and like you're taking good care of yourself are all good sensations. But fun, satisfaction, pleasure, joy, beauty—the things we sometimes dismiss as frivolous—need to be there too, because without them, we'll feel like something is missing.

As well, we might fall into the idea that the garden we are creating is for the benefit of others in our lives, rather than for our own benefit. One of my mentors in medical school, psychiatrist Dr. Nick Kates, once told me that many of his female patients who leave abusive situations do so for their children rather than for themselves. Indeed, in my own marriage, my decision to leave was driven primarily by my desire to protect my kids and give them a better future. Often, even our acts of courage are dependent on other people's well-being. But it's okay—even essential, I would argue—to take action for our own benefit. That's what I'm working on changing, and my first decision from that new mindset was to go to medical school. Part of me believed that the responsible thing to do, for the benefit of my family's financial security and my children's future, was to stay in finance. But wanting to pursue medicine to fulfill my own goals and desires was okay: it didn't have to be for the kids. It could be for me.

And as with a garden, we don't have to wait until the weeds take over to embark on self-care—just as we don't wait until our teeth start to fall out to think about brushing them! Self-care isn't just about tidying up on our bad days: it's about being proactive and deliberate in building care into our good days, so we can be better equipped to deal with life's rough patches.

Ask yourself:

- **What can I do to fill my inspiration bucket?** In the classic book *The Artist's Way: A Spiritual Path to Higher Creativity*,[16] author and teacher Julia Cameron advocates what she calls the artist date, an excursion or creative playdate for yourself that you preplan and do on your own, with the goal of engaging your creative, playful, ready-to-be-inspired self. Yes, it could be going to an art gallery or a concert—but it could just as easily be looking at buttons and ribbon at a sewing notions store, taking yourself bowling or visiting a local animal refuge.

- **What makes me grin?** Not just smile, but full-on, ear-to-ear grin? Maybe it's driving on the highway singing at the top of your lungs to your favourite megastar. Perhaps it's rewatching episodes of a favourite sitcom. Or taking your pup to the dog park. Pay attention to the things that make you so happy your cheeks hurt: add more of that to your week! I have a list for when I need these reminders.

- **What sense am I neglecting?** When it comes to adding joy to our lives, most of us default to one or two senses, often filling our ears or our eyes—or pleasing our taste buds. But what scents or textures might recharge your brain? Perhaps it's a spritz of perfume or some time spent inhaling the smell of a forest. Perhaps it's pulling on your coziest pyjamas or spending some time in a yarn shop.

- **Am I making room for "be time"?** It's easy to live in the land of constant "doing" while neglecting the value of "being." I remind myself to build my "be" muscles by literally scheduling "be time" in my calendar: fifteen-minute blocks when I commit to simply observing in the moment rather than planning, problem-solving or projecting myself into the past or future.

Take a look at your self-care garden: Where can you add a splash of flower power—and what form will it take?

What's in Your Bento Box?

Looking at the pieces in this way—as daunting as it might initially seem—allows us to step back and see the interconnections: how imbalance in one area can throw us out of whack in others, and how small positive changes can add up to benefits that seem proportionally bigger than we might expect. Self-care isn't a single bucket: it's a bento box with multiple compartments.

What we carry in our individual bento boxes can help fuel us for dealing with life's challenges—but there will still be influences outside the box that affect us. Being aware of our multiple compartments allows us to spot where we might be running low and encourages us to focus our efforts on what we can influence, rather than putting our energy into trying to control factors beyond our command. Put another way: being aware of both context and complexity helps us channel our energy away from trying to change the direction of the wind to focus instead on fuelling ourselves to flap our wings.

Start with One Thing

This is the point where a lot of us get stuck. We look into our bento boxes and think, *Well, that compartment is empty, that one is empty too, that one's got mould in it, that one—are those stale gummy bears? Oh yeah, and there's a carrot stick. Yuck.* It's a bit like when you go to get your kids' backpacks ready for the start of school in September—and discover June's last lunch growing there in the dark. You might be tempted to just zip it up and pretend you'd never even opened it in the first place.

We want to fuel ourselves well. And we might be tempted to try to come up with our perfect life plan. But while it can help to look at the big picture of our life (and we'll get to that in the Unconditioning Workbook section of this chapter), it can also be hard, simply adding to our stress-filled to-do list when we already feel depleted.

That doesn't sound like a good idea.

Try this instead: pick one small thing from the list below. And just start.

I'm going to warn you: the self-doubting, cynical part of your brain might look at the list and think, *These won't make a difference—they're too small.* Or *There aren't enough choices—the thing I really need to do isn't on this list.* To that part of your brain, say, with love and compassion, *I hear your concerns. Thank you for sharing. And now I'm going to trust the process and try just one of these things. Let's see what happens.*

Remember: just pick one. And for the next three weeks, try it.

1. **THREE THANK-YOUS:** After you brush your teeth at night, sit quietly before you go to sleep and jot down or record a voice note of three things you're thankful for. These could be thank-yous to specific people (to the driver who paused to let you merge onto the highway this morning), for specific circumstances (for your dog who makes you laugh every day) or for more general conditions (for today's sunshine).

2. **TAKE TEN, TWICE:** Look at your day and choose two roughly consistent points during your schedule when you will get up and go for a ten-minute stroll. If you can get outside, great, but even if it simply means you'll walk the halls at the office for a few minutes, that's also fine.

3. **GET CHATTY:** At your first opportunity each day, engage in positive small talk with a stranger or acquaintance. It could be the person you see at the bus stop every morning or someone on the subway platform you'll never see again, the gas station clerk or the admin assistant at the doctor's office. Say something nice to them (something you actually

mean): "That scarf's a great colour on you" or "Wow, that sun is nice and warm today!" If they chat back, great. If they grunt and turn away, that's fine too. Gauge success in the quality of the energy you put out, not the response you get. (You may also get an oxytocin hit—the hormone connected to parent-infant bonding and romantic attachment that also gets triggered in experiences related to being recognized or trusted.)

When your three weeks are up, complete the exercise in this chapter's Unconditioning Workbook section (page 281).

Whispered Wisdom

Chardikala: this ancient Punjabi word translates to "an optimistic mind," which is also supported by the neuroscience concept of "where focus goes, neurons grow." By keeping the mind in a positive place through gratitude, mindfulness, prayer and other similar practices, we can maintain brain health and resilience through adversity.

DR. SHIMI KANG, PSYCHIATRIST,

HEALER & BESTSELLING AUTHOR OF

THE TECH SOLUTION &

DOLPHIN PARENT

What Do I Need Right Now?

In 2022, my daughters and I moved into a new home in the suburbs outside Toronto. In the months that followed, I could feel that something was just a bit . . . off. The new house was closer to school for me, so my commute was shorter. We'd done a kitchen reno when we moved in, but that disruption was behind us. Still, I felt mildly out of sorts. And I couldn't figure out why.

Then, one Saturday morning, I met a friend downtown for brunch. I could feel my mood picking up as I drove into the city. After I parked and headed along Queen Street West to the restaurant, I felt energized, brighter. Brunch was filled with chatter and laughter, and then after, I strolled along the street, window-shopping and drinking in the energy of the busy weekend crowds. As I climbed back behind the wheel, I realized something: I missed the city!

In the past, I might have slipped immediately into doing mode, my thoughts flying from the emotional recognition of missing the city to a tumble of ideas about selling the house and moving back to the city core. This time, though, I focused on being mode, noticing when that "off" feeling struck me. I didn't feel it all the time, and in fact, there were stretches when I barely felt it at all. I was glad to not be fighting traffic as much at the end of my days in class. I was happy not to be dealing with a landlord anymore. Saarah was happy in her new school and Kinza was busy with her university courses as well, and we all enjoyed downtime at the house together. But still, there were moments when the suburbs felt, well, sleepy, and my energy dipped as well.

As I lingered in being mode, I realized I didn't need to upend our entire living situation to deal with a "sometimes" feeling. What was I missing? The crowds, connection and hum of the city. Did I need it 24/7? No. But how could I fit city-time into my already packed schedule? A solution bubbled to the surface: I spent hours each weekend reading and studying. Instead of doing it all at home, on Saturday mornings, I loaded my books into the car and headed downtown to a coffee shop. Tucked in a corner, I sipped a latté, caught up on my reading and absorbed the buzz of city energy, capping it off with a busy sidewalk stroll back to my car.

This might not look like self-care to everyone. But it was exactly what I needed.

Whispered Wisdom

You may be the first at a table, but don't be the last. I want to ensure all humans get a fair shot, regardless of postal code or genetic code.

CLAUDETTE McGOWAN,

FOUNDER & CEO OF PROTEXXA

Unconditioning Workbook

- Self-care involves our inner selves, our physical selves and our connected selves, and includes the steps we take to be well, stay well and cope well.
- Self-care isn't a single activity in a single area of our life. Self-care is like a bento box with many compartments. Your bento box order might look very different from mine—and may change over time.
- As women, we are often told that self-care is selfish, and our role is to be selfless and serve others. But we cannot love others fully without loving ourselves first. Taking care of ourselves is the most loving thing we can do for ourselves and for others.
- There may be circumstances beyond our control that deplete our inner, physical and connected selves. We need to be aware of context and focus our energy on what we can influence or control. You can't change the direction of the wind, but you can focus on fuelling yourself and flapping your wings.

"One Thing for Three Weeks" Follow-Up

See the instructions on pages 276–78 and enter the start date for your three-week challenge here: _____

When did you finish? Enter the date here: _____

I chose to do

        ___   Three thank-yous

        ___   Take ten, twice

        ___   Get chatty

What difference, if any, did adding one small self-care activity make for you? Consider your moods, energy level, ability to focus, sleep patterns or any other aspect where you noticed a change. Try not to assign a negative or positive assessment to the change—simply note where there was a shift you think was connected to the activity.

I noticed the following changes _____

_____

_____

_____.

Is this activity one you will continue with and why?_____

_____

_____.

What insights from this experience will you carry over as you consider other self-care steps?_____

_____

_____.

Reflection: What's Your Bento Box Order?[17]

To get a more complete picture of your self-care bento box, complete the following worksheets. You can do this in whichever way feels like a good fit for you: start with the section in which you feel strong already, choose the section that corresponds with the self-care area your three-week challenge targeted or target the area you feel most depleted in.

What's in Your Self-Care Bento Box Now?

Rate each using this scale:

    ✓   I do this well

    ~   I'd like to do this better

    ?   It never occurred to me to do this

    X   I don't think this is relevant to me

Inner Self

_____	*I have hobbies I enjoy.*
_____	*I make sure I unplug from technology.*
_____	*I express my emotions.*
_____	*I pay attention to my thoughts, attitudes, beliefs and feelings.*
_____	*I journal or take time for self-reflection.*
_____	*I appreciate my own skills, accomplishments and strengths.*
_____	*I learn about new things.*
_____	*I laugh about things.*
_____	*I take days off from work or rest days from responsibilities.*
_____	*I take holidays.*
_____	*I ask for help when I need it.*
_____	*I engage in interesting new tasks at work/school.*
_____	*I have work I enjoy.*
_____	*I pursue professional or work-related development.*
_____	*I feel comfortable saying no to unnecessary, uncomfortable or undesirable activities or tasks.*
_____	*I can set personal and professional boundaries.*
_____	*I engage in a religious or spiritual practice.*
_____	*I practise gratitude.*

_____ _I am open to inspiration._

_____ _I am hopeful and optimistic._

_____ _I am open to not knowing, not being in charge or not being the expert._

_____ _I allocate quiet time for reflection._

_____ _I appreciate beauty (art, music, nature, literature)._

_____ _I allow myself to cry._

_____ _I meditate._

_____ _I feel a sense of purpose in my life._

_____ _I feel like my values align with how I live my life._

_____ _I contribute to causes I believe in or express my values in social action, advocacy or other ways._

_____ _I do other things that support my emotional, mental and spiritual well-being._

Physical Self

_____ _I get enough sleep._

_____ _I drink enough water._

_____ _I eat regular meals._

_____ _I get regular exercise._

_____ _I spend time outdoors/connecting with nature._

_____ _I maintain good physical hygiene._

_____ _I eat healthy meals._

_____ _I take time to recover when I am sick._

_____ _I seek professional healthcare for prevention and necessary treatment._

_____ _My work environment is safe and pleasant._

_____ _I take regular work breaks (such as lunch)._

_____ _I wear clothing I like._

_____ _I engage in sexually pleasurable activities on my own or with others._

_____ _I do other things that support my physical health._

Connected Self

_____ *I spend time with people whose company I enjoy.*

_____ *I stay in contact with distant connections.*

_____ *I have mentally stimulating conversations/exchanges.*

_____ *I am part of a cultural, linguistic or ethnic community.*

_____ *I am part of a community of choice (a group I identify with because of shared interests or attributes).*

_____ *I do fun activities with others.*

_____ *I am intimate/romantic with another.*

_____ *I spend quiet/private time with others.*

_____ *I socialize or connect with co-workers.*

_____ *I make new friends/talk to new people.*

_____ *I spend time with my pets.*

_____ *I make time to reply or reach out with personal emails, letters and messages.*

_____ *I have people in my life whom I trust, with whom I can share a fear, hope or secret.*

_____ *I volunteer for a charity or in my community.*

_____ *I do other things that help me nurture my relationships.*

What Do You Want to Add?

As you reflect on these areas of your self-care bento box, where would you like to add new ingredients? Do you notice shifts that have occurred—areas you used to do more in that may be receiving less attention because of your current circumstances?

Inner Self

What are some of the specific self-care activities I am doing now to be well?_____

_____

_____

_____.

What are some new self-care activities I can add to stay well?_____

_____

_____

_____.

Are there self-care activities I need to add right now to cope well?

_____

_____

_____.

Physical Self

What are some of the specific self-care activities I am doing now to be well?_____

_____

_____.

What are some new self-care activities I can add to stay well?

_____

_____

_____

_____.

Are there self-care activities I need to add right now to cope well?

_____

_____

_____.

Connected Self

What are some of the specific self-care activities I am doing now to be well?_____

_____

_____

_____.

What are some new self-care activities I can add to stay well?_____

_____

_____

_____.

Are there self-care activities I need to add right now to cope well?____

_____

_____

_____

_____.

What Do You Need Less Of?

Are you using coping strategies in any of these areas that you would like to reduce or eliminate? These could be activities that tip from self-care to self-numbing, or that are actively harmful in some way. As you think about what you might want to reduce or eliminate, think also of what you might substitute for what you're removing.

Some activities I would like to eliminate include:

Activity   Possible substitute

_____   _____

_____   _____

_____   _____

That's a Pretty Big Bento Box Order!

You might look at your list and see a number of areas where you'd like to add a new ingredient to your self-care list. Don't try to do it all at once! Choose one activity in one area. How? Maybe you opt for something in the area that has the fewest things you do well (✓). Or perhaps you build on the "one thing for three weeks" exercise on page 276 and choose an area informed by that learning. Maybe you target an activity that you'd like to do better (~) or opt for something a little less negatively charged and go for something you never thought of (?). Whatever you decide: just choose one. And remember to dial down your inner perfectionist: even with the best of intentions, you won't be able to sustain a perfect record with your new activity. Aim for improvement, not perfection.

What now? Consider one small positive step or activity you can add to your routines that will shift your rating from a ? or a ~ to a ✓. Write it down and be specific: not "get more active" but "set an alarm on my phone for 11:00 a.m. and 3:00 p.m. and when it goes off, spend five minutes stretching."

What might help? Consider what author S.J. Scott calls habit stacking.[18] Take a habit you already have and stack the new habit on top of it. If you did the "three thank-yous" self-care challenge after you brushed your teeth each night, you've already habit-stacked, because you added the thank-yous to your daily dental care regime. Giving yourself a realistic timeline to make your new habit stick is also helpful. Three weeks is a popular target, but it's not necessarily true that every new habit can be cemented in just twenty-one days. One study of habit-forming found new habits can take anywhere from eighteen to 254 days to become automatic,[19] depending on factors such as ease, enjoyment, efficiency, craving and other factors.

When you're ready, go back to your list and consider adding a new specific self-care strategy. And another. Who knows? You may find self-care becomes habit-forming!

But What if It's Not?

We all face challenges as we try to improve our self-care. A shift in circumstances can derail an established habit: if you've buddied up with a pal to go to the gym and that friend moves away, you might find yourself needing a new anchor to hold your habit in place. New responsibilities or diminished resources—a change in income, time or other stressors that deplete our reserves—can shift our overall self-care equation. What can you do?

- Be realistic about the barriers that arise.
- Resist the urge to slide directly into "do mode." If possible, step back into "be mode": observe and reflect. Then, ask yourself "What step can I take that would help most right now?"
- Recognize there is no single equation for self-care that works for everyone, all the time. Check in and adjust what you're doing to what you need, now.

Whispered Wisdom

Don't iron out your quirks! They define your uniqueness and authenticity. Celebrating your quirky traits fosters creativity, innovation and genuine connections.

AMY RUDDELL, VICE-PRESIDENT, MACGREGOR COMMUNICATIONS

EPILOGUE:

A Girls' Getaway

lmost three years had passed since my Quebec road trip. In the house where my girls and I were now all students, the cycles of our varied school years rarely aligned: Saarah was nearing the end of the high school year but with a couple more months still to go. Kinza was wrapping up her final university classes before exams. And I was about to embark on another stretch of hospital rotations. But there on the calendar was a single weekend we could all clear: two days we could carve out for a girls' getaway, a weekend at a Nordic spa in Quebec's Gatineau region. We'd agreed—okay, I decreed, and the girls agreed—we'd limit our device time. Laptops would stay home. Phones would be used to share music selections only. We'd spa. We'd laugh. We'd eat. We'd spa some more.

The day before we left was Kinza's final day of classes in her journalism program. In the past few months, she'd come into her own, writing well-received articles and columns and using her design and photography skills as she worked on the university newspaper. It was late when she finally turned her car into the driveway after a wrap-up day with her newspaper colleagues. I heard the thump of her shoulder bag on the floor near the door, and then she landed on the couch, cuddling next to me with a wide smile on her face.

"You look happy!" I said as she hugged me.

"I am," she said as she shared the details of her day and the praise she'd received for her end-of-year work. "You know, Mom, when I was driving home, I was just thinking about how different our lives are, and how different my life is from what it would have been if you'd stayed with Dad. None of this would have happened. I wouldn't be who I am now. You saved yourself. But you saved us too."

"We saved each other," I whispered as we hugged.

The next morning, as we piled into the car for the five-hour drive to the spa, I handed Kinza the keys. Her journey would be different than mine had been, as Saarah's would be as well.

Writers use phrases like "my heart swelled," but here with my girls, it truly felt as if my heart was swelling. In the days after Saarah and I had looked at my wedding jewellery, bracelets and other finery made to fit a child bride's small frame, I had allowed myself to feel both the grief for what I had lost and my immense relief that my daughters' lives would be different, that my life now *was* different. I was strong enough to weather life's inevitable sadness. And I was brave enough to seek the happiness we all deserve.

In my heart, there was room for it all.

Just as your heart has room for all of you.

Acknowledgements

Much of what I know about living and loving unconditionally has been learned from my daughters, Kinza and
Saarah. You have been my companions, my motivation
and my inspiration. So many of my early decisions were made to
ensure that you would each have the life you deserve, with the freedom to soar and become all you want to be. Little did I realize that
the decisions I made to make your world bigger would fill my world
with so much joy and possibility as well! I am honoured to be on this
journey with you and am so enormously proud of the people you
have become.

To my co-author, Kim Pittaway: the words on these pages would
not have been as graceful without your understanding and skill. Our
conversations have enriched my thinking and helped me sharpen my
ideas. Thank you for your wisdom and friendship.

The enthusiasm and support of my publishing dream team at
HarperCollins has been a tremendous gift. Editor Julia McDowell's
steady hand and guidance have been more than I could have hoped
for. Thank you to production editor Natalie Meditsky, copyeditor
Catherine Dorton, designer Zeena Baybayan and the rest of the
team for the skill and care they brought to these pages.

My agent, Samantha Haywood, has believed in me from the very beginning. Sam, your insight and friendship continue to inspire me. Rob Firing, you saw my potential as a speaker before anyone else did, and your encouragement helped me to step onto that stage. I am grateful for the support of the entire team at Transatlantic Agency.

At Speakers Spotlight, Farah and Martin Perelmuter have continued to support me in sharing my message with the world. Thank you to Farah for whispering your wisdom onto these pages, to Farah and Martin for your guidance and professional support and to all of the agents I have had the pleasure of working with at Speakers Spotlight.

I consider myself enormously lucky to have found mentors who have both guided and challenged me. John Rothschild's belief in me has been life-changing. I would not have achieved what I have without his guidance and friendship. Harvey Botting, Professor Gordon Anderson and Justin Schurman have all been dear friends whose encouragement and wisdom continue to inspire me.

Thank you to the board of directors and team at Brave Beginnings for working with me to turn another of my dreams into a reality. Together, we are making a difference in the lives of women who have survived abuse, violence or oppression by matching them with trained mentors to help rebuild their lives through friendship and support. I am so excited about what we are creating!

To all of the amazing women who have whispered wisdom in my ear: Foluke Akinboyo, Dr. Andrea Alvarez, Jennifer Bernard, Elisabeth Burks, Elizabeth Charles, Jennifer Clark, Julie Fry, Alexandra Gillespie, Ann Gomez, Sheri Griffiths, Dr. Robyne Hanley-Dafoe, Emma Haraseth, Zabeen Hirji, Dr. Shimi Kang, Kelsey Komorowski, Margaret MacSween, Claudette McGowan, Sarah McVanel, Farah Perelmuter, Leila Rafi, Wendy Reed, Amy Ruddell, Tina Sarellas, Ayesha Shah, Harriet Thornhill, Halina Von Dem Hagen, Azadeh

Yaraghi, Karen Myhill-Jones, Sherri Stevens, Dr. Kathleen Hames, and Kelly MacDonald. Thank you for allowing me to share your inspiring words on these pages.

While I had long harboured the dream of becoming a doctor, I believed it was a dream that had passed me by. I am grateful to have been welcomed by McMaster University, which opens the door to medical education to non-traditional students like me. I especially wish to thank Dr. Nick Kates, Dr. Gary Chaimowitz, Dr. Suzanne Archie, Dr. Amanda Bell and Dr. Wendey Proctor for their guidance and support.

I began my journey to education—and freedom—at the University of Toronto as an undergraduate and then as a graduate student in economics. Later, during my time on the university's Governing Council, I learned essential lessons in leadership. Now, I am delighted to return to the university to complete my residency in psychiatry. It is like coming home! I wish to thank Dr. Sanjeev Sockalingam for his mentoring and support, and to thank my classmates, colleagues and professors with whom I am sharing this next adventure.

And a special thank you to brand designer extraordinaire Azadeh Yaraghi, for making me look good online.

Finally, to all of you who have attended my speaking engagements, read my books or shared your insights with me in person or online: thank you for your attention and your positive energy. I look forward to continuing this journey with you!

Notes

Prologue: Unlearning

1. Some confuse the terms *arranged marriage* and *forced marriage*. An arranged marriage can be as happy and emotionally healthy as a love marriage if both parties are consenting adults. But forced marriages involve coercion, where one party, almost always the woman, is emotionally, financially or physically manipulated into marrying. And any marriage involving someone who is a minor is by definition coercive because of their more limited ability to give full informed consent.

Introduction: Why I've Written This Book

1. Dr. Bessel Van Der Kolk, *The Body Keeps the Score: Brain, Mind, and Body in the Healing of Trauma* (Unabridged), read by Sean Pratt (Penguin Audio, 2021), Audible audio ed., 16 hr., 15 min.

2. Dr. Bessel Van Der Kolk, *The Body Keeps the Score: Brain, Mind, and Body in the Healing of Trauma* (Penguin Books, 2015).

3. Dr. Gabor Maté with Daniel Maté, *The Myth of Normal: Trauma, Illness and Healing in a Toxic Culture* (Alfred A. Knopf Canada, 2022).

4. Nedra Glover Tawwab, *Set Boundaries, Find Peace: A Guide to Reclaiming Yourself* (TarcherPerigee, 2021).

5. Shauna L. Shapiro, *Good Morning, I Love You: Mindfulness and Self-Compassion Practices to Rewire Your Brain for Calm, Clarity, and Joy* (Boulder, Colorado: Sounds True, 2022).

6. American Psychological Association, "What is Cognitive Behavioral Therapy?" *Clinical Practice Guideline for the Treatment of Posttraumatic Stress Disorder (PTSD) in Adults (2017)*, accessed January 4, 2024, https://www.apa.org/ptsd-guideline /patients-and-families/cognitive-behavioral.

7. CAMH, "What is Dialectical Behaviour Therapy (DBT)?," *Dialectical Behaviour Therapy (DBT)*, accessed January 29, 2024, https://www.camh.ca/en/health-info/mental-illness-and-addiction-index/dialectical-behaviour-therapy.

8. Steven C. Hayes, Kirk D. Strosahl and Kelly G. Wilson, *Acceptance and Commitment Therapy: The Process and Practice of Mindful Change,* 2nd edition (New York: The Guilford Press, 2016).

9. Richard Schwartz, *No Bad Parts: Healing Trauma and Restoring Wholeness with the Internal Family Systems Model* (Boulder, Colorado: Sounds True, 2021).

Chapter 1: You Are Here

1. Dr. Gabor Maté with Daniel Maté, *The Myth of Normal: Trauma, Illness and Healing in a Toxic Culture* (Alfred A. Knopf Canada, 2022), 23.

2. Maté, *Myth of Normal*, 25.

3. North Carolina Division of Social Services and the Family and Children's Resource Program, "How Trauma Affects Child Brain Development," Children's Services Practice Notes, accessed January 29, 2024, https://practicenotes.org/v17n2/brain.htm.

4. North Carolina Division of Social Services and the Family and Children's Resource Program, "How Trauma Affects Child Brain Development."

5. Dr. Bessel Van Der Kolk, *The Body Keeps the Score: Brain, Mind, and Body in the Healing of Trauma* (Penguin Books, 2014), 45.

6. Steven C. Hayes, Kirk D. Strosahl, Kelly G. Wilson, *Acceptance and Commitment Therapy: The Process and Practice of Mindful Change, Second Edition* (Guilford Press, 2016), 250–252.

7. "Oprah Talks to Maya Angelou," *O, The Oprah Magazine*, May 2013, accessed January 29, 2024, https://www.oprah.com/omagazine/maya-angelou-interviewed-by-oprah-in-2013/5#:~:text=I%20mean%20having%20enough%20courage,Maya%3A%20Indeed%20not.

Chapter 2: A Real Mother

1. L. Tomova, K.L. Wang, T. Thompson, et al., "Acute Social Isolation Evokes Midbrain Craving Responses Similar to Hunger," *Nature Neuroscience* 23, (2020): 1597–1605, https://doi.org/10.1038/s41593-020-00742-z.

2. G. Macdonald and M.R. Leary, "Why Does Social Exclusion Hurt? The Relationship Between Social and Physical Pain," *Psychological Bulletin* 131 no. 2 (2005): 202–23, https://doi.org/10.1037/0033-2909.131.2.204.

3. It's important for me to acknowledge here that with this and all other examples that involve my daughters, I have their permission to share these details with readers.

4. Maté, *The Myth of Normal*, 103.

5. Nedra Tawwab (@nedratawwab), "Things Adult Children Want to Hear," Instagram post, August 10, 2023, https://www.instagram.com/p/CvxFM8fOR9 -/?igshid=MTc4MmM1YmI2Ng%3D%3D.

Chapter 3: Superwoman in a Box

1. Marjorie Hansen Shaevitz, *The Superwoman Syndrome* (Warner Books, 1984).

2. C.L. Woods-Giscombé, "Superwoman Schema: African American Women's Views on Stress, Strength, and Health," *Qualitative Health Research* 20, no. 5 (May 2010): 668–83, https://doi.org/10.1177/1049732310361892.

3. Woods-Giscombé, "Superwoman Schema," 14.

4. Kevin Sneader and Lareina Yee, "One is the Loneliest Number," *McKinsey Quarterly*, January 29, 2019, https://www.mckinsey.com/featured-insights/gender-equality /one-is-the-loneliest-number.

5. McKinsey & Company and LeanIn.Org, "Women Are Doing Their Part. Now Companies Need To Do Their Part Too," *Women in the Workplace 2018*, accessed January 30, 2024, https://womenintheworkplace.com/2018.

6. Van Der Kolk, *The Body Keeps the Score*, 117.

7. RAINN, "The Vast Majority of Perpetrators Will Not Go to Jail or Prison," *The Criminal Justice System: Statistics*, accessed January 30, 2024, https://www.rainn.org /statistics/criminal-justice-system.

8. Richard Schwartz, *Introduction to Internal Family Systems* (Boulder, Colorado: Sounds True, 2023), Chap. 1, Kobo.

9. Schwartz, *Introduction to Internal Family Systems*, Chap. 1, Kobo.

10. Schwartz, *Introduction to Internal Family Systems*; Richard Schwartz, *No Bad Parts: Healing Trauma and Restoring Wholeness with the Internal Family Systems Model* (Boulder, Colorado: Sounds True, 2021); and Van Der Kolk, *The Body Keeps the Score*, Chap. 17.

11. Internal Family Systems—IFS Institute, "Dr. Richard Schwartz Explains Internal Family Systems (IFS)," uploaded March 5, 2019, video, 7:48, accessed January 30, 2024, https://www.youtube.com/watch?v=DdZZ7sTX840&t=464s.

12. Randy A. Sansone and Lori A. Sansone, "Rumination: Relationships with Physical Health," *Innovations in Clinical Neuroscience* 9, no. 2 (February 2012): 29–34, https://www.ncbi.nlm.nih.gov/pmc/articles/PMC3312901.

Chapter 4: Braveheart

1. Cathy J. Lassiter, "The Courage to Lead: Activating Four Types of Courage for Success," *Executive Leadership*, Texas Elementary Principals and Supervisors Association, accessed January 30, 2024, https://www.tepsa.org/resource/the -courage-to-lead-activating-four-types-of-courage-for-success/.

2. Jennifer Armstrong, "The Six Types of Courage," *Lion's Whiskers*, accessed January 30, 2024, http://www.lionswhiskers.com/p/six-types-of-courage.html.

3. Jenn Lofgren, "Four Skills You Need for Courageous Leadership," *Forbes*, January 10, 2019, https://www.forbes.com/sites/forbescoachescouncil/2019/01/10/four-skills -you-need-for-courageous-leadership/?sh=3f1138d13f38.

4. Angela Duckworth, *Grit: The Power of Passion and Perseverance* (Scribner, 2016).

5. Hazel Markus and Paula Nurius, "Possible Selves," *American Psychologist* 41, no. 9 (September 1986): 954–969, https://psycnet.apa.org/doi/10.1037/0003 -066X.41.9.954.

6. E.C. Murru and K.A. Martin Ginis, "Imagining the Possibilities: The Effects of a Possible Selves Intervention on Self-Regulatory Efficacy and Exercise Behavior," *Journal of Sport Exercise Psychology* 32, no. 4 (August 2010): 537–54, https://doi.org/10.1123/jsep.32.4.537.

7. A. Alimujiang et al., "Association Between Life Purpose and Mortality Among US Adults Older than 50 Years," *JAMA Network Open* (American Medical Association: May 24, 2019, electronic), https://doi.org/10.1001/jamanetworkopen.2019.4270.

8. C. Meilstrup et al., "Does Self-Efficacy Mediate the Association Between Socio-economic Background and Emotional Symptoms among Schoolchildren?," *International Journal of Public Health* 61, no. 4 (February 23, 2016): 505–512, https://doi.org/10.1007/s00038-016-0790-3.

9. RRC—Evaluation and Training Institute, "What is R2?," accessed January 30, 2024, https://r2.resilienceresearch.org/wp-content/uploads/2021/10/R2

-Summary.pdf. The other factors are gratitude, mindfulness, sleep, nutrition and physical activity.

Chapter 5: Love Lessons

1. Maté, *Myth of Normal*, 105–110.
2. Government of Canada, "Fact sheet: Intimate Partner Violence," accessed January 30, 2024, https://women-gender-equality.canada.ca/en/gender-based-violence /intimate-partner-violence.html.
3. Raquel Kennedy Bergen with contributions from Elizabeth Barnhill, "Marital Rape: New Research and Directions," VAWnet: National Online Resource Center on Violence Against Women, February 2006, accessed March 8, 2024, https:// vawnet.org /material/marital-rape-new-research-and-directions.
4. Bergen and Barnhill, "Marital Rape," 2006.
5. Bergen and Barnhill, "Marital Rape," 2006.

Chapter 6: The Perfect Imposter

1. Héctor García and Francesc Miralles, *Ikigai: The Japanese Secret to a Long and Happy Life* (Penguin Random House, 2017).
2. P.R. Clance and S. Imes, "The Imposter Phenomenon in High Achieving Women: Dynamics and Therapeutic Intervention," *Psychotherapy Theory, Research and Practice* 15, no. 3 (Fall 1978): 241–247, https://doi.org/10.1037/ h0086006.
3. P.R. Clance and M.A. O'Toole, "The Imposter Phenomenon: An Internal Barrier to Empowerment and Achievement" in E.D. Rothblum and E. Cole (Eds.), *Treating Women's Fear of Failure* (New York: The Haworth Press, 1988), http://paulineroseclance.com/pdf/ip_internal_barrier_to_empwrmnt_and_achv.pdf.
4. Clance and O'Toole, "The Imposter Phenomenon."
5. Manfred F.R. Kets De Vries, "The Dangers of Feeling Like a Fake," *Harvard Business Review*, September 2005, accessed March 8, 2024, https://hbr.org/2005/09/the -dangers-of-feeling-like-a-fake.
6. H.M. Hutchins, L.M. Penney and W. Sublett, "What Imposters Risk at Work: Exploring Imposter Phenomenon, Stress Coping, and Job Outcomes," *Human*

Resources Development Quarterly 29, no. 4 (November 2017): 31–48, https://doi .org/10.1002/hrdq.21304.

7. W.S. Crawford, K.K. Shanine, W.V. Whitman and K.M. Kacmar, "Examining the Imposter Phenomenon and Work-Family Conflict," *Journal of Managerial Psychology* 31, no. 2 (March 2016): 375–390, https:/doi.org/DOI:10.1108/JMP-12 -2013-0409.

8. P.L. Hewitt, and G.L Flett, "Perfectionism in the Self and Social Contexts: Conceptualization, Assessment, and Association with Psychopathology," *Journal of Personality and Social Psychology* 60, no. 3 (1991): 456–470, https://psycnet.apa.org /doi/10.1037/0022-3514.60.3.456.

9. K.G. Rice and S.A. Mirzadeh, "Perfectionism, Attachment, and Adjustment," *Journal of Counseling Psychology* 47, no. 2 (April 2000): 238–250, https://doi .org/10.1037/0022-0167.47.2.238.

10. See description of Personal Standards Perfectionism as opposed to Evaluation Concerns Perfectionism in T. Fang and F. Liu, "A Review on Perfectionism," *Open Journal of Social Sciences* 10, no. 01 (2022): 355–364, http://dx.doi.org/10.4236 /jss.2022.101027.

11. Fang and Liu, "A Review on Perfectionism."

12. H. Kearns, A. Forbes and M. Gardiner, "A Cognitive Behavioral Coaching Intervention for the Treatment of Perfectionism and Self-Handicapping in a Nonclinical Population," *Behavior Change* 24 (2007): 157–172, https://doi .org/10.1375 /bech.24.3.157; and S.J. Egan, T.D. Wade and R. Shafran, "Perfectionism as a Transdiagnostic Process: A Clinical Review," *Clinical Psychology Review* 31 (2011): 203–212, https://doi.org/10.1016/j.cpr.2010.04.009.

13. S. Melero, A. Morales, J.P. Espada, I. Fernandez-Martinez and M. Orgiles, "How Does Perfectionism Influence the Development of Psychological Strengths and Difficulties in Children?" *International Journal of Environmental Research and Public Health* 17, no. 11 (June 2020): 4081, https://doi.org/10.3390/ijerph 17114081.

14. Dr. Rumeet Billan, "The Tallest Poppy," Women of Influence+, accessed January 30, 2024, https://www.womenofinfluence.ca/tps/; Dr. Rumeet Billan, *The Tallest Poppy: How the Workforce Is Cutting Ambitious Women Down*, Women of Influence+, accessed January 30, 2024, www.womenofinfluence.ca/wp-content/uploads/2023/02 /tp-whitepaper.pdf.

15. Katherine May, *Wintering: The Power of Rest and Retreat in Difficult Times* (Riverhead Books, 2020), 236.

16. Oprah Winfrey, *The Path Made Clear: Discovering Your Life's Direction and Purpose* (Flatiron Books, 2019).

17. Michelle Obama interviewed by Oprah Winfrey in *The Light We Carry: Michelle Obama and Oprah Winfrey*, Netflix, April 25, 2023.

18. J.B. Heekerens and K. Heinitz, "Looking Forward: The Effect of the Best-Possible-Self Intervention on Thriving Through Relative Intrinsic Goal Pursuits," *Journal of Happiness Studies* (June 2019), https://link.springer.com/article/10.1007/s10902-018-9999-6; J.B. Heekerens and M. Eid, "Inducing Positive Affect and Positive Future Expectations Using the Best-Possible-Self Intervention: A Systematic Review and Meta-Analysis," *The Journal of Positive Psychology* (February 2020), https://doi.org/10.1080/17439760.2020.1716052.

Chapter 7: Tokenized

1. Manulife, "About Us," accessed January 30, 2024. https://www.manulife.ca/about-us.html.

2. BMO, "About BMO," accessed January 30, 2024. https://www.bmo.com/main/about-bmo/.

3. BBC News, "Maya Angelou: In Her Own Words," May 28, 2014, https://www.bbc.com/news/world-us-canada-27610770.

4. C. Pierce, "Psychiatric Problems of the Black Minority," in S. Arieti (Ed.), *American Handbook of Psychiatry* (New York: Basic Books, 1974), 512–523.

5. Gina C. Torino, David P. Rivera, Christina M. Capodilupo, Kevin L. Nadal, and Derald Wing Sue (Eds.), *Microaggression Theory: Influence and Implications* (John Wiley & Sons, 2018).

6. Ijeoma Oluo, *So You Want to Talk About Race* (Seal Press, 2019), 170.

7. Oluo, *So You Want to Talk About Race*, 172.

8. Ibram X. Kendi, *How to Be an Antiracist* (Penguin Random House, 2019), 47.

9. Melissa Moyser and Amanda Burlock, "Time Use: Total Work Burden, Unpaid Work, and Leisure," *Women in Canada: A Gender-based Statistical Report*, Statistics Canada, July 30, 2018, https://www150.statcan.gc.ca/n1/pub/89-503-x/2015001/article/54931-eng.htm.

10. Institute for Women's Policy Research, "Women Do 2 More Hours of Housework Daily Than Men," January 22, 2020, https://iwpr.org/women-do-2-more-hours-of-housework-daily-than-men/.

11. E.C. Willroth, G. Young, M. Tamir, I.B. Mauss, "Judging Emotions as Good or Bad: Individual Differences and Associations with Psychological Health," *Emotion* 23, no. 7 (March 13, 2023): 1876–189, https://psycnet.apa.org/doi/10.1037/emo0001220.

12. Tianqiang Hu, et al., "Relation between Emotion Regulation and Mental Health: A Meta-Analysis Review," *Psychological Report* 114, no. 2 (April 12014), https://doi.org/10.2466/03.20.PR0.114k22w.

13. A.I. Masedo and M. Rosa Esteve, "Effects of Suppression, Acceptance and Spontaneous Coping on Pain Tolerance, Pain Intensity and Distress," *Behavior Research and Therapy* 45, no. 2 (February 2007): 199–209, https://doi.org/10.1016/j.brat.2006.02.006.

14. L. Campbell-Sills, D.H. Barlow, T.A. Brown and S.G. Hofmann, "Acceptability and Suppression of Negative Emotion in Anxiety and Mood Disorders, *Emotion* 6, no. 4 (2006): 587–595, https://doi.org/10.1037/1528-3542.6.4.58.

15. Allison S. Gabriel, Joel Koopman, Christopher C. Rosen, John D. Arnold and Wayne A. Hochwarter, "Are Coworkers Getting into the Act? An Examination of Emotion Regulation in Coworker Exchanges," *Journal of Applied Psychology* 105, no. 8 (2019): 907–929, https://psycnet.apa.org/doi/10.1037/apl0000473.

16. S.A. Nixon, "The Coin Model of Privilege and Critical Allyship: Implications for Health," *BMC Public Health* 19, no. 1637 (2019), https://doi.org/10.1186/s12889-019-7884-9.

Chapter 8: Creating Your Team

1. University Of Michigan, "Low Sense of Belonging Is a Predictor of Depression," *ScienceDaily*, August 11, 1999, https://www.sciencedaily.com/releases/1999/08/990810164724.htm; Bonnie M. Hagerty and A. Reg Williams, "The Effects of Sense of Belonging, Social Support, Conflict, and Loneliness on Depression," *Nursing Research* 48, no. 4 (July/August 1999): 215–219.

2. Maya Rossignac-Milon and E. Tory Higgins, "Epistemic Companions: Shared Reality Development in Close Relationships," *Current Opinion in Psychology* 23 (2018): 66–71, https://doi.org/10.1016/j.copsyc.2018.01.001.

3. J. Jetten, N.R. Branscombe, S.A. Haslam, C. Haslam, T. Cruwys, J.M. Jones, et al., "Having a Lot of a Good Thing: Multiple Important Group Memberships as a Source of Self-Esteem," *PLoS One* 10, no. 5 (May 27, 2015): e0124609, https://doi.org/10.1371/journal.pone.0124609.

4. Nedra Glover Tawwab, *Set Boundaries, Find Peace: A Guide to Reclaiming Yourself* (TarcherPerigee, 2021), 142–143.

5. Julianne Holt-Lunstad and Bert Uchino, "Social Ambivalence and Disease (SAD): A Theoretical Model Aimed at Understanding the Health Implications of Ambivalent Relationships," *Perspectives on Psychological Science* 14, no. 6 (November 2019): 941–966, https://doi.org/10.1177/1745691619861392.

6. Julianne Holt-Lunstad, Bert Uchino et al., "Social Relationships and Ambulatory Blood Pressure: Structural and Qualitative Predictors of Cardiovascular Function during Everyday Social Interactions," *Health Psychology* 22, no. 4 (2003): 388–397, https://doi.org/10.1037/0278-6133.22.4.388.

7. Monica Anderson, Emily A. Vogels and Erica Turner, "The Virtues and Downsides of Online Dating," Pew Research Center, February 6, 2020, https://www.pewresearch.org/internet/2020/02/06/the-virtues-and-downsides-of-online-dating/.

8. "Outdoor Marriage Proposals Skyrocket in 2021, According to The Knot 2021 Jewelry & Engagement Study," *The Knot Worldwide*, December 2, 2021, https://www.theknotww.com/press-releases/2021jewelryandengagementstudy/.

Chapter 9: Questions of Faith

1. K. Shipps, "Leaving a High Demand, High Control Religion: What Is a Therapist's Role?" *Psychotherapy Networker* (January/February 2023), https://www.psychotherapynetworker.org/article/leaving-high-demand-high-control-religion/.

2. W.C. Roof, "Multiple Religious Switching: A Research Note," *Journal for the Scientific Study of Religion* 28, no. 4 (Dec 1989): 530–535, https://doi.org/10.2307/1386582.

3. Michael Lipka, "A Closer Look at America's Rapidly Growing Religious 'Nones,'" Pew Research Center, May 13, 2015, https://www.pewresearch.org/fact-tank/2015/05/13/a-closer-look-at-americas-rapidly-growing-religious-nones/.

4. Gregory A. Amsith, "About Three-in-Ten U.S. Adults are Now Religiously Unaffiliated," Pew Research Center, December 14, 2021, https://www.pewresearch

.org/religion/2021/12/14/about-three-in-ten-u-s-adults-are-now-religiously -unaffiliated/.

5. M. Bjorkmark, P. Nynas, and C. Koskinen, "'Living between Two Worlds': Experiences of Leaving a High-Cost Religious Group," *Journal of Religion and Health* 61 (2022): 4721–4737, https://doi.org/10.1007/s10943-021-01397-1.

6. M. Litalien, D.O. Atari, and I. Obasi, "The Influence of Religiosity and Spirituality on Health in Canada: A Systematic Literature Review," *Journal of Religion and Health* 61 (2021): 373–414, https://doi.org/10.1007/s10943-020-01148-8; L.K. George, C.G. Ellison, and D.B. Larson, "Explaining the Relationships between Religious Involvement and Health," *Psychological Inquiry* 13 (2022), 190–200, https://doi.org /10.1207/S15327965PLI1303_04; E.L. Idler et al., "Measuring Multiple Dimensions of Religion and Spirituality for Health Research: Conceptual Background and Findings from the 1998 General Social Survey," *Research on Aging* 25, no. 4 (July 2003): 327–365, https://doi.org/10.1177/0164027503025004001; and A.R. Sullivan, "Mortality Differentials and Religion in the United States: Religious Affiliation and Attendance," *Journal for the Scientific Study of Religion* 49, no. 4 (December 2010): 740–753, https://www.jstor.org/stable/40959060.

7. A.T. Banerjee, M.H. Boyle, S.S. Anand, P.H. Strachan, and M. Oremus, "The Relationship between Religious Service Attendance and Coronary Heart Disease and Related Risk Factors in Saskatchewan, Canada," *Journal of Religion and Health* 53 (May 2012): 141–156, https://doi.org/10.1007/s10943-012-9609-6.

8. D. Speed, C. Barry, and R. Cragun, "With a Little Help from My (Canadian) Friends: Health Differences between Minimal and Maximal Religiosity/Spirituality Are Partially Mediated by Social Support," *Social Science and Medicine* 265 (November 2020), https://doi.org/10.1016/j.socscimed.2020.113387.

9. A.R. Fisher, "A Review and Conceptual Model of the Research on Doubt, Disaffiliation, and Related Religious Changes," *Psychology of Religion and Spirituality* 9, no. 4 (2017): 358–367, https://psycnet.apa.org/doi/10.1037/rel0000088.

10. M. Bjorkmark, "'Living between Two Worlds.'"

11. M.V. Thoma, S.L. Rohner, et al., "Identifying Well-Being Profiles and Resilience Characteristics in Ex-Members of Fundamentalist Christian Faith Communities," *Stress and Health* 38, no. 5 (May 2, 2022): 1058–1069, https://doi.org/10.1002 /smi.315.

12. Available as a downloadable PDF at https://brenebrown.com/resources/dare-to -lead-list-of-values/.

Chapter 10: Care Package

1. Canadian Women's Foundation, "At This Stage of the Pandemic, New Survey Suggests Circumstances Have Not Improved for Caregivers: Mothers' Health and Careers Continue to be Impacted," May 5, 2022, https://canadianwomen.org /may-2022-pandemic-survey-moms-caregivers/.

2. Deloitte, "Women @ Work 2022: A Global Outlook," accessed January 31, 2024, https://www.deloitte.com/global/en/issues/work/women-at-work-global-outlook -2022.html.

3. McKinsey & Company and LeanIn.Org, "Women in the Workplace 2021," accessed March 8, 2024, https://leanin.org/women-in-the-workplace/2021/introduction.

4. Statistics Canada, "Working from Home, Satisfaction with Family Time, and Work-Life Balance," *Canadian Social Survey – Well-Being, Unpaid Work and Family Time,* February 21, 2022, https://www150.statcan.gc.ca/n1/en/daily-quotidien/220221 /dq220221a-eng.pdf?st=98d14-wd.

5. "Working Women Are Worried: Poll Shows Canadian Women Concerned that Pandemic Workplace Accommodations Won't Last," *The Prosperity Project,* June 15, 2022, https://blog.canadianprosperityproject.ca/working-women-are-worried/.

6. Deloitte, "Women @ Work 2022: A Global Outlook," accessed January 31, 2024, https://www.deloitte.com/global/en/issues/work/women-at-work-global-outlook -2022.html.

7. Rakesh Kochhar, "The Enduring Grip of the Gender Pay Gap," Pew Research Center, March 1, 2023, https://www.pewresearch.org/social-trends/2023/03/01 /the-enduring-grip-of-the-gender-pay-gap/.

8. Dr. Shauna Shapiro, *Good Morning, I Love You: Mindfulness and Self-Compassion Practices to Rewire Your Brain for Calm, Clarity, and Joy* (Boulder, Colorado: Sounds True, 2022).

9. J.M.G. Williams, "Mindfulness, Depression and Modes of Mind," *Cognitive Therapy Research* 32 (2008): 721–733, https://doi.org/10.1007/s10608-008-9204-z.

10. C.J. Lyddy and D.J. Good, "Being While Doing: An Inductive Model of Mindfulness at Work," *Frontiers in Psychology* 7 (February 21, 2017), https://doi.org/10.3389 /fpsyg.2016.02060.

11. World Health Organization, "Self-care Interventions for Health," June 30, 2022, https://www.who.int/news-room/fact-sheets/detail/self-care-health-interventions.

12. Samueli Integrative Health Programs and The Harris Poll, "Health and Self-Care: A Look Inside Patient and Physician Perspectives on Self-Care," Samueli Foundation,

Summer 2019, https://healingworksfoundation.org/wp-content/uploads /2019/07/2019_HarrisPoll_SelfCare_FNL.pdf.

13. E. Luis et al., "Relationship Between Self-Care Activities, Stress and Well-Being During COVID-19 Lockdown: A Cross-Cultural Mediation Model," *BMJ Open* 11, no. 12 (December 15, 2021), https://doi.org/10.1136/bmjopen-2020-048469.

14. E. Ayala et al., "U.S. Medical Students Who Engage in Self-Care Report Less Stress and Higher Quality of Life," *BMC Medical Education* 18, no. 189 (2018), https://doi .org/10.1186/s12909-018-1296-x.

15. P.F. Saint-Maurice et al., "Association of Leisure-Time Physical Activity Across the Adult Life Course With All-Cause and Cause-Specific Mortality," *JAMA Network Open* 2, no. 3 (2019), https://doi.org/10.1001/jamanetworkopen.2019.0355.

16. Julia Cameron, *The Artist's Way: A Spiritual Path to Higher Creativity, 30th Anniversary Edition* (TarcherPerigee, 2016).

17. Variations of the inventory are widely available online; I have adapted and expanded on these for use in this book. Many cite the original source as K. Saakvitne and L.A. Pearlman, *Transforming the Pain: A Workbook on Vicarious Traumatization* (W.W. Norton, 1996).

18. S.J. Scott, *Habit Stacking: 127 Small Life Changes to Improve Your Health, Wealth, and Happiness* (Amazon Digital Services LLC, 2017).

19. Lally, P. et al., "How Are Habits Formed: Modelling Habit Formation in the Real World," *European Journal of Social Psychology* 40 (July 2009): 998–1009, https://doi .org/10.1002/ejsp.674.